Small Woodworking
Projects

Small Woodworking
Projects

The Best Of Fine WoodWorking

The Taunton Press

Cover photo by White Light

First printing: April 1992

A FINE WOODWORKING Book

FINE WOODWORKING® is a trademark of The Taunton Press, Inc.,
registered in the U.S. Patent and Trademark Office.

The Taunton Press, Inc.
63 South Main Street
Box 5506
Newtown, Connecticut 06470-5506

Library of Congress Cataloging-in-Publication Data

Small woodworking projects.
    p. cm. – (The Best of fine Woodworking)
    "A Fine woodworking book" – T.p. verso.
    Includes index.
    ISBN 1-56158-018-X
    1. Woodwork.   I. Series.
TT180.S497   1991
684'.8–dc20
                             92-829
                                CIP

Contents

Introduction

There's nothing quite as satisfying as completing a small project. A huge rolltop desk or a set of cabinets is impressive, but it's impersonal. You have to stand back to view it; you can't pick it up, turn it over in your hands and examine it carefully, as you can a small-scale project.

Besides being impersonal, large projects can be frustrating. Usually, by the time I'm three-quarters of the way done, I've lost the original spark and just want to get the darn thing finished. Not so with small projects. They tend to be therapeutic. A small box, a lathe-turned bowl or even a small lap desk can be a great excuse to head for the shop on Saturday morning for a pleasant weekend of woodworking, with a good chance of being rewarded with a finished product on Sunday night.

The 35 articles in this book, reprinted from past issues of *Fine Woodworking* magazine, offer a huge variety of small-scale projects that won't bust your budget or take months of your spare time to complete. Many of them would make ideal gifts for friends or family, and any of them would provide reason enough for you to while away the weekend in the shop.

—Jim Boesel, executive editor

The "Best of *Fine Woodworking*" series spans issues 48 through 90 of *Fine Woodworking* magazine, originally published between mid-1984 and the end of 1990. There is no duplication between these books and the popular *"Fine Woodworking on..."* series. A footnote with each article gives the date of first publication; product availability, suppliers' addresses and prices may have changed since then.

Mack Truck Super Liner

Ten-wheel tractor for tiny truckers

by Richard Blizzard

British craftsman Richard Blizzard was inspired to build this Mack truck after seeing the massive 18-wheelers on American interstate highways. The mahogany cab, more than 2 ft. long, has the mirrors, lights, bulldog mascot, and sleeping cabin of the full-size rig.

When I visited the United States a couple of years ago, I was impressed by the size and power of the huge trucks that roared down the highways every hour of the day. One of my favorites was the monster Mack. We don't have anything quite like it in Europe today. When I returned home to England, I was determined to reproduce this giant of the American trucking scene.

I wanted my truck to be accurate, so I wrote to the company for brochures to help me draw the plans and develop the marvelous details created by the company's designers. If you'd prefer a toy instead of a model, you can use my overall dimensions and construction ideas to come up with a simpler truck that will inspire any child's imagination. On a toy, omit details like the rigid exhaust pipes, metal mirror supports and other small items that could be dangerous in young hands.

The truck's chassis is beech and the superstructure is mahogany. You can use other hardwoods, but the body looks best when it's made from a dark-colored wood. I turned the cylindrical parts on the lathe, but did most of the other work with hand tools. Assembly is pretty straightforward, but here are a few helpful hints.

As with any vehicle, begin by first constructing the chassis, the

foundation of the whole truck, then do the cab and superstructure. Don't glue the parts together until you've cut everything out and dry-fit all the parts, to make sure everything fits properly. Cut all the components and joints before doing any shaping. The parts are easier to work when they are flat on the bench, rather than fastened to a partly assembled cab or chassis. Pieces representing things like fuel tanks and fenders should be rounded over and sanded smooth, for a softly curved metal look. Every piece should be sanded or scraped clean before assembly.

With a complex model like this, always plan ahead. Parts that must be mirror images of each other, such as the long chassis supports and ladder uprights, should be taped or clamped together and marked out as a pair. Machine them together, if possible. Pieces like the ladder uprights can be drilled while they're fastened together. Try to do all the cutting, shaping and boring on each piece before assembly. On the long chassis supports this means cutting the front of the chassis for the axle crossbar, and boring holes for the dowel rods used to attach the fuel tanks.

The rear wheel carriage assembly really conveys a sense of the massive power of this machine. The two wood and metal suspension units look real, and allow one wheel to be raised while the

Photos: above, Linda Lane; facing page, Richard Blizzard

others remain on the ground. For this action to occur, the axle holes must be slightly elongated to oval shapes. I drilled the ovals by making pairs of overlapping holes, then cleaned up to the layout lines with a rat-tail file. The rear axle mounting blocks are fairly simple, but use a drill press to ensure that the holes shown are bored perpendicular to the surface of the blocks.

The steering assembly, shown in detail on p. 11, is a bit tricky. Cut the parts shown and chamfer the front axle block recesses so the stub axle units can turn freely. Smooth each of the small parts, so everything fits well, by rubbing the parts over sandpaper on a flat surface. After boring holes and inserting the metal axles, align the pieces as shown, tape everything together and drill right through the axle block and stub axle to ensure good alignment. This requires a good deal of care, so if the telephone rings, don't answer it!

Begin construction of the superstructure with the engine cab side panel. Since these panels are set at an angle, it's a good idea to draw them full-size on paper, then use the drawing to mark off the angles for the forward and rear spacers, which are mortised into the panels. To compensate for the angled "off-set" of these panels, plane the outside of the panels to the correct angle.

The massive radiator requires quite a lot of work. Use a knife to mark out the radiator recess on a wood block, then rout out the area. Next, glue the six small wooden strips across the recess. To create the three-dimensional look of a real radiator, narrow strips of aluminum mesh (the screens used in auto body shops to patch holes in cars) are glued in between the wooden strips, then a larger piece of aluminum mesh is shaped over the wooden strips and fastened with headed straight pins and narrow strips of wood glued at the top and bottom of the recess.

I carved the steering wheel by drilling holes to remove most of the waste and rough out the hub and two spokes, then shaped them with fine rasps. The windows are 1/16-in. clear Plexiglas, available from hobby and model shops. You can heat the plastic in an oven and bend it on a mold, but you'll likely end up with gobs of plastic all over the stove. It's safer to glue the plastic to the cab, then glue the window frame over the plastic. The curve of the frame will create the illusion of a curved windscreen.

The mirror and aerial assemblies on Mack trucks do so much to capture the look of the truck that they justify a little metalwork. Make the mirror supports from 1/16-in.-dia. brass wire. Paint the wires silver, and glue them into small holes bored into the cab's side wall and wooden frame. The mufflers are turned on the lathe. The narrow tenon left at the top fits into a piece of black plastic pipe. The mufflers are then covered with aluminum mesh, pinned together at the back, and screwed to the cab's rear wall. Another word of warning. If a youngster will be playing with the truck, fit flexible tubing to the tops of the mufflers, otherwise some very nasty accidents could happen. The truck's front fenders are cut from solid blocks of wood and glued to the cab. I cut the inside first, then clamp the block in a vise and file or sand off the saw marks. Then, I cut the outside shape and round the outer edges.

The ladders for the driver's bunk and the sides of the cabin are made by taping two 10-in. pieces of wood together, locating the rungs and drilling through both pieces at once. Separate the two halves and lightly countersink each hole on the inside faces. Glue all the dowel rods into one side first, start the dowels into the other side, then put the ladder in the vise and squeeze the sides together. Finally, cut the ladder into three sections.

If you'd like, you could build a flat-bed or closed trailer to go with the cab. It would be fun for you and your children to model it after a trailer you like. Add strips of wood, braces and wheel assemblies to match the trailer you've selected, much as you did in building the Mack. I'd suggest you build your trailer around a 1/8-in.-thick plywood bed about 42 in. long and 8¼ in. wide, and supported by 1-in. by 3/8-in. edging strips glued to the plywood edge. The chassis members should be hardwood strips 1½ in. wide and 7/8 in. thick, the same length as the bed. I cut half-lap joints along the length of the chassis members to house matching half-laps on the five 2½-in. by ¾-in. crossmembers. The crossmembers look very realistic if they're the same width as the bed and beveled at the ends to fit flush with the edging strips. If you want to build a closed trailer, rabbet the sides of the trailer panels to fit over the plywood instead of the edging strips, and insert the roof into rabbets cut on the top edges of the panels. To make it possible for the cab to tow your trailer, glue a block of wood, about the same size as the cab's fifth wheel, between the chassis members about 2 in. from the front of the bed. A ½-in. dowel pin in the block fits into the cab's hitch. Experiment with pin location and size to make sure the hitch works before you glue it in.

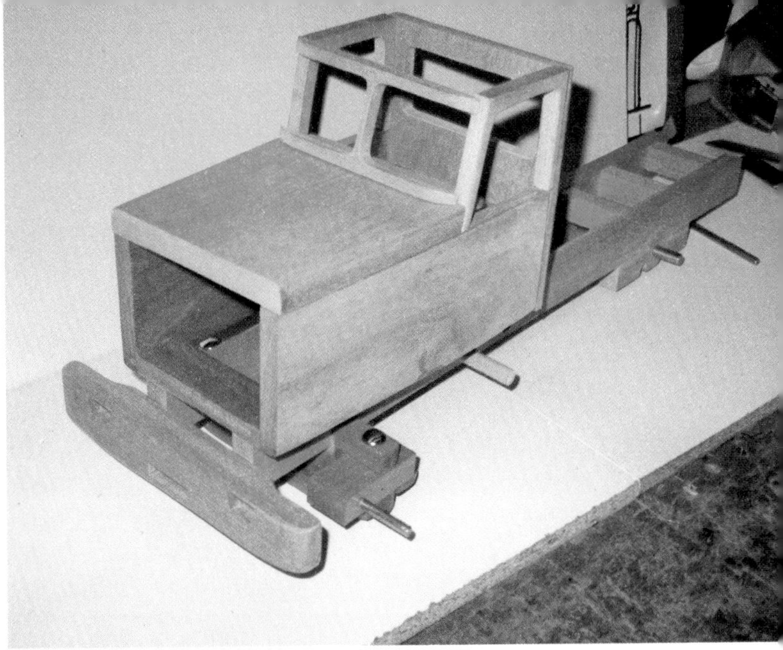

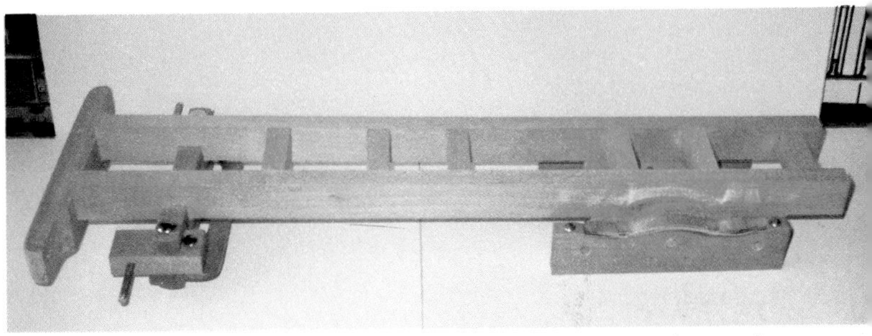

The front view of the partially assembled truck, top, shows the front spacer that sets the width of the cab and is screwed to the frame pieces. Also supporting the cab is a rigid chassis, above, a series of beech crossmembers mortised into two long frame pieces, which are, in turn, mortised into the front bumper.

I finished the model with four coats of polyurethane varnish rubbed on with a cloth, followed by a coat of wax polish. Then, I mounted the 4-in. wheels (available from Craft Supplies, Ltd., The Mill, Millers Dale, Buxton, Derbys., England SK17 85N) with ¼-in. mild steel rods and chrome-plated spring caps. No Mack truck would be complete without its bulldog bonnet mascot. I cut out the basic shape with a coping saw and shaped the dog with small chisels, gouges and wood rasps. I'm sure that other craftsmen will be able to fashion a far more bullish dog. □

Richard Blizzard is an author and designer, and host of a British Broadcasting Corp. television series on making toys.

Truck plans

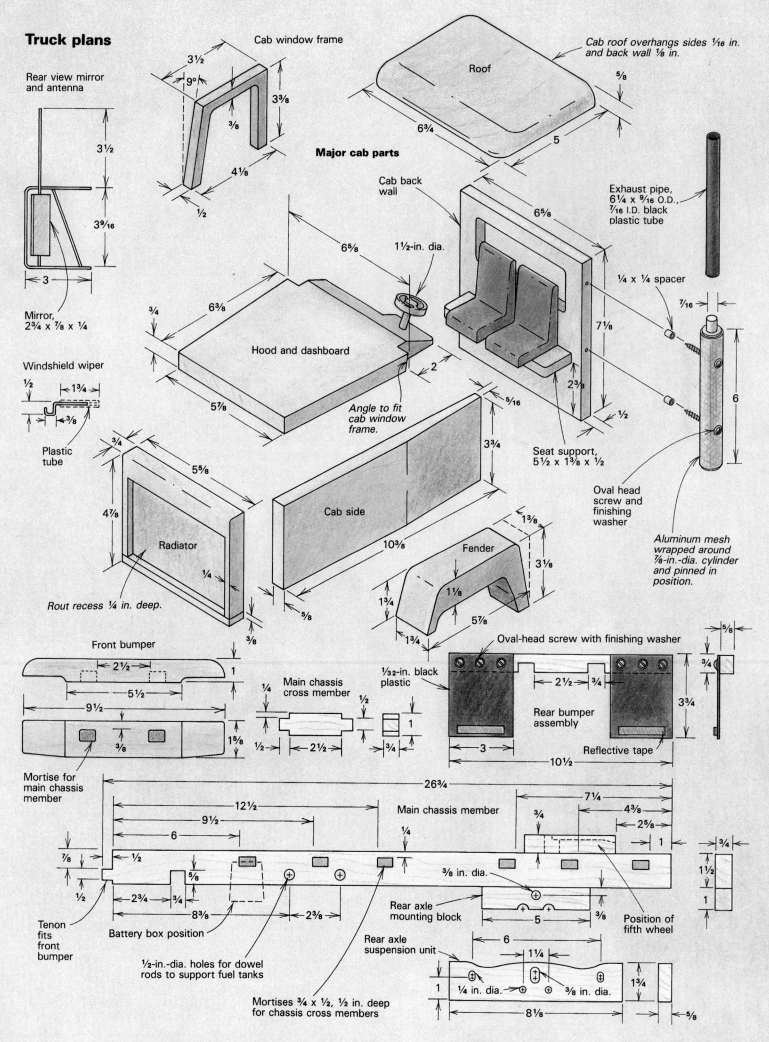

Rear view mirror and antenna

3½

3⁹/₁₆

3

Mirror, 2¾ x ⅞ x ¼

Windshield wiper

½

1¾

⅜

Plastic tube

Cab window frame

3½

9°

3⅜

⅜

4⅛

½

Major cab parts

Roof

Cab roof overhangs sides ¹/₁₆ in. and back wall ⅛ in.

6¾

5

⅝

Exhaust pipe, 6¼ x ⁹/₁₆ O.D., ⁷/₁₆ I.D. black plastic tube

Cab back wall

6⅝

1½-in. dia.

6⅝

6⅜

¾

Hood and dashboard

5⅞

Angle to fit cab window frame.

2

7⅛

2⅜

½

¼ x ¼ spacer

⁷/₁₆

6

Seat support, 5½ x 1⅜ x ½

Oval head screw and finishing washer

Aluminum mesh wrapped around ⅞-in.-dia. cylinder and pinned in position.

¾

5⅝

4⅞

Radiator

¼

Rout recess ¼ in. deep.

⅝

⅜

5/16

3¾

Cab side

10⅜

1⅜

Fender

3⅛

1¾

1⅛

1¾

5⅞

Oval-head screw with finishing washer

⅝

Front bumper

2½

5½

9½

1

Mortise for main chassis member

3/8

1⅝

¼

Main chassis cross member

½

½

2½

¾

1

¹/₃₂-in. black plastic

2½

¾

Rear bumper assembly

3

Reflective tape

3¾

¾

10½

26¾

Mortise for main chassis member

12½

9½

6

Main chassis member

⅞

½

5/8

2¾

¾

8⅜

2⅜

¼

Rear axle mounting block

¾

7¼

4⅜

2⅝

1

5

⅜

Position of fifth wheel

¾

1½

1

Tenon fits front bumper

½

Battery box position

½-in.-dia. holes for dowel rods to support fuel tanks

⅜ in. dia.

Rear axle suspension unit

6

1¼

¼ in. dia.

⅜ in. dia.

1

8⅛

1¾

⅝

Mortises ¾ x ½, ½ in. deep for chassis cross members

Drawing: Caren Mastranardi

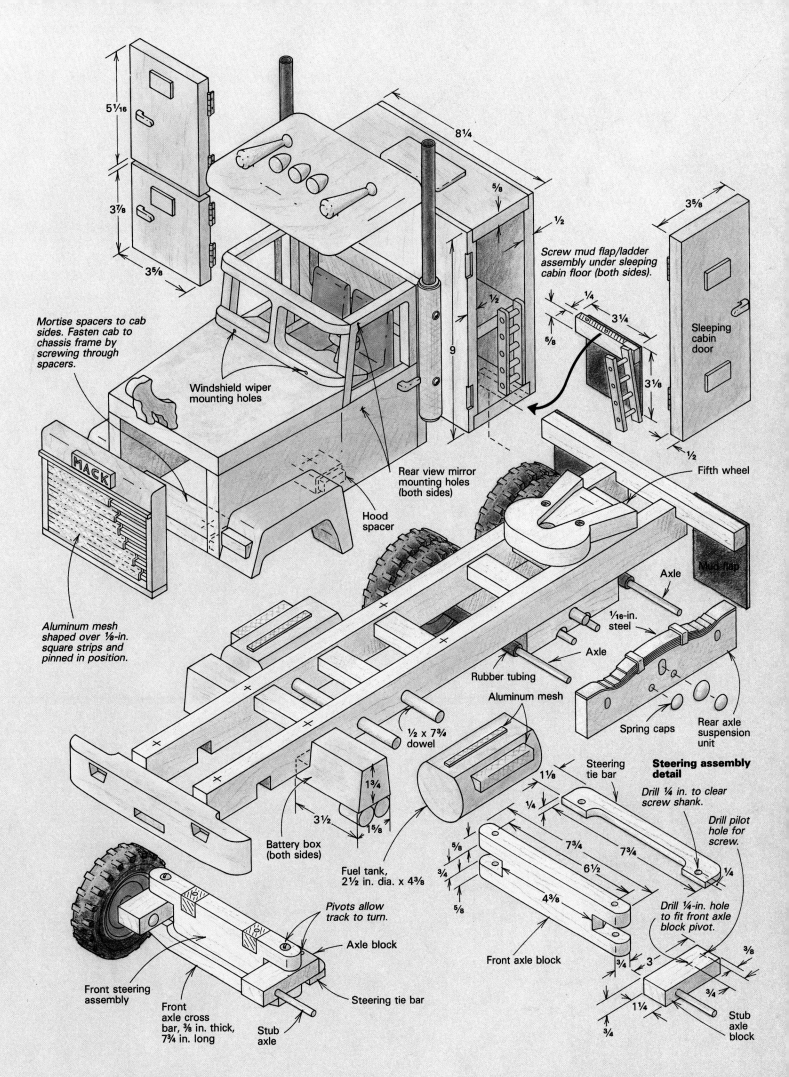

5 1/16

3 7/8

3 5/8

8 1/4

5/8

1/2

9

1/2

1/2

3 5/8

Screw mud flap/ladder assembly under sleeping cabin floor (both sides).

1/4

3 1/4

5/8

3 1/8

Sleeping cabin door

1/2

Mortise spacers to cab sides. Fasten cab to chassis frame by screwing through spacers.

Windshield wiper mounting holes

MACK

Rear view mirror mounting holes (both sides)

Hood spacer

Fifth wheel

Aluminum mesh shaped over 1/8-in. square strips and pinned in position.

Axle

Mud flap

1/16-in. steel

Axle

Rubber tubing

Aluminum mesh

Spring caps

Rear axle suspension unit

1/2 x 7 3/4 dowel

Steering tie bar

1 1/8

Steering assembly detail

Drill 1/4 in. to clear screw shank.

Drill pilot hole for screw.

1/4

7 3/4

7 3/4

1/4

5/8

6 1/2

3/4

Battery box (both sides)

1 3/4

3 1/2

1 5/8

Fuel tank, 2 1/2 in. dia. x 4 3/8

Pivots allow track to turn.

4 3/8

Front axle block

5/8

Drill 1/4-in. hole to fit front axle block pivot.

3/4

3

3/8

Front steering assembly

Axle block

Front axle cross bar, 3/8 in. thick, 7 3/4 in. long

Stub axle

Steering tie bar

1 1/4

3/4

3/4

Stub axle block

Building an Ahrens-Fox Fire Engine

A colorful classic in ¹/₁₆ in. scale

by Doug Kenney

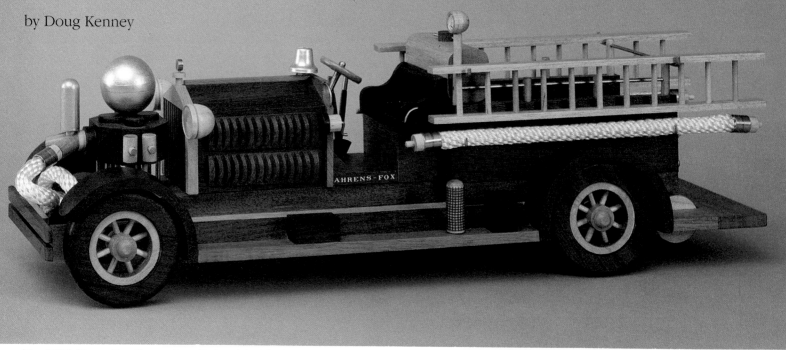

The 1928 Ahrens-Fox fire engine, distinguished by its silver pressure dome on top of the piston pump, is one of the most elegant fire engines ever built. The author's 16-in.-long model, above, is built from natural-color woods, including bloodwood, mahogany, maple and walnut.

Of the dozens of scale model vehicles I've built, few compare in class and elegance with the 1928 Ahrens-Fox fire engine. The front-mounted piston pump crowned by the shiny chrome pressure dome distinguishes it from all other fire engines. I built the Ahrens-Fox, shown in the photo above, from a full-scale engineer's drawing, mixing straight reproduction and artistic interpretation. Instead of assembling the fire engine piece by piece, I employed an assembly-line method: I constructed sub-assemblies, and then combined these to complete the model. The fire engine involves six units: the piston pump, the engine and cockpit, the rear bed, the chassis, the base and hose housings, the spoked wheels and final details.

Despite its complex appearance, the Ahrens-Fox isn't hard to build; the only special tools you'll need are a pin vise for working with tiny drill bits, several hole saws and a set of numbered drills. All the parts are either pinned in place or held with yellow glue, and I use different-color woods to enhance the beauty of the model. Many hardwood parts, such as the headlights and axle pins, are available from Toys and Joys, 407 Woodcreek Dr., Lynden, Wash. 98264; brass stock is available from your local hobby store.

Assembling the piston pump—The body of the pump is a block of ³/₄-in.-thick bloodwood or satiné, a bright red Brazillian hardwood, cut into an octagon and capped with a ¹/₈-in.-thick satiné cross. The other components are shown in figure 1 on pp. 14-15. The first step is to cut and fit the four pistons and mounting jacks, as shown in the drawing. The pressure dome is a 1¹/₄-in.-dia. hardwood ball wrapped with a strip of tape to simulate a metal seam. The dome is painted with Testor's chrome enamel before being doweled to the pump.

The Y-inlet at the front of the pump is made from two lengths of ³/₈-in. dowel, drilled down the center with a #30 drill. Cut a 60°

angle on one end of each, glue the angles to each other and sand the end of the Y-inlet flat so it can be glued to the two discs on the front of the pump, as shown in the drawing. Then, round over the end of a ⁷/₁₆-in. dowel and pin it atop the Y-inlet.

Gluing up the engine housing and cockpit—To save on expensive wood, I made the engine housing from a 1³/₄x2x3 pine block sheathed with ¹/₈-in.-thick satiné. Glue a thin strip of cherry to the ridge of the housing. The fire wall is a thin cherry panel, with quarter-round notches sawn out of the corners. Drill two ³/₆₄-in. holes in each notch. I hand-drill small holes like this with a bit in a pin vise. Then, bend the small grab bars from ³/₆₄-in. brass rod and press them in place before gluing the fire wall to the engine housing.

The radiator is ¹/₄-in.-thick mahogany. Start with a 2-in. by 6-in. strip and plow 10 lengthwise kerfs, ³/₃₂ in. wide, ¹/₁₆ in. deep and ³/₁₆ in. apart, with a thin-rim blade on a tablesaw. Crosscut the section to length, add the maple trim and complete the radiator, as shown. The four strips applied to the sides of the engine housing simulate vents. They are grooved using the above method, except the 13 kerfs are ³/₃₂ in. deep, crosscut with the saw's miter gauge set square and the blade tilted at a 45° angle. Before gluing the strips, put a radius on each by rocking it back and forth on a belt sander and clean up the kerfs with an emery board.

To complete the engine housing, drill a hole in the fire wall for the steering column. Start by drilling a pilot hole at 60° and reaming the hole with a #20 (0.161 in. dia.) drill. I make the steering wheel from three pieces: a rim, a spoke center and a ⁵/₃₂-in. brass rod column. The rim is a ¹/₈-in.-thick maple disc cut with a ¹/₈-in. hole saw. Mount the disc temporarily on a spindle. Then, round the disc's edges by spinning it as you rock it back and forth against a belt sander. Next, spot-glue the disc to a scrap of veneer to support it while drilling out the center with a ³/₄-in. brad-point bit.

Finally, pry off the veneer with a knife or by sanding. The spoke center disc is sliced off the end of a ¾-in. walnut dowel. To form the four quadrants shown in the drawing, press the disc against a ½-in.-dia. drum sander, but be careful to avoid sanding your fingers. Glue the spoke disc to the inside of the rim. Then, bore a center hole and slip the finished wheel on the column, leaving ⅛ in. of the brass rod protruding for the horn.

For the floor board, cut a ¼-in.-thick piece of satiné and rip the footrest strip at 45° on the tablesaw. Four pieces of ³⁄₁₆-in.-thick rosewood make the seat, with the sides shaped as shown. Glue the seat together first, and then glue it to a mahogany block. Drill holes for the grab bars and fit them to the sides as shown. Apply the "Ahrens-Fox" name to the floor board assembly with ⅛-in.-high white rub-on letter decals, available from an art supply store.

Making the rear bed—The sides of the rear bed are two ⁵⁄₁₆-in.-thick pieces of satiné glued to a mahogany end piece. The top edges of each bed side are bored with a #9 bit, located as shown, for dowel stanchions that support the brass rail. A ³⁄₃₂-in. hole is bored through each stanchion ¹³⁄₁₆ in. up from the bottom to house the brass rails and ladder hooks. Assemble the bed and stanchions with the rails in place, and mount the hose hooks in each bed side. I used yellow satinwood for the chemical tank, which mounts behind the seat. Before shaping the edges, either with a router or by sanding, bore a ⅜-in.-dia. hole in the top for the walnut fill cap. A ¹⁄₁₆-in. hole through the cap holds its brass rod handle. Drill the holes for the front ladder hooks, slip them in place and glue on the tank.

Boring axle holes—The chassis of the fire engine is a single maple board with a notch cut out in front for the hose box assembly. Bore four ⁷⁄₃₂-in. axle holes ½ in. deep, centered on the stock. The fenders are rings I drilled with two large hole saws: a 3⅝-in. saw for the outside diameter and a 3-in. saw for the inside. One ring makes the two forward fenders and one ring is needed for each rear fender. With the larger hole saw chucked up, set your drill press for 500 RPM and drill three holes ¹⁄₃₂ in. shy of drilling through (see the above, left photo). The remaining wood anchors the fender blank while you drill out each fender with the smaller hole saw. Remove the fenders by sanding away the bottom using a 50-grit belt on a stationary belt sander. Slice the rings as shown and round the front fenders on the belt sander.

The running boards are ⁵⁄₁₆-in.-thick mahogany strips, fit and glued between the fenders. Make the sloped step from a ⁹⁄₁₆-in. by ⁹⁄₁₆-in. satiné strip ripped in half at a 45° angle. Now, glue the fenders to the chassis, keeping the grain vertical to minimize cracking. The tail platform is three pieces of ⁵⁄₁₆-in.-thick mahogany lined up with the running boards and glued to the lower edges of the rear fenders. For detail, I glue a rosewood battery box and two tool/parts boxes to the running boards.

Mounting the base and hose housings—The base is a 3¼-in.-wide by ½-in.-thick mahogany board that fits on top of the chassis. Like the chassis, the front end has a notch for the hose box, with the top edges of the prongs rounded on the belt sander. Drill four holes for mounting the piston pump, which is attached later.

The booster hose reel is made from a square mahogany block with a 1-in. hole bored through its length and one corner cut away. Glued to the ends of the reel are two 1¼-in.-dia. discs cut with a 1⅜-in. hole saw, each with a counterbored hole in the center for the axle pegs, which secure the spindle at the ends. Round the outside of the housing, except for the corner to be glued to the underside of the base, on the belt sander until it matches the discs. Cut a window in the reel to make threading the hose easier. The bed,

Left: With a large hole saw chucked in the drill press, the author makes two concentric cuts to create rings from which he'll fashion the fire engine's fenders. The same method is used for making rims and tires for the spoked wheels. Right: To keep the holes for the spoked wheels aligned in the center hub and outer rim, a home-made alignment jig is used with the drill press. Eight brass tubes pressed into the walnut outer ring act as bushings to guide the drill bit, while a round maple spacer keeps the hub centered in the rim.

engine, cockpit and pump can now be glued to the base, and the base can be glued to the chassis. Then, the booster hose reel and front hose box with bumpers can be attached to the chassis.

Cutting out spoked wheels—The wheels have a separate rim, hub, tire and eight spokes. Tires and rims are fabricated with hole saws following the same process used for the fenders. The tire requires a 2¾-in. saw for outside cuts and a 1⅝-in. saw for inside cuts. Use 1¾-in. and 1¼-in. hole saws for the rims. I used Milwaukee brand hole saws; other brands may have a different wall thickness, so check their inside cutting diameters. The hubs are slices of ⁹⁄₁₆-in. dowel bored to accept ⅛-in.-dia. spokes.

I devised the jig, shown in the above, right photo, for boring the spoke holes through the rim and hub simultaneously on the drill press. The outer ring of the 4-in.-dia. jig has eight ⁵⁄₃₂-in. brass tubes that act as drill guide bushings. The inner jig has a spacer ring that centers the hub while the spoke holes are bored. Insert ⅛-in. brass rods in the holes to keep the parts from shifting. Number and mark the orientation on each pair of rims and hubs as you work.

To assemble the rim/hub, slip two opposing spokes at one time through the rim into the hub and seat them with a large pair of pliers—there's no need for glue. Then, sand any protruding spokes flush with the rim. To assemble the wheel, bead glue on the inside of the tire and when it turns tacky, slip the rim in. Apply a heavy coat of polyurethane to keep everything in place. When the wheels are dry, bore the hub for the axle, round the edges of the tire, just as with the steering wheel earlier, and attach the finished wheels.

Finishing touches—Hoses, ladders and lights add nice detail to the fire engine. For the hoses, I use three sizes of braided polyester rope, cut with a hot knife to avoid fraying. Each rope receives a ferrule or two, made from brass tubing, and couplers made from short lengths of dowel, as shown at the bottom of figure 1. The nozzle on the booster hose is an axle peg tapered to a blunt point in a pencil sharpener. Use 2 ft. of ⁵⁄₁₆-in. rope for the pressure hose stored in the rear bed. Three lengths of ⅜-in. rope make the suction hoses: a 12-in.-long "soft" suction hose, stored in the front hose box, and two 7½-in.-long "hard" suction hoses that mount on hooks aside the bed. Each hard hose is stiffened with a ³⁄₆₄-in. brass rod threaded through the center. The strainer for the soft suction hose is a ⅜-in. dowel, rounded on one end and wrapped with fiberglass window screening.

Each ladder is made by fitting 11, ⅛-in. dowels into two cherry rails. The headlights are pegged to the corners of the radiator. To

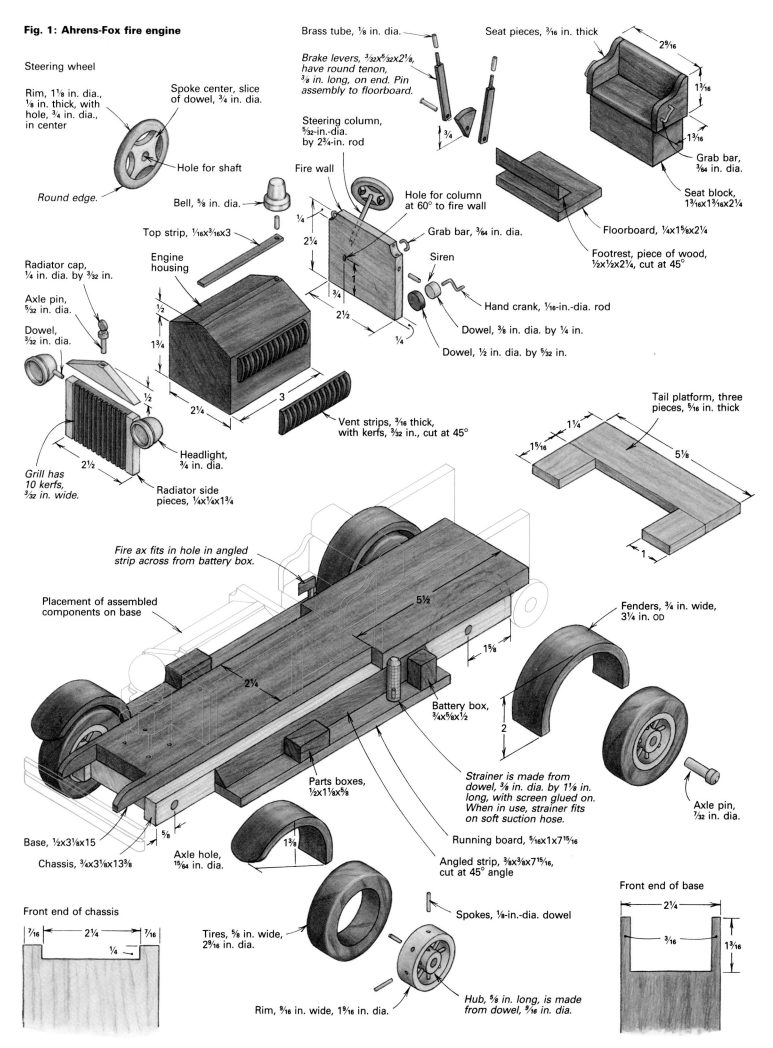

Fig. 1: Ahrens-Fox fire engine

Steering wheel

Rim, 1⅛ in. dia., ⅛ in. thick, with hole, ¾ in. dia., in center

Spoke center, slice of dowel, ¾ in. dia.

Hole for shaft

Round edge.

Brass tube, ⅛ in. dia.

Seat pieces, 3/16 in. thick

2 9/16

1 3/16

1 3/16

Brake levers, 3/32x5/32x2⅛, have round tenon, ⅜ in. long, on end. Pin assembly to floorboard.

¾

Steering column, 5/32-in.-dia. by 2¾-in. rod

Fire wall

Bell, ⅝ in. dia.

Top strip, 1/16x3/16x3

Hole for column at 60° to fire wall

Grab bar, 3/64 in. dia.

Grab bar, 3/64 in. dia.

Seat block, 1 3/16x1 3/16x2¼

Floorboard, ¼x1⅝x2¼

Footrest, piece of wood, ½x½x2¼, cut at 45°

Radiator cap, ¼ in. dia. by 3/32 in.

Engine housing

¼

2¼

¾

2½

1

¼

Siren

Hand crank, 1/16-in.-dia. rod

Dowel, ⅜ in. dia. by ¼ in.

Dowel, ½ in. dia. by 5/32 in.

Axle pin, 5/32 in. dia.

Dowel, 3/32 in. dia.

½

1¾

½

2¼

3

Headlight, ¾ in. dia.

Grill has 10 kerfs, 3/32 in. wide.

2½

Radiator side pieces, ¼x¼x1¾

Vent strips, 3/16 thick, with kerfs, 3/32 in., cut at 45°

Tail platform, three pieces, 5/16 in. thick

1¼

1 5/16

5⅛

1

Fire ax fits in hole in angled strip across from battery box.

Placement of assembled components on base

5½

1⅝

Fenders, ¾ in. wide, 3¼ in. OD

2¼

2

Battery box, ¾x⅝x½

Strainer is made from dowel, ⅜ in. dia. by 1⅛ in. long, with screen glued on. When in use, strainer fits on soft suction hose.

Axle pin, 7/32 in. dia.

Parts boxes, ½x1⅛x⅝

Base, ½x3⅛x15

Chassis, ¾x3⅛x13⅜

Axle hole, 15/64 in. dia.

1⅜

Running board, 5/16x1x7 15/16

Angled strip, ⅜x⅜x7 15/16, cut at 45° angle

Front end of base

2¼

3/16

1 3/16

5/8

Front end of chassis

7/16

2¼

7/16

¼

Tires, ⅝ in. wide, 2 9/16 in. dia.

Spokes, ⅛-in.-dia. dowel

Rim, 9/16 in. wide, 1 9/16 in. dia.

Hub, ⅝ in. long, is made from dowel, 9/16 in. dia.

Drawing: Lee Hov

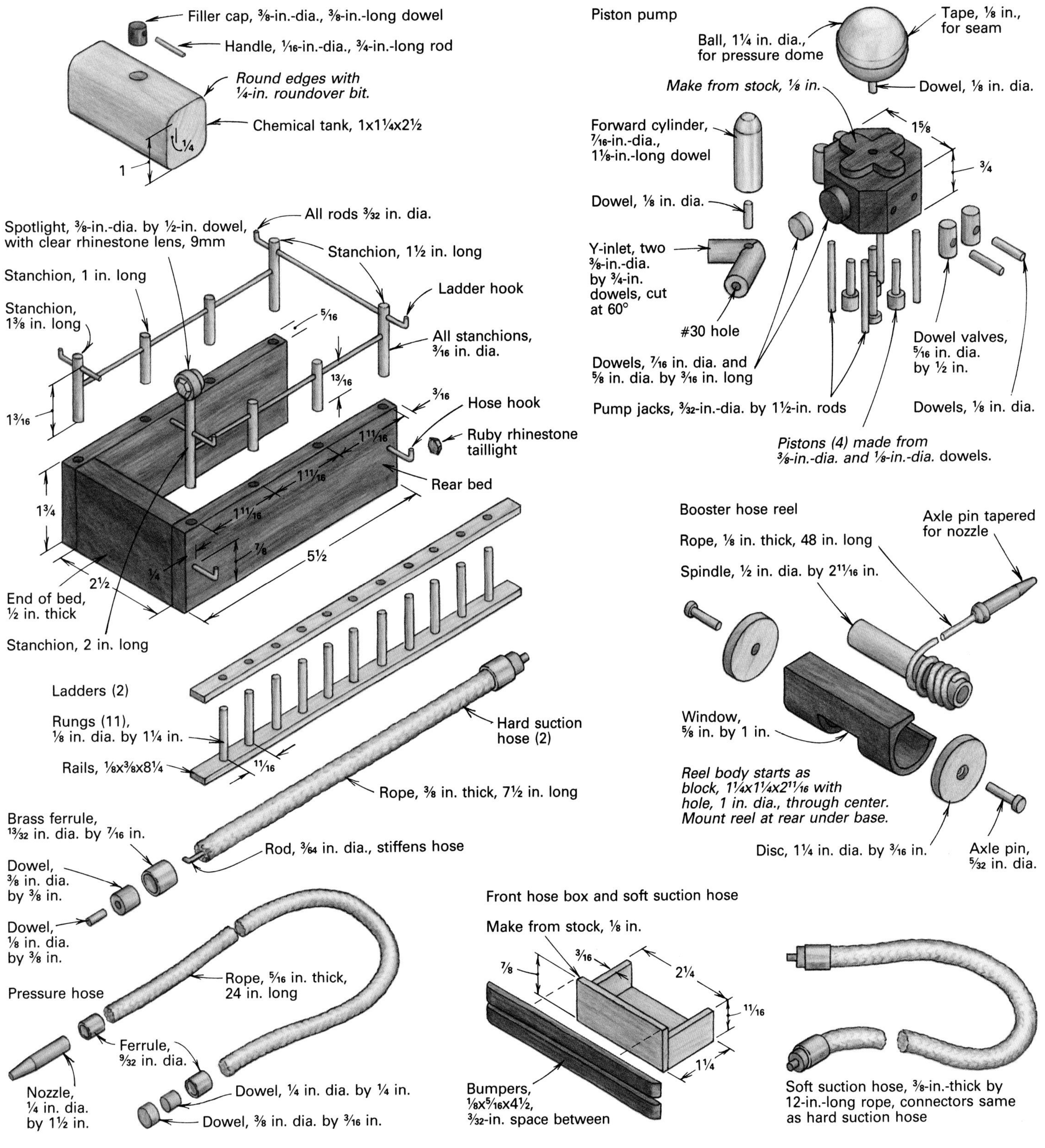
Filler cap, 3/8-in.-dia., 3/8-in.-long dowel
Handle, 1/16-in.-dia., 3/4-in.-long rod
Round edges with 1/4-in. roundover bit.
Chemical tank, 1x1 1/4x2 1/2
1/4
1
Piston pump
Ball, 1 1/4 in. dia., for pressure dome
Tape, 1/8 in., for seam
Make from stock, 1/8 in.
Dowel, 1/8 in. dia.
Forward cylinder, 7/16-in.-dia., 1 1/8-in.-long dowel
1 5/8
3/4
Dowel, 1/8 in. dia.
Y-inlet, two 3/8-in.-dia. by 3/4-in. dowels, cut at 60°
#30 hole
Dowels, 7/16 in. dia. and 5/8 in. dia. by 3/16 in. long
Dowel valves, 5/16 in. dia. by 1/2 in.
Pump jacks, 3/32-in.-dia. by 1 1/2-in. rods
Dowels, 1/8 in. dia.
Pistons (4) made from 3/8-in.-dia. and 1/8-in.-dia. dowels.
Spotlight, 3/8-in.-dia. by 1/2-in. dowel, with clear rhinestone lens, 9mm
All rods 3/32 in. dia.
Stanchion, 1 1/2 in. long
Stanchion, 1 in. long
Ladder hook
Stanchion, 1 3/8 in. long
5/16
All stanchions, 3/16 in. dia.
13/16
1 3/16
3/16
Hose hook
1 11/16
Ruby rhinestone taillight
1 11/16
Rear bed
1 3/4
1 11/16
7/8
5 1/2
1/4
2 1/2
End of bed, 1/2 in. thick
Stanchion, 2 in. long
Ladders (2)
Rungs (11), 1/8 in. dia. by 1 1/4 in.
Rails, 1/8x3/8x8 1/4
11/16
Hard suction hose (2)
Rope, 3/8 in. thick, 7 1/2 in. long
Brass ferrule, 13/32 in. dia. by 7/16 in.
Dowel, 3/8 in. dia. by 3/8 in.
Rod, 3/64 in. dia., stiffens hose
Dowel, 1/8 in. dia. by 3/8 in.
Pressure hose
Rope, 5/16 in. thick, 24 in. long
Ferrule, 9/32 in. dia.
Nozzle, 1/4 in. dia. by 1 1/2 in.
Dowel, 1/4 in. dia. by 1/4 in.
Dowel, 3/8 in. dia. by 3/16 in.
Booster hose reel
Rope, 1/8 in. thick, 48 in. long
Axle pin tapered for nozzle
Spindle, 1/2 in. dia. by 2 11/16 in.
Window, 5/8 in. by 1 in.
Reel body starts as block, 1 1/4x1 1/4x2 11/16 with hole, 1 in. dia., through center. Mount reel at rear under base.
Disc, 1 1/4 in. dia. by 3/16 in.
Axle pin, 5/32 in. dia.
Front hose box and soft suction hose
Make from stock, 1/8 in.
7/8
3/16
2 1/4
11/16
1 1/4
Bumpers, 1/8x5/16x4 1/2, 3/32-in. space between
Soft suction hose, 3/8-in.-thick by 12-in.-long rope, connectors same as hard suction hose

make the spotlight, bore a concentric hole with a 3/8-in. brad-point bit into a 1/2-in.-dia. mahogany dowel. Slice 3/8 in. off the bored end, slip a 4-in. length of 3/8-in.-dia. dowel into the hole, for a handle, and round the back side of the disc. Glue a 9mm rhinestone (available at a hobby shop) in the hole and pin the spotlight atop the bed stanchion with a 3/64-in. brass rod. Glue two 8mm ruby-color rhinestones to the rear edge of the bed for taillights.

The radiator cap is a 5/32-in. axle peg and a slice of 1/4-in. brass rod. Shorten the peg by 1/4 in., and then sand the head to 3/32 in. high. Slice a 3/32-in. disc from the brass rod, glue it to the peg and fit it atop the radiator. A small silver bell, about 5/8 in. in diameter (available from a craft supply store) is pinned or glued atop the fire wall.

To make the brake/shift lever assembly, whittle a 5/64-in.-dia. round tenon on two walnut sticks and slip on a brass tube handle. The lever base is a triangular piece of 1/8-in. maple with a radius cut on the shortest side. Secure the lever assembly to the floor board with a brass pin. The siren is two pieces of dowel glued together with a 1/16 in. brass rod hand crank and pegged to the fire wall. A miniature ax (item #756) on the right running board is available from Sir Thomas Thumb, 914 Landis Ave., Lancaster, Pa. 17603. To complete the fire engine, brush a satin finish on the wood and apply clear nail polish on the brass parts to prevent tarnishing. □

Doug Kenney builds wooden model vehicles in South Dennis, Mass.

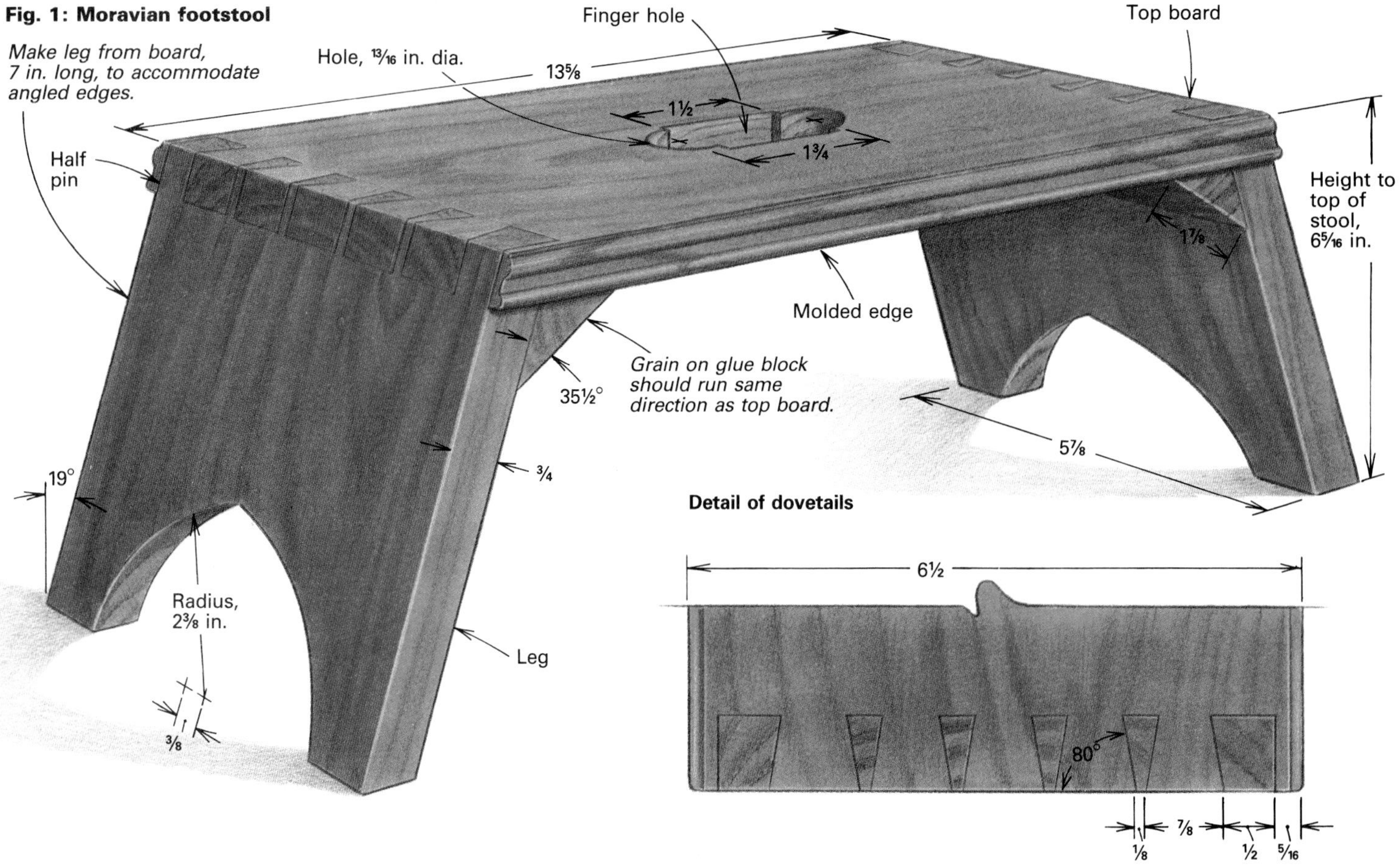
Fig. 1: Moravian footstool
Make leg from board, 7 in. long, to accommodate angled edges.
Hole, 13/16 in. dia.
Finger hole
13⅝
Top board
1½
1¾
Half pin
Height to top of stool, 6 5/16 in.
1⅞
Molded edge
Grain on glue block should run same direction as top board.
35½°
5⅞
19°
¾
Detail of dovetails
6½
Radius, 2⅜ in.
Leg
⅜
80°
⅛
⅞
½
5/16

A Moravian Footstool

Angled dovetails for strength and beauty

by David Ray Pine

Cutting angled dovetails isn't any more difficult than cutting dovetails that meet at right angles, even though they look as if they would be. And angled dovetails can make very strong and attractive joints, as in the footstool shown in the drawing above. The stool is a reproduction of one that was very popular in the old Moravian town of Salem, N.C., in the late 1700s. The single-board top is joined to the two legs with through dovetails so the legs splay at 19° from perpendicular. This sturdy little stool is an excellent example of joinery that's been applied correctly to meet a specific function both visually and structurally. Visually, the angled dovetails present themselves nicely on the obtuse corner of the stool. Structurally, the splay of the legs keeps the stool from racking side to side and the shape of the tails cut on the top resists the outward force on the angled legs as weight is applied to the top of the stool.

All you need to build this stool is one ¾-in.-thick hardwood board, 30 in. long by 6½ in. wide. This will be the finished width of the top. The legs will be ripped down to 5⅞ in. wide after they're crosscut from the board. The ⅝-in. difference in width between the top and legs allows a 5/16-in. overhang for the molded edges on the top (see figure 1 above). For crosscutting the top and legs to length, tilt the sawblade to 19°. The angles on the opposite ends of the top both splay away from the upper face so that when the top is viewed from the edge, it's a trapezoid. Conversely, the opposite ends of each leg should angle in the same direction, forming a parallelogram when viewed edgewise. If the finished length and height of your stool is critical, cut the parts a bit long, 1/32 in. for legs and 1/16 in. for the top, so you can cut the pins and tails to protrude 1/32 in. past their mating surfaces when the joint is pulled up tight. Cutting the parts a little long is a common practice with dovetails because it's much easier to plane the ends of the pins and tails flush with the faces of the boards after glue up than it is to plane the faces flush with slightly undercut pins and tails.

Drawing: Bob La Pointe

The first step in making 90° dovetails is scribing a line around the end of each piece with a marking gauge set to the length of the tails and pins. But, with angled dovetails, a standard marking gauge won't work because the ends of the workpieces aren't square with the fence of the gauge. If you're only cutting one or two joints, you can use a square to scribe lines on the boards' faces and an adjustable T-bevel to transfer the angle across the edges. However, since I build these stools 6 or 12 at a time, I made a marking gauge specifically for 19° angle dovetails on ³/₄-in.-thick stock. By making the gauge with an obtuse angle (109° for the stool), I can use it to scribe the acute side as well by holding the beam of the gauge down on the surface of the board and running the inside corner of the gauge's angle along the acute angle on the end of the board (see the top photos at right). If you make a marking gauge for angled dovetails, don't forget that the depth of the pins and tails is measured along the angle so it will be greater than the thickness of the stock. My gauge for the footstool actually scribes a line ²⁷/₃₂ in. from the end of the board to allow for the angle plus ¹/₃₂ in. for the pins and tails to extend as mentioned earlier. Joining boards of two different thicknesses requires two gauges that have scribing points at different distances from the angle.

Next, lay out the ends of the pins on the legs just as you would a 90° joint, with a half-pin at each edge and the other pins evenly spaced between. Square the pin lines down to the scribed length, and then saw them with a backsaw, stopping at the scribed lines. If you love handwork, or only have a few joints to cut, you can chop out the waste between the pins with a mallet and chisel. As with any dovetail, chisel from both sides toward the center, to avoid splitting out the grain on the board's face, and slightly undercut toward the center of the board. Here's another place where I use a fixture to speed the work for the stools. I made a "pitchboard," which presents the pins at 19° to my bandsaw blade, so I can saw most of the waste away, as shown in the bottom photo at right. In this way, I have only to chisel out the triangular piece left alongside each pin and pare the bottoms of the tail sockets cleanly to the scribed lines. Be sure to make the ramp of your pitchboard long enough so that you can also use it to bandsaw the tails on the stool's top, which is the next step.

After the pins are done, lay out for the tails by standing the pins on the inside of the top board with the wide end of the pins on the scribed line. Now, trace around the pins with a knife, and square the lines from the pins across the end of the board. You can saw the tails out by hand for just a few joints, but if you're making multiples and you already have the pitchboard, you can use it to bandsaw the waste from between the tails. In either case, finish up the tails by paring to the scribed stop lines with a chisel and the joint is ready for assembly. Depending on how confident you are about your dovetail skills, you may need to test-fit the joints and fine-tune them.

All that's left are the finishing touches. Cut the molding profile on the edges of the top with a molding plane or shaper and lay out for the finger hole. Drill two ¹³/₁₆-in.-dia. holes, 1¾ in. apart, and then with a coping saw or scroll saw, cut out a 1-in. by 1½-in. rectangle to connect them, as shown in figure 1. Draw and bandsaw the 2³/₈-in.-radius gothic arch on the bottom of each leg and clean up the cut using a drum sander or by hand-sanding.

Now you can glue up the dovetails. Spread glue on all mating surfaces and, bracing the legs of one end piece against a stop fixed to the workbench, drive the top onto the pins with a rubber mallet. The original Moravian footstools, which this stool was patterned after, had triangular glue blocks nailed behind each joint for added reinforcement. Unfortunately, the grain of the blocks ran cross-grain to the stool's top and legs, leading to problems when the

A shopmade marking gauge makes it easy to scribe lines for the pin and tail depth. Two blocks are glued and screwed together at the angle of the stool's joint and a nail scribes the line. The gauge's obtuse angle makes it possible to mark the same distance from the end on both sides of the board.

The author bandsaws most of the waste from between the pins using a pitchboard to support the leg at a 19° angle. The pitchboard can also be used to saw the tails on the stool's top board by removing the stop block that's screwed halfway up the ramp.

stool's boards expanded or contracted. On the reproductions that I build for Old Salem, I cut the blocks so their grain coincides with that of the stool, and glue and clamp them in place immediately after assembling the stool. Clamping from the base of the triangle to the outside corner of the stool ensures that when the glue sets, both legs will be at the prescribed 19° angle at which the triangles are cut. However, because angled dovetails are so mechanically strong, you might want to assemble your stool before gluing it up and give it a weight test. If your joints are well made, you may decide that the glue blocks are unnecessary. □

David Ray Pine builds period reproductions in Mt. Crawford, Va., and is the only person licensed by Historic Old Salem, Inc. to make this footstool for resale. However, a full-scale plan for the Moravian footstool, drawn by Carlyle Lynch, is available for personal use from T. Bagge Merchant, the museum store in Historic Old Salem, 626 S. Main St., Winston-Salem, N.C. 27101.

Fireplace Bellows

Wood and leather conjure up a breeze

by Glenn Elvig

I didn't plan on going into the bellows-making business. It started about 10 years ago when a friend asked if I would make her a fireplace bellows with a horse's head carved in it. I suggested it would be easier to buy a nice, plain wooden bellows and just carve the horse's head. But the local stores selling fireplace equipment offered only poorly built, imported bellows that didn't work very well. Carving a horse's head on such a poor product seemed inappropriate at best.

I decided to make a bellows from scratch. The design I came up with worked well and was surprisingly easy to build, and I soon realized that a line of fireplace bellows would complement the wood sculptures and carved signs we were making in my studio. Today, we make more than 200 bellows a year for fireplace stores, gift shops and galleries. They range in price from $75 to $350.

Bellows first appeared sometime in the Middle Ages when blacksmiths used large ones to speed up combustion in their forges. It probably wasn't long after that someone figured a smaller bellows would increase the heat from a cooking fire. By the 17th century, craftsmen were building ornate hand-bellows, inlaid with pewter and mother-of-pearl, for the homes of the rich. But, no matter how fancy the outside of a bellows may be, they all work the same way.

In its simplest form, a bellows is nothing more than an inflated bag with a nozzle at one end. Squeezing the bag expels the air. I once saw a Mongolian nomad employ the same principle by trapping air in a goat skin and then expelling the air through the neck of a broken bottle aimed at her cooking fire. The bellows I make, however, are more attractive and slightly more complicated. They consist of two pear-shape boards joined at their edges by a leather apron, which forms a chamber. The leather apron is widest at the heel of the bellows and tapers at the nose, where it acts as a hinge to hold the two boards together. The leather apron folds loosely when the bellows collapses and expels air; the leather stretches open as the bellows is inflated. A small piece of leather wrapped around the nozzle makes the bellows chamber airtight and reinforces the hinge.

One of the boards has a hole in its center, which is sealed on the inside by a leather flap that forms an inward-opening, one-way valve. Opening the bellows creates a vacuum in the chamber that sucks in the leather valve, breaking the seal over the hole and letting air flow into the chamber. Collapsing the bellows pressurizes the chamber, closing the leather valve. As the bellows collapses, the air is expelled through the nozzle.

I make both small and large bellows, as you can see in the photo below. The pear-shape sides can be easily modified to accommodate a variety of designs. One thing I've found, however, is

The author's leather-and-wood bellows can be built in any size, although overall weight should not be more than about 2 lbs. The smaller bellows here, made from butternut, has a sculptured inlay. The larger partridge-wood bellows has cut-out sides backed up with leather-covered lauan plywood to reduce weight.

Fig. 1: Bellows construction

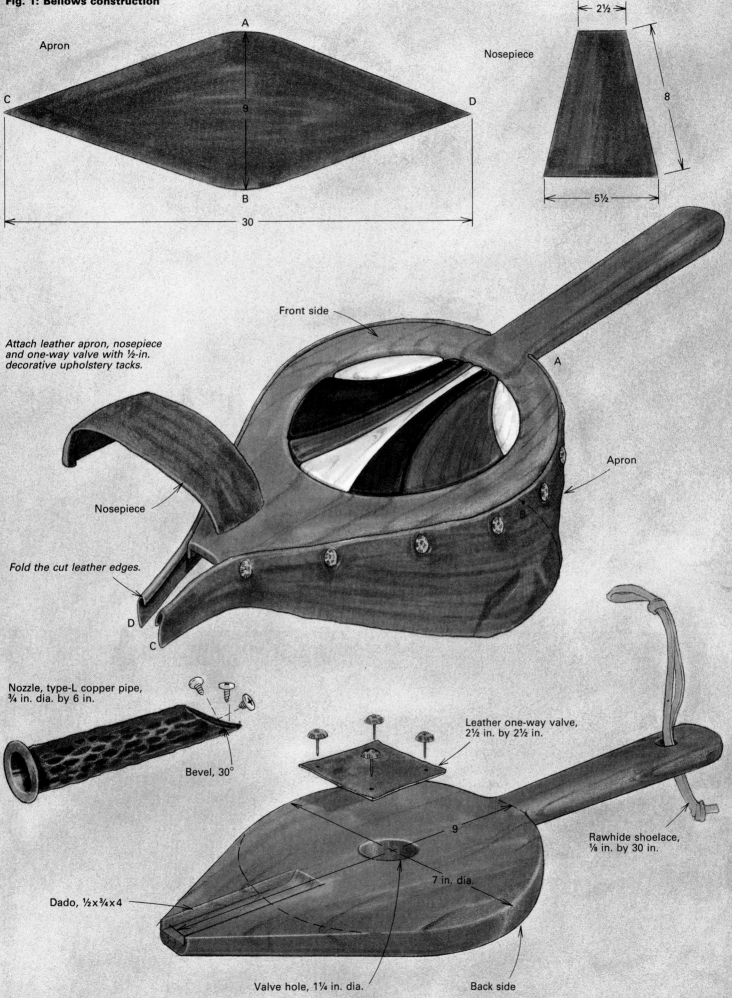

Apron

A

C

D

9

B

30

2½

Nosepiece

8

5½

Front side

Attach leather apron, nosepiece
and one-way valve with ½-in.
decorative upholstery tacks.

A

Apron

B

Nosepiece

Fold the cut leather edges.

D

C

Nozzle, type-L copper pipe,
¾ in. dia. by 6 in.

Bevel, 30°

Leather one-way valve,
2½ in. by 2½ in.

9

Rawhide shoelace,
⅛ in. by 30 in.

Dado, ½ x ¾ x 4

7 in. dia.

Valve hole, 1¼ in. dia.

Back side

that people don't like lifting heavy bellows. That's why the large partridge wood bellows shown has cutout sides. Partridge wood is very heavy, but by cutting out the sides and backing them up with leather-covered 1/8-in. lauan plywood, I reduce the weight of the large bellows until it's only 12 oz. more than the smaller bellows. Ideally, a bellows should weigh no more than about 2 lbs.

You might be tempted to build a large bellows right off, but I recommend you start with a 7-in.-dia. bellows. This size provides just about the right amount of forced air to fan the flames in the average fireplace without blowing ashes all over the room.

Making the sides—You'll need two pieces of 7-in. by 17-in. stock, planed 3/4 in. thick, for the sides. The smaller bellows shown is butternut, but you can use any hardwood. Before bandsawing the sides, I dado a slot in the center of each board just wide enough to accommodate the nozzle, as shown in figure 1 on the previous page. I lay out the pear-shape sides so the nose area on each of the mating halves surrounds its dado. After bandsawing the sides, I sand the sawn edges perfectly smooth and square. I also drill the hole shown for the one-way valve and drill and countersink a 1/4-in.-dia. hole in the handle for a leather thong.

I round over the outer edges of the main body with a router and 3/8-in.-dia. roundover bit, but I leave the inner edges square. The leather apron will cover the inner edges, and the square edge provides a wide surface to drive the tacks into. I round all the edges of the handles to create a comfortable grip, as well as round the edges of the valve hole on the inner and outer surfaces of the bellows sides. After finish-sanding the sides, I lacquer or varnish them.

Making the nozzle—I make the nozzle from a 6-in. length of 3/4-in.-dia. type-L copper pipe (available from building- and plumbing-supply outlets). The first step is to cut one end of the pipe at a 30° angle. (Later, this beveled end will be fastened to the dado with three small sheet-metal screws.) I peen the nozzle's entire surface, to give it the look of hand-forged iron, and flair its end on an anvil made from a 3/4-in. lag bolt. To make the anvil, saw the threaded end from the lag bolt, then file and sand the sharp edges of the head. Now clamp it horizontally in a vise. Slip the nozzle over the anvil and make small indentations by hammering the surface with the round end of a ball-peen hammer. The nozzle has been peened sufficiently when the indentations begin to overlap and flow together. Place the front end of the nozzle over the anvil's edge at about 30°. Then, carefully peen the metal to flare the final 1/8 in. of the nozzle. The nozzle is painted flat black.

To fasten the nozzle to the dado in the back side, I drill three 1/8-in.-dia. holes in the angled end of the pipe, and place it in the dado, angle-side-up. Then, using the holes in the pipe as a guide, I drill three starter holes to keep the wood from cracking and secure the nozzle with three pan-head sheet-metal screws.

Cutting and fastening the leather—Bellows leather must be soft and supple enough to fold accordian-like when the bellows collapses yet be strong enough to avoid tearing. Leather is classified by ounces per square foot, which correlates directly to its thickness (1 oz. equals 1/64 in.). I've found that 3-oz. to 3 1/2-oz. soft cowhide works best for bellows.

The bellows discussed here require about 3 sq. ft. of leather. I buy my leather by the half hide—about 20 sq. ft. to 25 sq. ft.—partly because I build so many bellows, but also because that's the only way most leather suppliers will sell it. Buying smaller amounts may be difficult, but some leather outlets, like Tandy

Leather Co., occasionally sell scraps. To find a Tandy leather outlet in your area, call (800) 433-5546.

I start my leather work by cutting out the one-way valve flap, the bellows apron and the nosepiece to the dimensions shown in the drawing. Each of the pieces is attached with 1/2-in. decorative upholstery tacks. Begin by tacking the one-way valve in place. It should be mounted loosely enough so it can pull away from the hole as the bellows expands. If the leather is stretched tightly over the hole, the valve won't open. Air, soot and possibly embers will get sucked back into the nozzle. Simply laying the leather on the hole and tacking the four corners creates just the right amount of slack to allow the valve to function smoothly.

The next step, upholstering the leather apron to both sides to form the bellows chamber, is the most difficult part of building a bellows. You must pay close attention to several things simultaneously: First, the apron must be mounted symmetrically or the handles will be skewed. Second, the apron must narrow gradually toward the nozzle until the noses are held tightly together. Third, the cut edges of the leather must be folded under to give the bellows a finished look. Fourth, the tacks must be spaced evenly and aligned with each other from side to side.

After building hundreds of bellows, I've found it easiest to fasten the apron in place while sitting on the ground, holding a bellows side between my knees. For your first bellows, however, it would be better to clamp the side in a vise. The upholstery tacks are spaced about 1 5/8 in. apart. Work with a tender touch as you install the leather, and locate the tacks correctly the first time. Making additional holes by relocating tacks just invites rips later on. I tap the tacks home very lightly with a rawhide mallet to avoid marring the leather and the tack heads. You'll find that the tacks tap easily into the endgrain at the back of the bellows, but the job gets harder in the edge-grain as you work your way around.

Begin by clamping the back side, nose-down, in a cloth-covered vise so the inside of the bellows faces you. You'll notice the widest points of the leather apron (marked A and B in the drawing) fasten directly under the handles. The narrow points (marked C and D) fasten to the nose. Begin by folding the edge of the leather over about 1/2 in. to hide the cut edge at point A. Then, holding the leather with point A directly under the handle, attach the leather with a tack on each side of the handle. Now remove the side from the vise, fold the rest of the leather edge over on each side of the handle and form the leather around the edge of the bellows. Pinch the leather together at points C and D, as shown in the top, left photo on the facing page. While holding the leather in this position, drive in a few tacks—enough to hold the apron in place—symmetrically around the edge.

Now, remount the side nose-down in the vise, but this time, turn the bellows so the outside is facing you and the leather is facing away. Align the handle of the front side with the handle of the back side. Fold the leather to finish the edge at point B and locate point B under the front-side handle in line with point A, as shown in the bottom, left photo on the facing page. Attach point B with a tack on each side of the handle, then flip the bellows over so the back-side handle is now held in the vise. Fold the cut edges of the leather over on both sides of the handle and wrap the leather around the front side of the body in the same manner that you did the back side.

Before attaching the leather all the way around with tacks, make sure the nose of each side is touching the other and the leather between the two nose sides is taut; otherwise, the hinging action at the nose of the bellows will be loose and the bellows won't work properly. If the leather is not taut between each side of the nose, fold a little extra leather under until the material is taut.

From *Fine Woodworking* magazine (September 1988) 72:66-69

Attaching the leather—*After the apron has been tacked to each side of the handle and the leather has been folded over ½ in. to finish the edge, the apron is wrapped around the body and pinched together at the nose while tacks are installed, as shown in the above photo. In the photo below, the back side of the bellows is placed nose-down in a vise. The two handles are lined up and the leather apron is ready to be tacked on both sides of the front-side handle. To seal the front of the bellows, the narrow part of the nosepiece is tacked to the back side of the bellows. Then, the leather strip is wrapped around the nose until its widest section covers the tacks that anchor the leather on the wood, as shown in the photo at right.*

Once the leather is tacked all around, remove the bellows from the vise and trim off any leather hanging out past the last tacks.

With the apron now in place, you can wrap the leather nose-piece around the nozzle. Fold the leather along the short edge of the nosepiece, then, avoiding the dado, tack the two corners of the narrow portion near the center of the nose on the back side. Fold the remaining edges under, as you did with the apron, and wrap the nosepiece around the nozzle to seal the hinge area and to conceal the tacks, as shown in the top, right photo above. Secure the nosepiece with three or four tacks around the edge.

Decorative treatments—My bellows are often decorated with carved designs or sculptured inlay. To create the sculptured inlay shown in the photo on p. 18, I scroll-sawed a 5⅝-in.-dia. circle from the front side and routed the outer edge of the opening with a ⅜-in.-dia. roundover bit. To lay out the pieces for the inlay, I traced the circle on paper, then drew arcs across the circle with a french curve to form puzzle-like shapes. I cut out the paper shapes and traced them on various species of different colored woods. It is important to consider grain orientation, color and compatibility in the design. I scroll-sawed these wooden

pieces, leaving the pencil mark so the pieces would be slightly oversize. The individual pieces were then sanded until they fit tightly together. I used a belt sander to sand convex curves and various sizes of drum sanders to sand concave curves. Once the shaped pieces fit together nicely inside the circle, I rounded the tops of the pieces with the belt and drum sanders to create a pillowy effect. (Needlenose pliers are real finger-savers when sanding small pieces.) All of the shaping operations were done with 100- to 120-grit sanding belts and drums. Then all the pieces were hand-sanded with 150- to 180-grit paper to remove any machine marks.

To attach the puzzle pieces to the bellows, I glued a piece of ⅛-in. lauan plywood on the inside of the opening, then glued the shapes onto the lauan.

Regardless of whether you make your bellows fancy or plain, you'll find that this shopmade fireplace bellows will provide a healthy amount of air, giving new life to dying embers. ☐

Glenn Elvig is a sculptor and makes fireplace bellows at his studio in Minneapolis, Minn. The specific designs shown in this article have been copyrighted by the author.

Walnut lap desk features a durable, lacquered writing surface and storage for every correspondent's necessities. The decorative corners are tablesawn finger joints. Beneath the hinged top, right, are compartments for legal-size paper, envelopes and pencils.

Walnut Lap Desk
Cutting corners with finger joints

by Kelly Mehler

When my partner and I went into business about ten years ago, we found that most people at craft fairs couldn't afford a trestle table or chest of drawers. If we were going to survive, we knew we had to offer accessories—affordable and easily transported items like quilt racks and boxes. My partner, Peter Blunt, designed and built the prototype of the lap desk described here and shown above. This functional object, made of nicely finished, highly figured hardwoods, was very successful. People called them Shaker desks because of the simple design, but Peter wasn't copying any style. These desks are an old idea, with many variations.

Lap desks are ideal for small-shop production runs. They don't require much wood, so you can afford good walnut or cherry. The distinctive finger joints can be cut efficiently on the table-saw, and the grooves for the bottom and shelves are all routed. In addition to being easy to cut, the fingers and slots in the joints

interlock so snugly that the box virtually squares itself up during assembly. And the large glue-surface area offered by the inter-locking components makes the joints incredibly strong. We usually made runs of 10 desks at a time. Leftover parts from one run became guides for setting the jigs for the next run. Now, I build two basic desks: the large one shown in figure 2 and a smaller one, just large enough for writing paper and envelopes.

Because grain is such an important design feature of a small object like this, I cut the stock for each desk body from a single 1½-in.-thick, 4-in.-wide plank for continuity of grain and color all the way around. The grain leads your eye around the piece, something that won't happen if a dark piece butts with a light piece or straight-grain patterns run into wild grain. I begin by crosscutting a 36-in.-long section for the body parts. I resaw the 1½-in.-thick stock into full-width, ½-in.-thick slices, plane the pieces to ⅜ in. thick and then cut out the back, front, two sides,

Drawings: David Dann; photos this page: Michele Russell Slavinsky

two dividers and shelf. Before continuing with the body, I resaw the stock for the top from a 2x5½x18½-in. plank and edge-glue the three pieces, each nearly ¾ in. thick, so the glue will have time to cure. Grain patterns are critical because the top is the most closely scrutinized surface. Quartersawn lumber is better than plainsawn, both for figure and to avoid warping. Whenever possible, I arrange the boards so all the grain patterns run in the same direction to avoid tearout when the top is surfaced.

Cutting finger joints—Large lap desks are joined by finger joints, which are made by cutting a series of equally spaced interlocking slots and fingers into the ends of mating pieces. For the pieces to interlock, the joint of one piece must begin with a finger; the joint of the mating piece must begin with a slot. Smaller desks can be made with a tongue-and-rabbet joint, shown in figure 3. To ensure accuracy and consistency from batch to batch, I've made a series of jigs for crosscutting the pieces to length, cutting the joint itself and tapering the sides.

I begin by ripping the pieces to the proper width, then crosscut them to length with the L-shaped stop jig shown in figure 1. Because the jig is attached to the saw table at an angle behind the miter fence, I have room to cut one end of the board square, move the miter gauge back, flip the piece over and butt the squared-off end against the stop, then cut again. You can adjust the jig to accommodate larger or smaller pieces.

My jig for cutting the finger joints is a simple, shop-built, fence-and-spline arrangement, shown in the photos on the next page. Basically, the jig provides a guide for stepping off the fingers and slots as you move the stock through the blade. I square

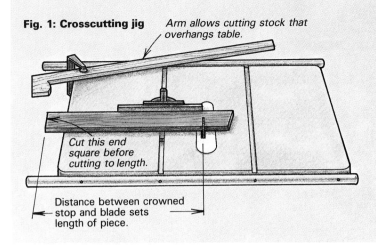

Fig. 1: Crosscutting jig — *Arm allows cutting stock that overhangs table.*

Cut this end square before cutting to length.

Distance between crowned stop and blade sets length of piece.

up a piece of stock, fit it with a spline that's exactly the width of my sawblade and screw or clamp the assembly to my tablesaw's miter gauge. Jig height isn't critical—2 in. to 4 in. is adequate for supporting the side, front and back pieces when they are held upright for the endgrain cuts. Adjust the blade so it protrudes from the table slightly more than the thickness of the stock being joined. Then, cut a slot through the miter gauge board and insert the spline.

The trick is to locate the fence so the spline is exactly one sawkerf away from the blade. You may have to do some fiddling to get it right. Sometimes the setup goes very fast, other times it seems an impossible task. The adjustment is a matter of micro-millimeters. Even a slight error compounds across the width of a

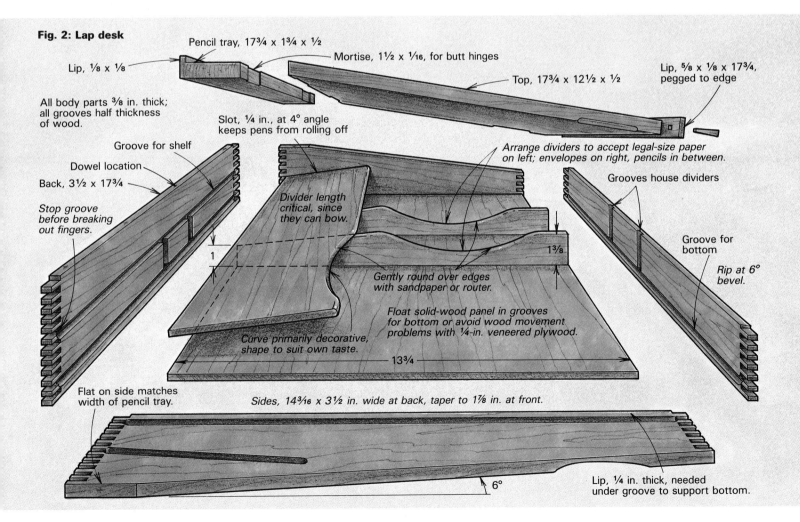

Fig. 2: Lap desk

Pencil tray, 17¾ x 1¾ x ½

Lip, ⅛ x ⅛

Mortise, 1½ x 1/16, for butt hinges

Top, 17¾ x 12½ x ½

Lip, ⅝ x ⅛ x 17¾, pegged to edge

All body parts ⅜ in. thick; all grooves half thickness of wood.

Slot, ¼ in., at 4° angle keeps pens from rolling off

Groove for shelf

Dowel location

Back, 3½ x 17¾

Arrange dividers to accept legal-size paper on left; envelopes on right, pencils in between.

Grooves house dividers

Stop groove before breaking out fingers.

Divider length critical, since they can bow.

Groove for bottom

Rip at 6° bevel.

1 3/8

Gently round over edges with sandpaper or router.

Float solid-wood panel in grooves for bottom or avoid wood movement problems with ¼-in. veneered plywood.

1

Curve primarily decorative, shape to suit own taste.

13¾

Flat on side matches width of pencil tray.

Sides, 14 3/16 x 3½ in. wide at back, taper to 1⅞ in. at front.

6°

Lip, ¼ in. thick, needed under groove to support bottom.

The finger-joint jig locates the spline one sawkerf from the blade so each cut leaves a finger equal to the blade width.

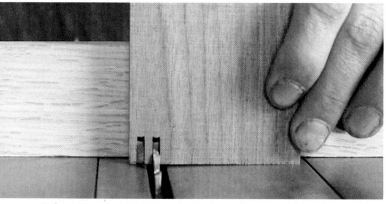

Before the next slot is cut, the board is moved so the previous slot fits over the spline. The process is repeated until fingers and slots are cut across the width of the board.

The first half of the joint begins with a finger, so the mating piece must begin with a slot. The initial finger on the first piece becomes a stop for cutting the first slot on the mating piece. After the slot is cut, the sequence is the same as described above.

Minor miscalculations can be rectified by ripping the pieces narrower so each joint ends with the same element it began with—a full-width slot or finger. This makes the ends interchangeable, and pieces can be flipped to hide a defect or pitch pocket.

board to create a no-go situation. Here is where your test pieces come in. Cut a few fingers on ends of scrap and see if they fit together. If not, move the jig one way or the other.

Because the fit is so precise, I remove the piece after each cut before retracting the miter gauge for the next cut. Blade choice varies, too. I use a regular 50-tooth combination blade, which leaves slight crown at the top of the slots. A 30-tooth rip blade or specially sharpened blade would probably leave a flatter surface, but I don't think the crown detracts from the joint's visual appeal.

Ideally, each joint should start and end with the same element, either a slot or a finger. This isn't absolutely necessary, but it lets you flip each piece end-for-end and cut both sides at the same time with the same setup. I always cut the first piece so the joint begins with a finger. That way you can butt the piece against the spline, as shown in the top photo at left, and the positive stop of the spline eliminates having to align the stock with the kerf in the support board the first time the jig is used. After cutting the first slot, which simultaneously creates the first finger, I move the board so the new slot can be slid down on the spline and the next slot-finger pair can be cut. The process is repeated until the fingers and slots extend across the width of the board. After completing the joint half that began with a finger, I use the first finger on the piece as a stop, as shown in the third photo at left, to cut the first slot on the mating piece.

You should size your stock to get full-width fingers or slots across the board, especially with fingers only a kerf wide. You can check the dimensions before you begin by dividing the board's width by the sawkerf's width. With larger joints cut with a dado setup instead of a sawblade, you can adjust the width of the cutter before you begin so the slots and fingers will cover the whole board. With a project like this, where the dimensions aren't critical, you have a little more flexibility if the setup is a little off and leaves a partial slot or partial finger—just rip again to remove the partial element.

After I cut all the joints, I dry assemble the basic frame to check the fit and mark the sides as left and right, to avoid cutting the taper the wrong way. Initially, we experimented with different taper angles before deciding the 6° angle looked best. I cut the taper with the jig shown in figure 4. The length of the jig isn't important as long as it doesn't interfere with the fence. What is important is adjusting the fence so the rip cut leaves the proper flat at the top and the height of the sides matches the width of the front, as shown in the drawing. I always test the setup with scrap pieces.

I cut the grooves for the bottom, shelf and dividers with an overarm router, but a table-mounted router fitted with a fence and stops would work. I dislike cutting stopped grooves on the tablesaw, because I've never felt comfortable dropping stock on a spinning blade. And even with a router, it is easy to break off the fingers at the end of the cut. When a finger does pop off, I often cut one of the scraps used for test cutting and glue it in place. Finger joints are so strong that the joint won't be significantly weakened by the patch.

I cut the angled grooves for the shelf with a pin router, again using a taper jig as I did for the sides, but this time with a 4° angle. The angle isn't critical, as long as it's the same on both sides, but the slope should be great enough to keep pencils from rolling off. The 5¼-in.-wide shelf is large enough to be functional, yet still allows a clear view of what's in the desk. The cutout also allows more hand room for picking up paper, as do the cutouts in the dividers. Before shaping the dividers, I taper them on the jig used to cut the shelf groove to ensure all the angles match.

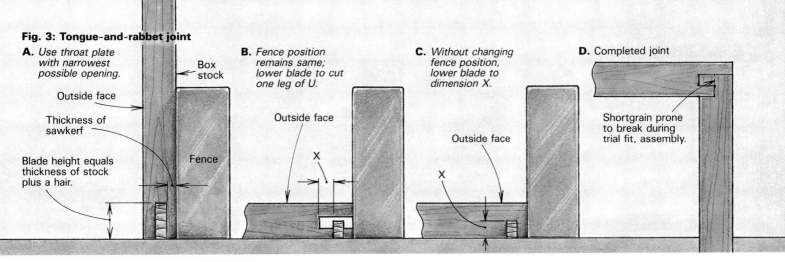

Fig. 3: Tongue-and-rabbet joint

A. *Use throat plate with narrowest possible opening.*

Box stock

Outside face

Thickness of sawkerf

Fence

Blade height equals thickness of stock plus a hair.

B. *Fence position remains same; lower blade to cut one leg of U.*

Outside face

X

C. *Without changing fence position, lower blade to dimension X.*

Outside face

X

D. Completed joint

Shortgrain prone to break during trial fit, assembly.

Assembly—I assemble the finger joints with Franklin Liquid Hide Glue. It's easy to clean up and its slow setup time is welcome with all the little pieces that must be tapped into place. The sequence for assembly is to sand or scrape the inside faces of all the components, join a side and back to form a corner, then insert the bottom and shelf. The other side and the dividers are next. The front goes on last. Excess glue is wiped off with a damp cloth as soon as it appears. Between the bottom and the tight-fitting finger joints, the box just about pulls itself square, but I do check it with a framing square and adjust if necessary. I generally don't clamp the piece unless I have a problem squaring it.

As shown in the photo on page 22, a section of the top is cut to form a pencil tray. To provide enough stock for the tray, I plane the glued-up top to ⅝ in. thick, then rip off a 1¾-in.-wide section before planing the remaining part to about ½ in. thick. Then I rabbet the thicker section with a single tablesaw cut, as shown at right, and pop off the waste to create the ⅛-in. ledge. The pencil groove is cut with a router and cove bit. The groove, which is a little longer than a new pencil, is usually located slightly above the midsection of the tray.

Before hinging the tray and top together, I take a bevel gauge and set the sawblade to the same angle as the side taper and rip a slight bevel on the upper edge of the top. This bevel allows the hinges between the tray and top to close properly. I mortise for the hinges and attach them so I can fit the tray and top to the box as a unit. Before attaching the top, however, the handholds visible on the edges of the top are routed with a 60° chamfer bit. Each handhold is about four fingers wide.

The first step in fitting the tray-and-top unit is to drive a series of brads into the top edge of the back and the flats of the sides, leaving the brads proud of the surface. Next, I clip off their heads, center the assembly on the box and force it down to mark locations of ⅛-in. dowels. After removing the brads, I bore the holes, insert the dowels, spread white glue onto the mating edges and clamp the tray down so the joint will fit tightly. The final step is to sketch out a gently chamfered recess on each side, directly under the handholds on the top, and shape them with chisels and sandpaper. Finally, the pencil catcher can be attached to the front edge with glue and little pegs.

After scraping and sanding the exterior, I spray it with one coat of sealer and two coats of lacquer. The inside gets one coat of sealer and one coat of lacquer. People like lacquer—it's durable, doesn't need to be maintained and really sets off the grain patterns of the broad writing surface. □

Kelly Mehler builds custom furniture and operates the Treefinery Gallery in Berea, Ky.

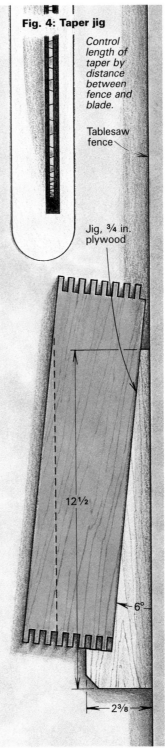

Fig. 4: Taper jig

Control length of taper by distance between fence and blade.

Tablesaw fence

Jig, ¾ in. plywood

12½

6°

2⅜

The ledge on the pencil tray is formed by rabbeting the tray on the tablesaw. A single cut, ⅛-in.-deep, into the face of the board establishes the ledge, above; any remaining waste can be broken off. Push sticks are essential on such a small piece. The pencil tray, below, is joined to the body with glue and ⅛-in. dowels, then clamped together.

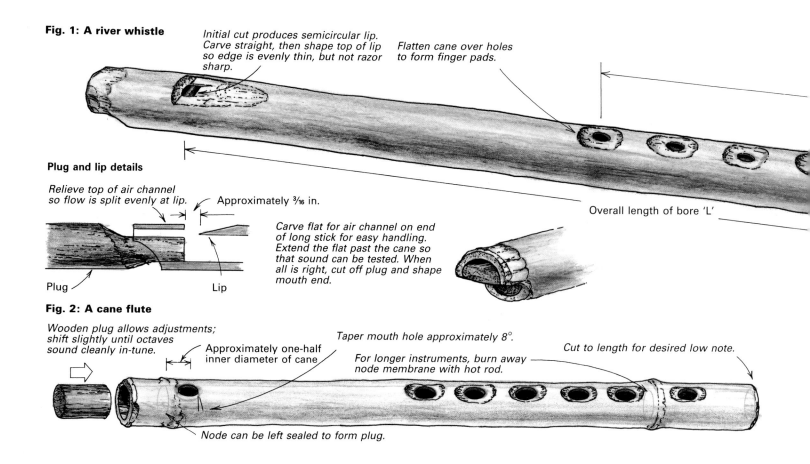

Fig. 1: A river whistle

Initial cut produces semicircular lip. Carve straight, then shape top of lip so edge is evenly thin, but not razor sharp.

Flatten cane over holes to form finger pads.

Plug and lip details

Relieve top of air channel so flow is split evenly at lip.

Approximately ³⁄₁₆ in.

Carve flat for air channel on end of long stick for easy handling. Extend the flat past the cane so that sound can be tested. When all is right, cut off plug and shape mouth end.

Plug

Lip

Overall length of bore 'L'

Fig. 2: A cane flute

Wooden plug allows adjustments; shift slightly until octaves sound cleanly in-tune.

Approximately one-half inner diameter of cane

Taper mouth hole approximately 8°.

For longer instruments, burn away node membrane with hot rod.

Cut to length for desired low note.

Node can be left sealed to form plug.

River Whistles and Cane Flutes
Pastoral pipes for plaintive tunes

by Delbert Greear

Music is a child of many parents, and surely many forces must conspire to bring forth a musical instrument. I like to think that the flute was born in a cane patch—inspired by the wind rustling the hollow reeds and brought to being by the essential spark of human inspiration.

In fact, the origin of the flute is a matter mostly of conjecture. The oldest known flutes are made of bone and date from prehistory. Pipes of hollow reed must also have been developed in the Stone Age, as they're common in the Stone-Age cultures of which we've unearthed traces. Perhaps the antiquity of the reed or cane flute helps explain why it is associated with magic and why it has been a symbol of the rustic pleasures of pastoral life since the days of ancient Greece.

Then too, a flute of reed, cane or some other sort of hollowed-out wood is light in weight and takes rough treatment well. These qualities helped make it, before the days of harmonicas (and transistors), a traditional instrument of shepherds, travelers and country revelers.

River cane—The river cane I use for making whistles and flutes is a bamboo that grows in dense groves along rivers and streams throughout the southeastern United States, ranging as far north as New Jersey and as far west as Oklahoma and Texas. It looks just like the cane seen in Chinese ink drawings.

Mature canes can be harvested any time with just a sharp knife, but watch for snakes in warm weather. The plant has little economic value, and most landowners are not jealous of a few canes—but of course, it's polite to ask.

I'm told that in parts of the country where cane doesn't grow, you might try gardening centers and even junk shops. Cane was once widely used for garden stakes and fishing poles—and is hardly ever thrown away—so it's worth a look. In fact, don't be surprised if you find that you have a suitable piece stashed away forgotten in your attic, basement or garage. For those without such resources, small quantities of suitable bamboo can be ordered from Bamboo and Rattan, 470 Oberlin Ave. S., Lakewood, N.J. 08701; (201) 370-0220.

Drawings: J. Willard Whitson

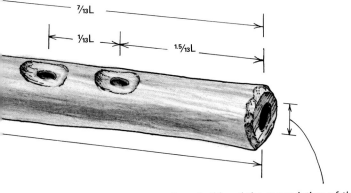

The river whistle is tuned by ear. The 'rule of thirteenths' is an approximation based on small finger holes and a bore slightly constricted at the open end. Increasing the diameter of a hole raises its pitch, as does positioning it farther up.

Length 'L' and the constriction of the bore at the lower node determine the fundamental (lowest) note of the whistle.

The river whistle – River cane is a hollow tube that's sealed at each node with a thin, hard membrane. A river whistle is typically made from a single "joint." Cut the cane into pieces just above, or right through, each nodal membrane. You can do this with a knife or a small backsaw. I generally use the upper end of the joint for the mouth, because the cane is more evenly round at this end: Use a small sharp knife to ream the membrane out of the node until its diameter is the same or slightly larger than the inside of the cane. At the other end, leave enough of the node so the tube is slightly constricted.

The next step is to cut a notch about ⅝ in. to ¾ in. from the end of the joint, as shown in figure 1. The upper end of this notch should be square with the end. The lower end of the notch is at a shallow angle, forming a rounded lip where it intersects the inner diameter of the cane. For good results, the sharp lip thus formed must now be squared off with respect to the upper end of the notch and then trimmed to an even thickness and taper. This means the top of the lip needs to be contoured to match the curve of the inside of the cane. This lip should be fairly thin and free of fibers at its leading edge, but a super-sharp edge is not desirable – it tends to create shrill overtones. The inside of river cane is fragile, so it's not a bad idea to back up the lip while shaping it with a round piece of wood inserted into the cane.

The distance from the square edge of the notch to the lip is important. If it's too small, the whistle will lack power and refuse to play the low note. If this space is too great, the little whistle will be raspy and won't play its high notes. The distance varies with the cane diameter. For a cane with an inside diameter of ½ in., a good average distance is about ⁵⁄₃₂ in. to ³⁄₁₆ in. If a longitudinal crack develops in the lip, or if something else goes wrong at this stage, it's best to discard the blank and start fresh.

The lip needs to extend down into the air channel of the mouthpiece. It will draw down into the cane a little as the cane dries, but usually one needs to scrape a little off the top of the inside of the mouthpiece, thus inletting the air channel into the cane (figure 1).

The lower side of the air channel is formed by a round plug of wood flattened on the upper side. I like to experiment with different shapes of air channels – tapering the wood to concentrate and direct the air or carving a little chamfer at the inner end – but a simple straight passage will suffice; the objective is to form a smooth stream of air that is split evenly by the lip.

Of course, before the air channel is formed, the plug must first be carved to fit snugly in the end of the cane. Plug stock may be split out of a small cut of hardwood. Walnut and maple make good whistle plugs because they don't seem to expand and contract a lot with moisture changes, and they have close, even grain as well. Carving the plug on the end of an 8-in. to 10-in. piece of wood saves the obvious hassle of holding the small plug while you carve it. Carving the flat that forms the air channel back a little past the end of the cane makes it possible to test the whistle before you cut the plug off its stock.

A smooth, soft breath should cause the river whistle to sound its low note, or fundamental. Blowing just a little harder should make it jump to its second harmonic. Harder yet and it should play its third and fourth harmonics. When you're satisfied with the response and tone of the whistle, cut the plug off at the end of the cane and shape the mouthpiece. I never glue the plug into place until the whistle is well-seasoned, as the air channel usually needs reshaping. Beeswax can be used to seal any gaps.

Tuning a whistle – The fundamental, or low note, is determined principally by the overall length of the instrument. If you want to tune a river whistle to a particular pitch, it must be done before any note holes are made. Gradually cut out the remains of the node at the open end until the whistle sounds the note desired. If this doesn't bring the note up to the pitch you want, gradually shorten the length of the tube.

The traditional, and still the best way to make the finger holes, is to burn them. I use a ¼-in. steel rod about 20 in. long, which is ground to a point. Heated in a fire to a red glow, this tool has no trouble burning through the cane. In fact, a dull rod would burn through almost as well, but the taper allows me to size the holes according to how deep I push the point.

Such a tool can inflict a serious burn and must be handled with care. One safety tip is to make a pilot hole with a knife point to prevent the rod from slipping off the cane. One could use a knife or drill for the whole job, but this leaves splinters that dull the tone, whereas the scorched edge is clean. Also, the hot steel can be used to clean and scorch the inside of the cane (any tiny loose fibers inside the tube can dull the tone) and can be used to burn out nodes as well, should you want a longer pipe.

The proportions for tuning in the drawing above are approximate. In practice, each hole should be burned out small at first, then widened until the desired pitch is reached. Essentially, each higher hole shortens the effective length of the whistle, and the shorter the whistle, the higher the note. Six holes are sufficient to produce the eight-note octave, because the eighth note can be achieved by closing all the holes and blowing a little harder.

The transverse flute – The river whistle is a pleasant companion, but it does have some shortcomings. For one thing, its volume is limited by the small size of the air passage. Also, its two-piece construction makes it prone to fall apart when it gets too dry or choke up when too moist. Once you're comfortable with the burning rod, you may want to attempt a regular transverse flute.

Generally speaking, the transverse flute is a more powerful instrument whose simplicity belies its elegance. This same simplicity also hides some difficulties. Location, size and shape of the mouth hole, or embouchure, are of prime importance in fashioning this flute. For myself, I must admit, these subjects are more a matter of constant experimentation than of strict rules. The proportions given here are therefore only a general guide.

Because the embouchure needs to be small relative to the bore, it's best to choose fairly large canes for transverse flutes. I like to saw the cane an inch or two above the node so the embouchure can be located close to the node, yet still be comfortable for the lips. A good alternative is to ream out both ends of the cane, burn the mouth hole a comfortable distance from one end and fill the end with a wooden plug. This allows some measure of control over the distance from mouth hole to plug, which can be fine-tuned for best response. By the way, if the plug is too far from the mouth hole, the flute will still play its low register, but it won't play well in its second octave.

The embouchure must also be undercut, tapered wider toward the inside of the cane. A very small amount of trash or fuzz in the hole is enough to keep the instrument from sounding. As with the river whistle, it pays to be sure the flute works well in its fundamental mode before attempting to supply it with finger holes for additional notes. Finger holes are made as they were for the river whistle. It's a little harder to make this style of flute jump to its second octave, so you may wish to furnish it with a few extra holes for additional notes (but of course, no more than you have fingers for).

The transverse flute is a difficult instrument to master. Sometimes I think it's the source of the old saying, "You're not holding your mouth right," as an explanation for a failed endeavor. And indeed it does require more skill to obtain a pure tone from this instrument than from the river whistle: I hope you'll enjoy both the practice and the making. As with most true handcrafts, monetary profits in the flute business are somewhat elusive. For a camp-fire craft, however, and pleasant hours on the riverbank, cane flutes and whistles are hard to beat. □

Delbert Greear lives in Sautee, Ga.

Twig whistles

by John Marcoux

Whistle making is a wonderful, magical experience for children. I know, because my grandfather taught me how to make whistles in Vermont when I was very young. I made them for years as a child, but as I grew older, I forgot how.

I was vaguely disquieted about this for a couple of years: I kept asking people about whistles, hoping to meet someone who knew about them and remembered how to make them. One day my wife, Alice, brought home a library book with instructions, and the process was just as my grandfather had shown me. That was six years ago, and every spring now we have three or four whistle-making sessions at our house with friends, their children and our grandchildren.

The drawings show the process. I have made successful whistles from alder and white ash, and I'm told that willow works well, too. There's not much effort involved, so experiment with whatever woods are convenient. I can tell you from experience that some woods don't work,

because you can't get the bark off in one piece, but many woods do work fine.

Spring is about the only time of year when there's enough sap under the bark for it to slip off. Clip off a section of branch with pruning shears, then whittle the stick as shown. Next, tap and rub the bark with something smooth and hard, such as the handle of a table knife, to help it break loose. Close your whole fist around the bark section and try to twist it. If it seems to stick, tap and rub some more, but not so much that you damage the bark. If there are any splits or cracks, the whistle won't work.

Gradually whittle the flat to size until you get a pleasantly surprising noise. If it doesn't work, try again with different proportions. Infinite variations are possible; both of the whistles in the photo have pleasant tones. Try various shapes and you'll soon discover that the larger and longer a whistle, the lower its note.

Sometimes whistles last very well and work for a long time, but more often,

Fig. 3: Making a whistle

A. Cut branch, whittle end angle at small end and notch as shown.
70° to 80°
¾ in.
45° to 60°
¾ in. maximum

B. Slice around bark, then tap and rub gently with hard, smooth object to loosen. Sap appearing at cuts indicates progress. Slide bark off.

C. Cut flat on mouthpiece, then cut away center of stick and discard.
¾

Approximate proportion of opening
⅛

Flat

Discard

D. Reassemble whistle and blow softly; adjust depth of flat for clear tone.

they don't whistle for more than a day or two. The bark dries out and splits, and the openings' sizes change. You can extend a whistle's life by keeping it in a sealed plastic bag, but this defeats the concept somewhat. Give your whistle to a child, who'll make the most of it for as long as it lasts and remember it a good while longer. □

To give a sense of scale, the larger whistle is ¹¹/₁₆ in. in diameter and 6 in. long.

John Marcoux lives in Providence, R.I.

Bandsawn Boxes from Burls

Diamonds from the rough

by Jeffrey Seaton

Wild-figured western burlwoods are the raw material for Jeffrey Seaton's band-sawn boxes, like the tall, nesting boxes shown above.

When I first met Bruce Byall in 1973, I was a frustrated finish carpenter living in Mendocino, Calif. Byall, a creative artist working in wood, had been making wonderful little free-style bandsawn boxes from chunks of local redwood burl. I was enchanted by the speed, simplicity, and, most of all, the creative freedom of working with the bandsaw. I'd been looking for an alternative to the redwood burl tables that I'd been making part-time, and the bandsawn box offered the obvious advantages of being a marketable small object that was intrinsically more interesting to make than a burl table.

I still have my first crude, poorly sanded redwood burl box. Although my designs and quality have improved during the last decade, my basic techniques have remained the same. In a nutshell, a bandsawn box is a container cut from one solid piece of wood, including the box bottom and the lid. Whether made from burl or a thick board, the box's outside shape is bandsawn first, then the lid is sawn off, the center plug is removed and the kerf is glued closed. This technique allows the grain to flow between the lid and box, resulting in a visual unity difficult to achieve in a conventional box made from separate pieces of wood.

Since I earn my living making boxes, I've tooled up to produce them in large numbers. I own two Rockwell (now Delta) 14-in. bandsaws, one of which is fitted with the extension kit (part #28984, $63.85) that increases the saw's depth of cut to

12½ in. I keep a ½-in. 4 tooth-per-in. blade on the older saw, with which I usually make the flat, primary cut for the bottom of each box. On the other saw, I use a ³⁄₁₆-in. 4-tpi blade, which can saw to the radius of a nickel. The smaller blade allows great maneuverability, an essential element in competent bandsawn box making. The guides on my saws are standard Rockwell issue. However, I recommend 3M silicone spray to lubricate the blade and the guides. This will also help when cutting abrasive woods.

For me, the most satisfying stage of creating a box is the actual design. Over the years, I've developed several distinct styles that fall into two rough categories. The more refined styles usually have a finished appearance, like the tall set of nesting boxes shown above. These boxes are usually drawn out on paper and exact measurements made before committing an expensive piece of exotic wood to the saw. The other style, which is the most fun, is more free-form and spontaneous, and incorporates some of the natural exterior surface of the burl or root section. I look for natural features like a branch, a knot, an interesting arch or a balanced space between these features to be the focal point of the box. Around this focal point, I cut a graceful curve, aiming to give the piece a harmonious, flowing line for the eye to follow.

Virtually any burl wood, or any large chunk of wood for that matter, is suitable for a bandsawn box. Some of my favorites are Californian mountain lilac, desert ironwood and redwood, all of

From *Fine Woodworking* magazine (March 1987) 63:70-72

Ornery burls are made manageable by gluing on scrap-wood wedges, forming a flat base that allows the burl to be safely bandsawn without danger of the blade grabbing. To make a perfect-fitting inner lid for his boxes, Seaton saws off a thin slice of the center plug and glues it to the outer lid, bottom photo.

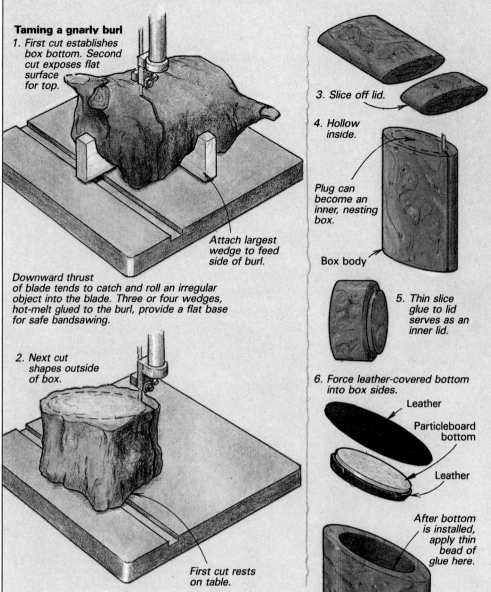

Taming a gnarly burl

1. First cut establishes box bottom. Second cut exposes flat surface for top.

Attach largest wedge to feed side of burl.

Downward thrust of blade tends to catch and roll an irregular object into the blade. Three or four wedges, hot-melt glued to the burl, provide a flat base for safe bandsawing.

2. Next cut shapes outside of box.

First cut rests on table.

3. Slice off lid.

4. Hollow inside.

Plug can become an inner, nesting box.

Box body

5. Thin slice glue to lid serves as an inner lid.

6. Force leather-covered bottom into box sides.

Leather

Particleboard bottom

Leather

After bottom is installed, apply thin bead of glue here.

which I obtain from sources in northern California. Burlwood might not be available in your area, so you might try perusing the classified ads section of this magazine for a source. One company that sells burls is Cal Oak Lumber Co., P.O. Box 689, Oroville, Calif. 95965.

Bandsawing an irregularly shaped burl is an adventurous, if not dangerous, task. It's definitely not recommended for beginning shop classes. But there is a way to do it safely. Since the blade moves downward, a roughly round object will be pulled toward the blade, spinning it downward, perhaps dragging a misplaced finger into the blade. Once the cut is past the center, the force suddenly reverses, and the block tries to turn the other way. *Always* keep your hands well to either side of the blade's line of cut. The best way to keep a round burl from rolling uncontrollably is to give it a flat surface on which to rest. I do this by hot-melt gluing three or four scrap wood wedges onto the front, side and back of the burl, as shown in the top photo and in figure 1. I bandsaw these wedges in various sizes and generally in two shapes: convex and concave. I use whichever shape fits that particular burl best, aiming for the broadest flat surface. Glue the largest wedge you can in front of the burl so there's no chance of the blade catching and pulling it up and over the base of the wedge. To ensure a good bond, I clean off any dirt or bark with an awl and compressed air before gluing the wedges. A wire wheel

on an electric drill will work if compressed air is not available.

To begin, first visualize the bottom and top of the box-to-be. Glue on the wedges, then use a ½-in. blade to make the bottom cut as straight as possible. This is a great time to check for moisture content. I use my hand to feel for any dampness. If you can feel moisture, you know the wood is too damp to work into a finished box right away. So, I shape out the rough burls into form and store them inside my shop, where the constant air flow from my ventilation fan helps dry them. Mountain lilac burl, my best-selling burlwood, dries at about 1 in. to 2 in. in thickness per year. I use a clear acrylic spray to seal the endgrain to minimize end checking.

When the wood is dry, and the bottom surface flattened, proceed with sawing the main body of the box. Pick a spot free of cracks and trim a chunk off the rough top surface to expose some figure and see that the wood is structurally sound. Then, with the wedges firmly intact, slowly cut the lid free. On a 12-in.-long box I usually cut a lid ⅝ in. thick, or whatever feels balanced to the rest of the box. The next cut, as shown in figure 2, defines the outside surfaces of the box.

One of the most frequently asked questions is: "How do you hollow them out?" There are two methods. The most involved is to thread a cut bandsaw blade through a ³⁄₁₆-in. hole bored through the box's center, then weld and grind the blade. This

As an alternative to his refined boxes, Seaton includes textural, run-of-burl edges in some of his designs.

shortens the blade life and requires a welder/grinder unit, preferably on the bandsaw. It's much easier to bandsaw directly through the side of the box, gluing the kerf closed later.

I look for a solid, check-free area at the narrowest end of the box. I saw straight in before turning to saw counterclockwise around what will become the inside of the box until I reach the entry cut. By cutting counterclockwise, the majority of an oblong box is always on the outside of the blade, giving you more throat clearance on larger boxes. Now stop the saw and back out of the open kerf. The center plug should fall right out. To cut the inner lid that holds the lid in place on this hingeless box, glue wedges to the plug and saw off a slice about ¼ in. to ½ in. thick.

I glue the inner lid on with yellow glue, applying a light coat to both parts. Take care to precisely align the outer lid with the body. Turn the box upside down and drop the inner lid down through the hole in the bottom, then position it so there's equal saw-kerf distance on all sides. Carefully lift off the box body and clamp the work for 24 hours. To glue up the seam left by the blade entry, I squirt glue into the kerf with glue injectors (available from Woodworker's Supply, 5604 Alameda N.E., Albuquerque, N.M. 87113). A combination of a band clamp and a bar clamp works well on round or oval forms. Let the box sit for a week, if possible, to acclimate. If the lid is going to warp at all, it will do so now. The warp can be sanded out later.

More than 60% of the time that goes into my bandsawn boxes is given over to sanding. My employee, Mark Wietstock, does most of the sanding. The extra effort he expends makes the difference between an ordinary production item and an heirloom. The first step is to sand the bottom completely flat on a stationary belt sander. I use the Jet Equipment and Tools combination sander, which has a 6-in. by 48-in. belt (25-grit silicon carbide) and a 12-in. disc sander (40-grit silicon carbide). The Jet is far cheaper than the Delta equivalent and for the last two years I've had no complaints. To shape, sand and bevel curved surfaces, the disc sander is the best tool for the job. Once the bottom is flat, I wire brush all the burly surfaces with a 6-in. #11-gauge wire wheel for hardwoods and a softer wheel for redwood, buckeye, or any spalted woods. I've mounted the wheels on an arbor-and-pulley setup that consists of a ½-in. chuck powered by a 1½-HP, 3,400-RPM motor stepped down to 2,600 RPM.

My rough burl boxes require no further shaping, but my more refined designs are sanded beginning with a 40-grit silicon car-

bide sanding disc mounted onto an 8-in. rubber-backed disc (available from Power Pad, 1223 W. 256th St., Harbor City, Calif. 90731, #8H50) with 3M feathering adhesive, #51135. Ideally, only bandsaw marks have to be removed at this point, but there may be a few bumps and valleys to even out. You can, if you wish, do more shaping on the disc. Subsequent sanding on an 80-grit disc will remove the deep scratches left by the 40-grit paper. Next, I switch to a 5-in. disc (Sears #28419) on a flexible shaft, sanding first with 120-grit garnet, then 180 and followed by 320-grit silicon-carbide paper. My "secret" finish is just the patience to continue on with 400-grit and 600-grit wet-or-dry paper.

After blowing off any sawdust with compressed air, I dip the entire box (including the lid) into a vat of clear Watco oil. The excess oil is blown out with compressed air and the box is hand wiped with a cotton cloth. Because of the noxious fumes, I strongly recommend a dual-cartridge organic vapor respirator and rubber gloves to minimize your exposure to the oil. I let the wood air out for three or four days before installing the bottom.

I used to slice the box bottoms off the center plug but found that these warped too much, so now I make the bottoms of ¼-in. particleboard. I simply trace the outline of the box interior right on the particleboard and bandsaw it, sanding off any rough edges. For tall, top-heavy work, I sandwich a ¼-in. layer of lead sheet between two layers of particleboard. My wife, Katrine, takes care of gluing leather to the box bottoms. I find that garment-grade, split-suede leather works best because it cuts easily, is flexible, and has a quality look to it.

Trace the outline of the particleboard bottom onto the leather, leaving ³⁄₁₆-in. surplus around the circumference. Spread a thin layer of yellow glue, apply the leather and then press the box down over the bottom. After the glue has dried overnight, trim the excess leather away with a sharp, single-edge razor blade.

To bring up a lustrous sheen on the wood, I use an 8-in. circular cotton hard pad (available from J.H. Lowe, Box 292, Old Bethpage, N.Y. 11804) mounted on a 1-HP, 3,400-RPM motor. A slight charge of tripoli compound on the wheel removes excess oil. On a second motor, I use an 8-in. lamb's-wool bonnet to apply hard carnauba wax for the final satin luster. Then, the sanded inner lid is signed and dated with a hand-held Dremel tool. □

Jeff Seaton sells his boxes at shows and in galleries. He works in Goleta, Calif.

Above left: Laurel Bernini gets ready to demonstrate the zigzag marble roll she built as a sixth grader in one of the author's classes.
Above right: Topher Wilkins uses a gouge to make a marble channel
in a piece of pine. When this section of track suits him, he'll glue it
in place on the plywood backboard. Masking tape provides the
clamping power for odd-shape pieces used for tracks or guardrails.

Making Marble Rolls
A crooked path to fun and physics

by Richard Starr

Ideas in my middle-school shop drift about like dandelion
seeds looking for fertile soil. The seeds may stay aloft for years,
but when they finally settle and take root, the blossoms
abound. So it has been with marble rolls. Even in this age of radio-
controlled cars, computer games and VCRs, kids still delight in
making these simple structures, which use gravity to propel marbles
in ingenious and amusing ways. In the process, they learn the value
of patience and care, which results in pride of accomplishment as
well as the ability to deal constructively with the frustration of
things going wrong.

Building a marble roll is an enjoyable trial-and-error exercise in
engineering and physics, a painless way to learn about motion,
friction, gravity and momentum. The photos and drawings accompanying this article illustrate the basic constructions and some of
the devices—I call them "events"—we've experimented with in
class. If you build a marble roll, you should experiment with dimensions, making adjustments as you go along. Shapes and sizes
aren't critical. The point of this project is not to follow a plan, but
to boldly roll where none has rolled before.

Zigzags—The easiest-to-build marble roll is the traditional zigzag,
like the one shown above, left. Sloping U-channel tracks made
from thin strips of pine are glued and nailed at each end to L-shape
uprights. A ¾-in.-dia. exit hole is drilled near the bottom end of
each track section and sawed through to the end so the marble can
drop through to the track below. The uprights support the tracks
and redirect the rolling marbles onto the top end of the lower

track segment. At the bottom of the zigzag, marbles are collected
in a scrapwood corral. For additional support, the uprights are fastened to a flat base. To decide how many tracks, how high and
how wide the roll will be, a child can sketch the project full-size
and take measurements from the drawing. The actual construction
is simple, requiring only hand tools, white glue and small brads.

A nifty variation is the double-track marble race shown in figure 2
on the facing page. Make your upright posts exactly as wide as two
tracks side by side. Lay out the first set of tracks and then place the
second set of tracks alongside the first, but tilted in the opposite
direction so the tracks cross in the middle.

Automatic starter—You can add to the excitement and validity of
the race with a simple mechanism for starting two marbles at the
same time. This automatic starter is made from three ¾-in.-thick
pine boards that fit between the uprights. Drill them as shown in
figure 1 on the facing page so the holes in the top piece are the
same distance apart but offset from those in the bottom and middle
pieces. The top and bottom pieces fit between the uprights, with
the middle piece, which is ¾ in. shorter, trapped between them.
When the middle piece is slid side to side, its holes line up either
with the top holes, letting a marble drop into and be trapped in
the center section; or with the bottom holes, letting a trapped marble drop onto the track. Carve sloping channels on the top board,
directed toward each hole, so several marbles can be lined up and
fed to the tracks. It's amazing to see dozens of colored glittering
balls clunk and zoom down the tracks on their way to the finish line.

From *Fine Woodworking* magazine (March 1989) 75:78-81

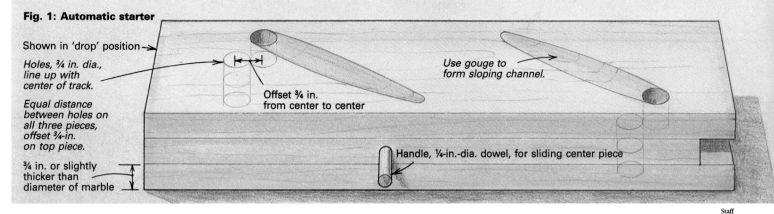

Fig. 1: Automatic starter

Shown in 'drop' position →

Holes, ¾ in. dia., line up with center of track.

Equal distance between holes on all three pieces, offset ¾-in. on top piece.

Offset ¾ in. from center to center

Use gouge to form sloping channel.

¾ in. or slightly thicker than diameter of marble

Handle, ¼-in.-dia. dowel, for sliding center piece

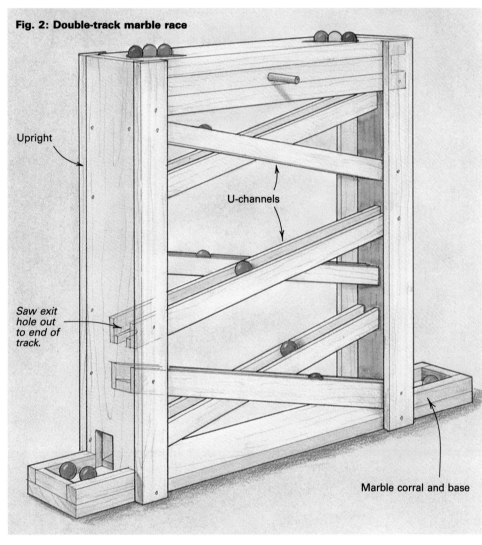

Fig. 2: Double-track marble race

Upright

U-channels

Saw exit hole out to end of track.

Marble corral and base

The author built this three-dimensional marble roll to show his students what is possible when basic 'events' are combined within, on and around a simple framework. Rube Goldberg, eat your heart out!

Chutes and ladders–After mastering the zigzags, many kids move on to building chutes-and-ladders marble rolls on a piece of plywood mounted vertically in a simple stand (see the top, right photo on the facing page). Although they begin as two-dimensional constructions, paths often run out from the board and sometimes bore through it. The backboard is a less restrictive structure than the uprights of the zigzags, offering more opportunity for experimentation. Sometimes we miter the U-channel track for the zigzag rolls into curves, steps and even spirals by gluing segments end to end and using masking tape to hold the pieces until the glue dries.

As imaginations run rampant, students raid the bandsaw scrap box for odd-shape pieces that can be glued to the backboard to alter the marble's path. A gouged path in a block of wood or a guardrail in just the right place keeps the marble on track. And

a small wedge at the start will add to the marble's speed, enabling it to overcome obstacles farther down the line.

Three dimensionals–If building a backboard marble roll is like composing a quick and amusing scherzo, three-dimensional rolls are a symphony. There is less structure to fasten things to, but room for much more to happen. The framework is four upright ½-in.-dia. dowels glued in holes bored at the corners of an H-shape base. We use U-channel tracks mitered and glued into various shapes and doweled to the uprights. Begin at the top and work your way down. Think of strange things you can make the marble do. To encourage the kids, I built the marble roll shown in the photo above. It is 3 ft. high, with three separate paths. Several different events cause the marbles to accelerate, slow down, spin wildly, rumble or fall abruptly along the way. An automatic switch-

Drawings: Kathleen Creston

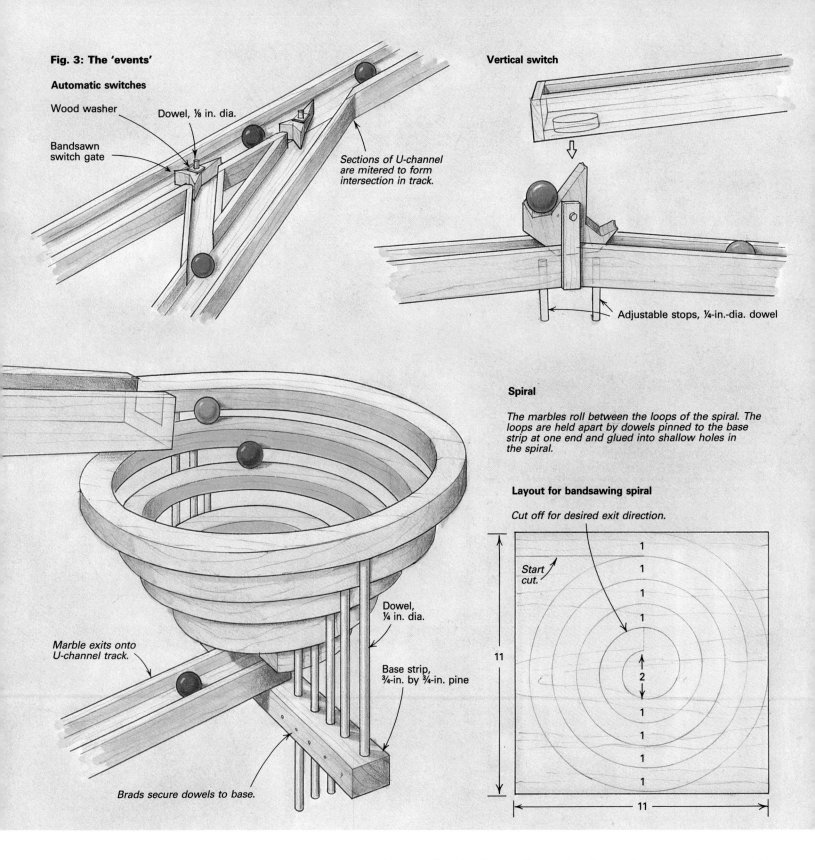

Fig. 3: The 'events'

Automatic switches

Wood washer

Dowel, ⅛ in. dia.

Bandsawn switch gate

Sections of U-channel are mitered to form intersection in track.

Vertical switch

Adjustable stops, ¼-in.-dia. dowel

Marble exits onto U-channel track.

Dowel, ¼ in. dia.

Base strip, ¾-in. by ¾-in. pine

Brads secure dowels to base.

Spiral

The marbles roll between the loops of the spiral. The loops are held apart by dowels pinned to the base strip at one end and glued into shallow holes in the spiral.

Layout for bandsawing spiral

Cut off for desired exit direction.

Start cut.

11

11

1
1
1
1
2
1
1
1
1

ing system feeds marbles to the various paths in sequence, and at the bottom, a marble pulls a lever that starts another at the top. The major events on this machine can be used together or alone on rolls as simple or complex as you care to build.

Switches—Any marble can be directed to a variety of paths by using intersections and automatic switches. Furthermore, several switches can be used together to introduce an element of surprise. A simple switch gate is shaped like a three-point star and swivels on a dowel inserted in the track floor where two tracks intersect, as shown in figure 3 above. The gate swivels until its long leg hits the sidewall, opening one path and closing the other. A marble

rolling by the gate hits a short leg in the open path, causing the switch to swivel to its alternate position. Beveling the bottom edges of the gate will keep it from hanging up on the track surface. A small piece of scrapwood acts as a nut to hold the gate on the dowel.

The basic principle is the same for a vertical switch. When a marble drops onto a vertical switch through a hole in the track above, it is directed to one of two paths, and the position of the switch is simultaneously reversed. Dowels located in the floor of the track limit the gate's tilt. To ensure that the marble doesn't roll off the side of the switch, you can hollow out the edge of the switch slightly with a gouge and cup the lip where the marble exits. Or, you can make the switch with a narrow sidewall to contain the marble.

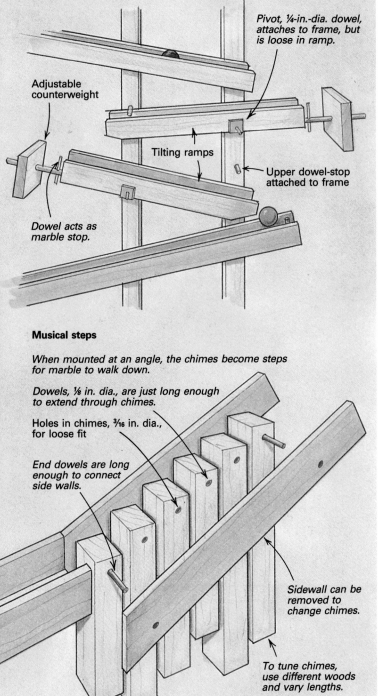

Tilting ramps

Weight of marble tilts ramp down until it hits ramp below. When marble rolls off end of ramp, the counterweight brings ramp back up against upper dowel-stop.

Pivot, ¼-in.-dia. dowel, attaches to frame, but is loose in ramp.

Adjustable counterweight

Tilting ramps

Upper dowel-stop attached to frame

Dowel acts as marble stop.

Musical steps

When mounted at an angle, the chimes become steps for marble to walk down.

Dowels, ⅛ in. dia., are just long enough to extend through chimes.

Holes in chimes, ³⁄₁₆ in. dia., for loose fit

End dowels are long enough to connect side walls.

Sidewall can be removed to change chimes.

To tune chimes, use different woods and vary lengths.

Spiral – In this event, the marble should accelerate dramatically, making a whirring sound as it races down the spiral path. A spiral is an unusual shape for wood, but it's easy to make. Select an 11-in. square of ¾-in.-thick white pine with clear, straight and flat grain. Bandsaw this square by eye, with successive loops about 1 in. apart, leaving a straight tongue tangent to the circle and parallel with the grain as an entrance (see figure 3 on the facing page). Then decide which side will be up, thus determining whether it will be a left- or right-handed spiral when stretched open. On the bottom surface, draw a line perpendicular to the grain and drill ¼-in.-dia. holes, almost through the board, on the line at each turn of the spiral. Glue an 8-in.-long piece of ¼-in. dowel in each

hole. On a ¾-in. by ¾-in. strip of pine, which will support the spiral, mark the position of each dowel and drill ¼-in.-dia. holes clear through. With this strip in a vise, use a hammer to gently tap the spiral above each dowel until each one is through the base strip.

To expand the spiral to its funnel shape, start at the center and drive the first pair of dowels through the base strip about ½ in. Moving outward, drive each successive pair of dowels through a little less than the previous set. Return to the center and repeat this process until a funnel shape is fully formed. The loops should be spaced so a marble is just barely retained by the next track up. You'll find the wood is stiffer near the bottom and can't be spread as far without breaking. As you approach full depth, test the track: Start a marble at the top with a little push so it'll cling to the rim. If it slows down anywhere along the path, drive that section of the spiral down slightly and try it again. When you're satisfied with the run, pin each dowel in the base strip with a small brad.

A spiral makes a fine beginning for any marble roll. If you install the spiral some distance from the starting point, you may need to use an entrance ramp to ensure the marble has enough speed to take the long, sweeping, ever-accelerating path, instead of walking down the funnel's steps.

Tilting ramp – The rhythmic, cascading motion provided by a series of tilting ramps contrasts nicely with the faster, swirling motion in a spiral. Short ramps give a rapid, herky-jerky motion; longer ones dip and rise more slowly in a less frantic way. Figure 3, left, shows how these tilting ramps are made. At the end of a section of U-channel, where the marble enters, a ¼-in. dowel is inserted to hold an adjustable wooden counterweight. Another small dowel is installed to prevent the marble from escaping. The bottom of the other end is beveled to increase the distance the ramp can tilt. The ramp pivots on a dowel about one-third the distance from the counterbalanced end. When a marble drops onto the inclined ramp, it rolls toward the exit end, tilting the ramp more as it rolls. When it falls off the ramp, the counterweight causes the ramp to snap back to its original position. I call the tilting ramps "click-clocks," because of the regular beat they produce as they dip, hit the underlying ramp and then rise and hit the upper dowel stop.

Musical steps – One of my favorite events is the musical steps shown at left. Marbles march down a set of stairs, creating an entertaining percussive sound. To make the steps, mark out and drill equally spaced holes (one for each step) in a ½-in. by 1-in. strip of wood, which will be one of the sidewalls. On the other sidewall, drill just the two end holes. Glue a ⅛-in. dowel in each hole on this sidewall. The dowels at each end should be long enough to run through and support the other sidewall. For the stairs, which will be the chimes, cut varying lengths of ¾-in.-thick pine, drill a hole near the end of each strip and hang one on each dowel. They should fit loosely. Drill two ⅛-in.-dia. holes in the other sidewall, and install it in place on the long end dowels from the first sidewall. Finally, hang the stairs on the framework of the marble roll at an angle that allows a marble to drop from step to step. Different kinds of wood give different tones. The chimes can be tuned by adjusting their lengths, and the scale can be changed by removing the sidewall and rearranging the chimes. □

Richard Starr teaches woodworking at Richmond Middle school in Hanover, N.H. He is also the author of Woodworking With Your Kids; *1990 (The Taunton Press, Box 5506, Newtown, Conn. 06470-5506). All photos are by the author, except where noted.*

Bentwood boxes have been used in Norway for centuries. These two variations are known as "tine" or "laup." The larger one is made of ash; the smaller one, pine.

Norwegian Bentwood Boxes

A leisurely soak eliminates steaming

by Johann Hopstad

Hopstad's boxes are bent around a wooden form bandsawn from a laminated blank. To anchor the box sides during bending, the ends are tucked into a notch cut in the side of the form and are held fast by a metal plate. A block nailed to the bottom of the form allows it to be held in a vise.

The soaked box side is bent around the form freehand and then pulled tight with a quick-action clamp. A curved block distributes clamping pressure across the face of the overlap. A heavy black line is marked on the form to designate the center of the long side that will become the box's front.

From *Fine Woodworking* magazine (March 1988) 69:84-87

Bentwood boxes have a long and illustrious history in Europe, spanning at least 3,000 years. In Norway, examples dating from A.D. 840 were unearthed in a Viking ship found in Oseberg. These boxes were used by rich and poor alike for storing anything from their most valuable possessions to cargo as humble as a day's lunch.

The boxes came in a variety of sizes and shapes—oval, round, triangular or heart-shaped. Some resembled baskets with solid-wood sides, while the sturdier versions had handles lashed to their lids and were used as suitcases. The box discussed here is known as a "tine" or "laup." It's about 9 in. long, 6⅝ in. wide and 3½ in. deep. The ³⁄₃₂-in.-thick sides, as well as the lid, handle, bottom and clasps are ash. These small, decorative boxes hold delicate objects such as needle and thread, but in years past, larger versions displayed farm produce in markets.

The engineering of these boxes is marvelous in its simplicity. The bentwood body doesn't even require steam bending; soaking the wood in water makes it pliable enough to bend around a form. Then, the two ends are fastened together with a little glue, birch-root lacing and wood pegs.

Building a box—Norwegian bentwood boxes are shaped around a solid-wood form, in this case an oval, as shown on the opposite page. To build the form, I make a paper pattern of the shape and trace it onto a block of wood a couple of inches thicker than the height of the box. The block can be solid wood or a plywood or solid-wood lamination. After bandsawing the oval shape, I hollow the form with a large auger bit or a router. The hollow allows room for a clamp head. The block nailed to the form's bottom is for clamping the form in a vise when the wood is bent around it. The center of one long side of the oval is marked to designate where the center of the overlap should fall when the body is clamped around the form. To accommodate the thickness of the overlapping ends, the form must be notched and fitted with a piece of sheet metal to form a lip, as shown in the left photo below. One end of the body is tucked under the sheet-metal lip and held in place as the body is bent around the form.

I resaw the ³⁄₃₂-in. ash for the body on a bandsaw, but you can do it on a tablesaw, making two rips on each edge of the board and then finishing the cut with a handsaw. Either quartersawn or flatsawn stock can be used, but I prefer flatsawn because it's less likely to break when bent. Straight-grain boards bend better and are less likely to split than figured wood. After crosscutting the resawn stock into sections equal to the circumference of the box plus a 3-in.-long overlap on each end, I plane or belt sand the sections. It's not necessary to make the pieces perfectly smooth at this point, though, because soaking will raise the wood grain, which will necessitate further sanding.

Bending sides—I soak the wood for 24 hours in cold water, then just before I bend it, I dunk each piece in warm, not hot, water for five minutes to increase its pliability. Steam bending would make the wood pliable much faster, but the steam-bent wood must be clamped within seconds of being removed from the steam box or its pliability is greatly reduced. My method, however, doesn't require an elaborate steam setup and allows me to work at a more leisurely pace.

I clamp the wood to the form with fast-action clamps, as shown in the center photo below. A piece of scrapwood caul cut to the outside curvature of the box distributes the clamping pressure on the overlap. I put the box aside for four or five days to let it dry before removing it from the form. Next, I sketch the heart and decorative fingers on the face of the outside overlap. I suspend the box from a piece of scrap clamped to the workbench top and drill out the perimeter of the heart and the circles between the bases of the decorative fingers (see right photo below). The waste is cut out with a sturdy sheath knife. Cutting out the fingers and the heart this way looks difficult, but the knife quickly splits off the waste and it's the only way to accurately align these decorative touches on the side of the box. If the heart and fingers are sawn before the box is bent, they may end up being incorrectly positioned, because it's impossible to predict exactly how much the wood will spring back once the box is removed from the form. You can't use a saw to shape the body after bending because there isn't enough room to work it.

I lightly chamfer the outside of each decorative finger with a file or knife, smooth the heart with the knife tip and then slip a peacock feather between the mating surfaces of the overlap so

The outlines of the decorative fingers and the heart are drilled out and then finished with a sturdy woodworking knife. The box's body is suspended from a board clamped to the workbench.

Photos of finished boxes: Michele Russell Slavinsky

To cut the rabbet in the bottom, the author first marks the back of the rabbet by tracing along the body from inside the box. He then marks the bottom of the rabbet by drawing a line on the outside edge using his hand as a marking gauge. He saws on this line around the box's edge with a dovetail saw, then pares along the kerf, working down to the first line.

With the lid of the box notched to fit over the clasps, the lid's profile is traced from the body. The pencil is wrapped in tape, thus creating space for an overhang around the box.

it's framed by the heart cutout. Peacock feathers have been used as decorations in Scandinavia for hundreds of years (available from Aardvark Adventures, Box 2449, Livermore, Calif. 94550). If you don't want to use a peacock feather, you can use red fabric or carve some sort of decoration into the overlap behind the heart. The next step is to spread a thin film of glue over the mating overlapping surfaces and squeeze them together. A single quick-action clamp and the curved caul are all that's needed to secure the box while the glue dries.

Attaching the bottom—The ⅜-in.-thick bottom is rabbeted to fit inside the box body. I prefer cutting the rabbet freehand, but you can use a router fitted with a rabbeting bit and ball-bearing pilot. To cut a rabbet freehand, trace the outside and inside perimeters

of the box onto the bottom, being sure to mark the overlap. Then, bandsaw the outside perimeter. Stand the bottom edge up in the vise and using your hand and a pencil as a marking gauge, trace a line around the center of the edge. Cut down ³⁄₃₂ in. to the inside perimeter mark with a dovetail saw. Saw around the perimeter of the bottom, turning the board after each cut. Next, with a chisel, pare down to the bottom of the kerf, as shown in the photo at left, and chisel out the notch to seat the overlap. Test fit the bottom to the body and pare accordingly. Do not peg the bottom in place until it has been mortised to accept the clasps for the lid and the lacing is completed.

I draw the profiles of the box clasps on a piece of cardboard, cut them out and transfer the marks to the wood blocks, which are about ⁹⁄₁₆ in. thick. The clasps' shapes aren't critical as long as they have a slight curve along the edge to make them attractive and are notched to fit the lid. The clasps are slotted, slid over the edge of the box body and pinned in place. The pin and the thinness of the body allows them to flex slightly when the lid is removed or pressed in place. When shaped, as shown in the drawing at right, the lid should fit with a satisfying snap. With the clasps pegged and glued in place, trace their outline on the box bottom, then chop mortises for the clasp ends.

Fitting the lid—The box lid is cut from a blank that's about ¾ in. thick, ½ in. wider than the box's width (the narrow length) and long enough to accommodate the length of the box and clasps, plus a ¾-in. overhang beyond the clasps. Locate the center of the blank's width and mark a line along its length, then slot the blank evenly on each side of the centerline to accommodate the clasps. Test fit the lid and trim the clasp slots as necessary. Wrap a pencil with tape and trace the outline of the box on the lid blank. The tape holds the pencil away from the box side so the lid will have an even amount of overhang. I freehand draw the bevel of the lid on the endgrain of the lid blank and plane down to the line with a jack plane. The lid is hollowed slightly from underneath. This can be done quickly with a scrub plane and then faired down with gouges and sandpaper. The oval lid is sawn out and its edges sanded smooth. Finally, I cut the handle from a ½-in.-thick piece of wood and peg it to the lid.

Since the overlap has been glued, the lacing is purely decorative, adding charm and character to the box. The lacing is gathered from the roots of young birch trees about 6 ft. high growing on high ground. The location of the tree makes a difference. Trees from high ground send out an extensive root system to gather moisture and are thus more likely to produce a plentiful supply of the small-diameter (about ⅛ in.) roots necessary for lacing. Trees that grow in damp areas produce thick, stubby roots. Gather the roots when they are most pliable, from May through September, and don't take too many from one tree, lest you kill it. I've taken lacing from just about every variety of birch (white, black and yellow) and find they all work fairly well. If there aren't birch trees where you live, you can easily substitute cane for lacing.

After rinsing off the roots, I store them bent in a ring. Soaking them in cold water for about five hours will make them pliable again. Once they're pliable, I wipe off the excess moisture with a rag, bend them around a wood block and work them back and forth in a buffing motion. This removes the roots' skin and polishes them. Next, I split each root in half along its length with a pocket knife and sharpen the tips so I can poke the roots through the holes more easily.

The lacing pattern is more easily illustrated than described (see figures 2 and 3). The two rows of lacing, on both sides of

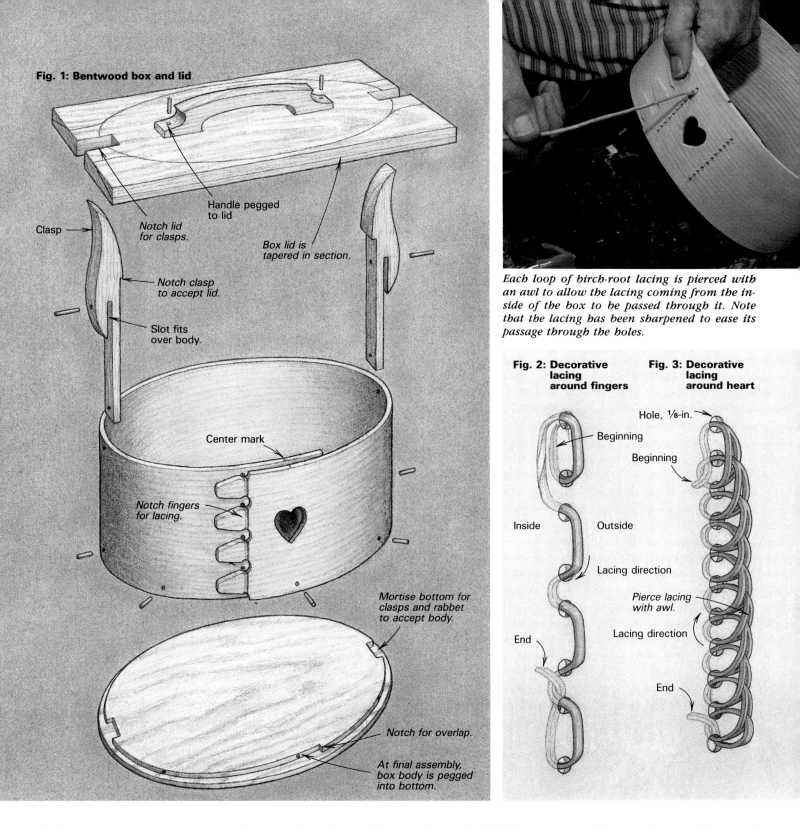

Fig. 1: Bentwood box and lid

Clasp

Notch lid for clasps.

Handle pegged to lid

Box lid is tapered in section.

Notch clasp to accept lid.

Slot fits over body.

Center mark

Notch fingers for lacing.

Mortise bottom for clasps and rabbet to accept body.

Notch for overlap.

At final assembly, box body is pegged into bottom.

Each loop of birch-root lacing is pierced with an awl to allow the lacing coming from the inside of the box to be passed through it. Note that the lacing has been sharpened to ease its passage through the holes.

Fig. 2: Decorative lacing around fingers

Fig. 3: Decorative lacing around heart

Hole, 1/8-in.

Beginning

Beginning

Inside

Outside

Lacing direction

Pierce lacing with awl.

Lacing direction

End

End

---

the heart, are started inside the box. If you start from the outside, the decorative pattern will be formed inside the box. The lacing around the fingers is also started inside the box. Mark a reference line for the lacing by butting a try square against the top edge of the box and drawing two lines, square to the top edge on either side of the heart. Bore 11 1/8-in. holes evenly spaced along the two lines for this lacing. No layout line is necessary to bore the holes for the lacing on either side of the fingers, just bore eight holes, two at the base of each of the four fingers. Use an awl to poke the lacing through when coming from the inside of the box. To make the knots at the ends of the rows, and to snug up loose areas, use the awl as a lever, sliding it under the lacing and pulling up with lacing between the awl and your thumb.

When the lacing is finished, secure the box's bottom with sev-

eral round whittled pegs. Drive the pegs into evenly spaced holes bored through the outside of the box into the rabbet in the box bottom. Be careful not to tip the drill while boring these holes; you could easily pierce the top surface of the bottom.

The box can be left plain, given a light coat of wax or finished with a 50/50 coat of linseed oil and turpentine. The latter gives the box a golden, mellow hue as it ages, making it hard to distinguish from boxes of antiquity. □

Johann Hopstad builds traditional bentwood and staved boxes in Bodo, Norway. He also teaches summer classes in the United States. For information, contact the Norwegian American Museum in Decorah, Ia., (319) 382-9681, or Augustana College in Sioux Falls, S.D., (605) 336-0770.

A Cabinetmaker's Baskets

In the Nantucket tradition

by Charles H. Carpenter, Jr.

Some lightship basket variations: The large photo shows an oval purse basket (8¾ in. by 7¼ in., 6 in. high) of oak and mahogany, which Hilbert made in 1977. The caning in each half of the double lid is inlaid into a recess. The open-top basket at top left has ear handles of bent oak and a turned mahogany bottom. The lid of the other small basket is fully caned, and the mahogany rims were bricklaid of many small pieces for stability. The basket, with its ivory finial, is at the Museum of Fine Arts, Boston.

Harry Hilbert is a former antique dealer from southern Connecticut with a great love of American decorative arts. He is also a woodworker of considerable skill. He has made his share of reproduction furniture over the past 45 years—tea tables, corner chairs, chests of drawers, children's furniture and so on. It is his baskets, however, that give Harry Hilbert a special place in the American craft scene.

In 1974, while visiting with my wife, Mary Grace, and me on Nantucket Island, Hilbert studied Mary Grace's collection of old Nantucket baskets and said: "I'm going to make one of those." In the years since, he has made dozens, no two exactly alike and none made for sale. Hilbert makes baskets solely for the joy of it.

In the 19th century, Nantucket baskets were made on board the lightships anchored in the dangerous shoals off Nantucket, hence the name lightship baskets. They are a distinctive type of American handicraft that came out of the maritime cooperage

tradition. The process entails as much woodworking as it does basketry—the staves are related to the staves of a Nantucket cooper's whale-oil barrel.

In the old Nantucket baskets, the bottom of the basket is usually solid pine, but sometimes a hardwood. A groove is cut into the edge of the bottom and then oak or hickory staves (water-soaked to make them supple) are fitted into the groove and shaped around a form. When the staves have dried they more or less retain the form's shape. The staves are then interwoven with fine cane in a plain or decorative pattern. Small ear handles like those in one of Hilbert's first baskets (photo above, top left) are a typical way to finish up. Other baskets had flat wooden lids attached by leather-thong hinges wrapped with cane. Although some of the early lightship baskets had bottoms with turned scratched lines for decoration, many bases were so plain that they didn't even have beveled bottom edges. The lightship-

From *Fine Woodworking* magazine (November 1985) 55:84-87

basket tradition continued in the 20th century, mostly in the form of open-top baskets, round or oblong. The round baskets were sometimes made in nests of six or seven. After World War II, lidded baskets became popular as purses and a cottage-industry grew up to produce them.

Hilbert, with his high-style cabinetmaker's instincts, has continued to refine the basic designs, adding features such as shop-made brass hinges instead of leather and all sorts of inlaid and applied decoration on the lids and tops.

Not all of Hilbert's refinements are purely decorative, as the small basket with pagoda-like lid in the photo on the facing page illustrates. If the mahogany rims of this basket had been turned from solid wood, they would constantly "move" with changes in relative humidity, becoming slightly oval, then round, then oval again. To ensure that the top and basket rims would stay round regardless of the weather, Hilbert laminated them from numerous thin pieces of wood in a bricklaid fashion. This also eliminates short-grain from the rims, greatly strengthening them. Functional as this basket is, it may also be considered a work of art. In fact, it was recently acquired by the Museum of Fine Arts in Boston and a similar one is now in the Art Museum of Yale University in New Haven.

Making a basket purse—The accompanying step-by-step photographs and drawings show how Hilbert makes one of his basket purses. The top photo at right shows two partially finished baskets with materials in the foreground. Hilbert makes the 6½-in.-long oak staves by splitting a wedge of oak from his own land, then bandsawing it into thin radial slices that resemble ⅛-in.-thick veneer. He then bandsaws these into staves that taper in width from about ⅜ in. at the top down to ¼ in. at the bottom. He handplanes these smooth, to a final thickness of about ¹⁄₁₆ in.

The weaving cane is a grade called superfine chairseat cane, which can be bought from many hobby shops or mail-ordered from general suppliers such as Constantine. One bundle of cane is enough for about six baskets. The top photo also shows the oval base of cherry or other hardwood, and brass ears sawn from ¹⁄₁₆-in. stock. The brass ears will serve to attach the lid, and can be made in whatever size is appropriate.

The next photo shows an oval basket mold, 5¾ in. by 8½ in. by 5½ in. high (about 1 in. higher than the finished basket). Hilbert makes molds by bandsawing four layers of 1⅜-in.-thick fir. He saws the top oval first, tilting the bandsaw table about 3° so the sides of the oval will taper. Then he traces the next oval from the bottom of the first, and so on. After glue-up, Hilbert rasps and files the lower edge to a graceful curve and sands the mold smooth. The dowel at the top will serve as an axle, allowing Hilbert to rotate the work in a simple benchtop jig while weaving.

The staves will be glued into a ¹⁄₁₆-in.-wide sawkerf around the edge of the base. The bottom photo shows Hilbert cutting the groove with a 1¾-in.-dia. sawblade in his drill press. The kerf is one-third down from the top, and the shopmade fence is set so the kerf is about ³⁄₁₆-in. deep. The kerf could also be cut with a handsaw, which is undoubtedly how they did it in the old days. The base is a 2⅞-in. by 4⅞-in. oval, ⅜-in. thick.

To shape the outside bottom rim of the base, Hilbert uses a router bit in the drill press. The top of the base is next shaped by hand to remove the sharp corner at its edge. Hilbert uses a spokeshave and file to gently round the top surface to blend down to the sawkerf, as shown in the drawing on p. 43. The base will be completely smoothed and sanded before weaving begins.

Hilbert next traces the base onto the bottom of the mold, and

Top photo shows two partially finished baskets and the makings of another—hardwood oval base, oak staves, superfine chairseat cane and shopmade brass 'ears' as anchor points for the hinges. The middle photo shows the built-up wooden form that controls the shape. At bottom, Hilbert cuts a groove in the base for the staves, using a small circular sawblade in a drill press.

routs a recess in the mold to accept the base. The recess brings the sawkerf in the rim of the base flush with the bottom of the mold. He then screws the base into position.

In the top photo on this page, weaving is under way. To get to this point, Hilbert first softens the staves by soaking them in water for three days, then inserts them into the slot one at a time, bending each to conform to the mold. A rubber band around the top of the mold keeps things in position as he proceeds. The staves were originally tapered on the bandsaw to allow space between them for the cane, and some of them must be tapered some more at this time, particularly where there are tight curves. The objective is to keep the gap between staves more or less uniform—it should be a little more than ⅛ in. at the top, and a little less than ⅛ in. at the bottom. After all the staves are inserted (as with any basket, always end up with an odd number), Hilbert wraps them tightly with cord and allows them to dry for 24 hours.

Hilbert advises gluing the staves in place after the shape has set. He pulls the bottom of each stave from its slot, applies a dab of glue, and reinserts it. He then starts the cane (which has been soaked in water) by drilling a small hole next to the center stave on one side, as shown in the drawing. From there, he weaves the cane around alternate staves, keeping it pulled taut to the mold and straightening and pushing each row down toward the base with the tip of a screwdriver, being careful to keep the rows of cane straight and even. In weaving, Hilbert suggests that instead of trying to push the cane under and over the staves in a straight line, as if sewing, it is much more efficient to slip the cane down from the top of the staves. Until the basket has been well started, this tends to spread the staves out from the form. Hilbert has devised a loose oval collar (of plywood and an inner tube) that fits around the top of the form. This prevents the staves from springing out too far, yet is loose enough for him to work the cane over and under the tops of the staves.

When Hilbert reaches the end of the first strand of cane, he interweaves a new piece (also shown in the drawing). Hilbert emphasizes that the staves should be kept vertical as weaving proceeds. He marks vertical reference lines at places around the sides of the mold as a guide.

When the weaving is within about 2½ in. from the top of the form, Hilbert marks a level line all the way around the top of the staves, gauging down about 1 in. from the top of the mold, and cuts the staves to the left and right of the center staves to final length with a sharp chisel (the rest of the staves will be trimmed when weaving is finished). He then makes a pair of brass ears to fit the basket and rivets these to the inside with No. 18 brass escutcheon pins (from Constantine). Hilbert removes the basket from the form while riveting the ears, then puts it back to continue weaving. The cane goes right over the brass, to within about ¼ in. of the gauged line.

A bentwood rim fits just above the last row of cane and binds the staves together. Hilbert planes, scrapes and sands two 5⁄16-in. half-round oak strips (one for the inside, one for the outside), soaks them in water for three days, then boils them for 30 minutes before wrapping them into a pair of bending forms, as shown in the center photo. Drying takes three days. Then the inner rim is dry-fitted to the basket, stretching it as much as possible before marking it for cutting. Both ends of the strip are feathered to make a scarf joint, as shown in the drawing, overlapped and glued. Hilbert then does the same with the outer rim, but this time he makes the joint on the other side of the basket, diagonally opposite the first.

When the glue is dry, he positions both rims on the basket and

Successive rows of cane that have been straightened and pushed toward the base with the tip of a screwdriver. To keep rows even, apply slightly more pressure on the sides than at the ends.

Half-round oak rims—one for the inside, one for the outside—are boiled, then wound into shopmade bending forms for drying.

Hilbert reinforces the wood at the hinge points by epoxying brass strips into saw kerfs. Lid is bandsawn oval after fitting.

marks and trims the staves so they will be flush with the top of the rim. He then drills and rivets the rims clear through every third or fourth stave, making sure that a rivet goes through each glued scarf joint to secure it. The drill bit is simply a No. 18 steel brad with the head clipped off. Hilbert places the brass pins in the holes as he goes along, cutting off the head and any excess length on the inside with pliers. He smooths the nipped ends with a file, leaving enough for final riveting with a ball-peen hammer. He then files the riveted ends even with the oak, covers the upper edges of the stave-ends with a single strip of medium cane, and binds around the top with weaving cane, as shown in the drawing. If you don't have medium cane, Hilbert suggests that you can plane down the strip of heavier cane that suppliers routinely tie around the chairseat cane.

He next bends the oak handle around a horseshoe-shaped ply-

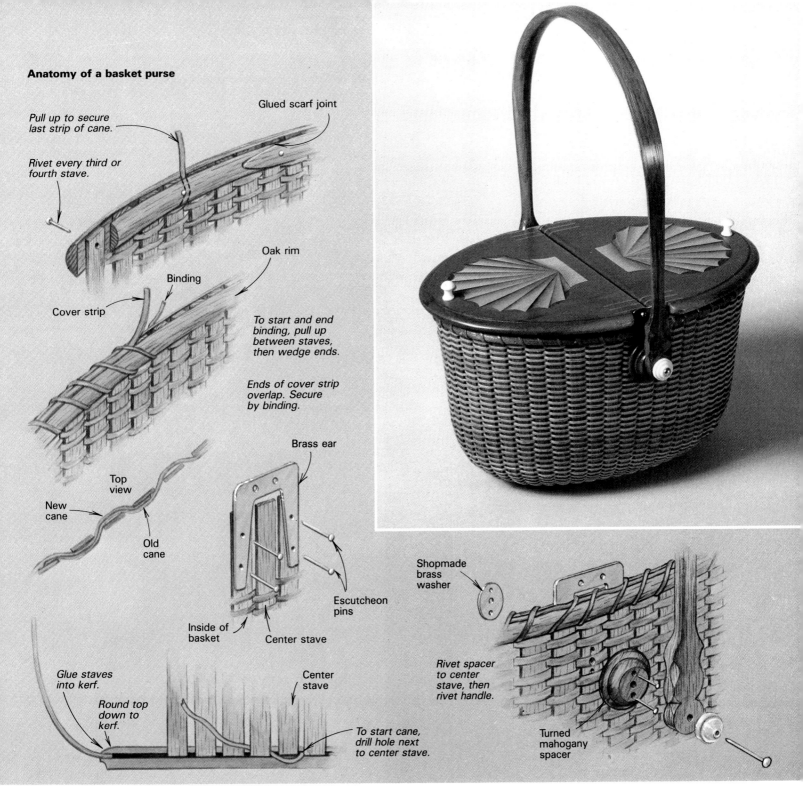

Anatomy of a basket purse

Pull up to secure last strip of cane.

Glued scarf joint

Rivet every third or fourth stave.

Cover strip

Binding

Oak rim

To start and end binding, pull up between staves, then wedge ends.

Ends of cover strip overlap. Secure by binding.

New cane

Top view

Old cane

Brass ear

Inside of basket

Center stave

Escutcheon pins

Glue staves into kerf.

Round top down to kerf.

Center stave

To start cane, drill hole next to center stave.

Shopmade brass washer

Rivet spacer to center stave, then rivet handle.

Turned mahogany spacer

wood form and clamps it in place to dry for three days. He has had his best success working with green oak, soaked in water for three days, then boiled for 30 minutes. After drying, the handle can be shaped with spokeshave, rasps and files. Hilbert suggests that it is much easier to shape the inside surface of the handle if the bent blank is clamped in a U-shaped plywood cradle held in a vise—if you try to do it freehand, it's like wrestling with a snake. Each craftsman tends to shape handles differently, something of a personal trademark.

Hilbert hinges the double lid by means of 1-in. No. 2 brass wood screws through the ears. He reinforces the wood by epoxying thin strips of brass into bandsawn kerfs (bottom photo, facing page). With the lid blanks hinged in place, he marks the profile by tracing the basket's rim, then removes the lid, bandsaws it to shape, and proceeds with edge treatment and decoration.

This particular basket has shell inlays made of 14 pieces of satinwood, charred on one edge in hot sand to create shading, and 13 pieces of crescent-shaped mahogany. Turned mahogany spacers keep the handle from contacting the lid. They are riveted to the center stave with No. 18 escutcheon pins, as shown in the drawing, then the handle and its decorative ivory knobs are riveted through with No. 12 escutcheon pins. Finishing touches include turned ivory knobs on the lids and a finish of one coat of thin shellac and two coats of satin varnish, applied to the cane as well as the wood. The basket is then waxed and buffed. □

Charles Carpenter is an author and art historian who lives part of the year on Nantucket Island. For more on bending wood for baskets and other purposes, see FWW on Bending Wood, *which is a collection of articles from back issues of* FWW.

Making a Message Center
Apprentice project develops woodworking skills

by Luca Valentino

At first glance, the message center in the photo below looks like a very simple project. And in some ways it is. But there's more to it than meets the eye. Developed as a project for cabinetmaking apprentices at the Labor Technical College in Manhattan, N.Y., the message center involves a wide range of woodworking operations. As such, it's a neat project for those who want to hone their skills while producing a functional item. There are many ways to build the piece, but here I'll present only the apprentices' method, so you can work along with them and see how students learn to build accurately from detailed plans.

Projects like the message center are part of a four-year program for cabinetmakers. The apprentices attend four hours of classes one evening each week, while working full time in union shops that sponsor their school training. By the end of their fourth year, each apprentice should have mastered the major aspects of the trade, including drafting, reading blueprints and using both hand and power tools, and will have worked on some fairly complex projects, such as a flight of stairs and a French provincial commode.

The construction plans for the message center, which I drew as an apprentice, are shown in figure 1 on the facing page. Basically it's a wall-hung shelf unit with a cork-veneered, backing board for tacking notes and a small drawer between the two lower shelves. All three shelves are tongued into stopped dadoes in the case sides. Sounds simple enough, doesn't it? But notice that even the radii of the curves on the case sides and crest rail are specified. The challenge for the students is to build the piece *exactly* as specified on the plan, and this requires the use of patterns and templates.

Making the patterns/templates—To ensure that the curved case sides and the crest rail will precisely match the specs on the plan, it's necessary to make full-scale patterns for these parts from ¼-in. tempered Masonite. The patterns serve a dual purpose. First, they're traced around for laying out the parts on the wood and then later they're used as template guides for final trimming the curves with a bearing-guided flush-trim router bit. With these templates, it's a snap to consistently reproduce the curves, whether you're making 2 parts or 200 parts. To aid in making the patterns so they match the specs exactly, draw a 1-in. grid on the Masonite. Swing the required arcs with a compass from the centers shown in figure 2 on p. 46 and connect these arcs with tangent lines. Mark the locations of the shelf dadoes and the template attaching screw holes. You should also mark on the case-side pattern for the locations of the shelf dadoes that will be routed on the inside of each side. Then, cut the patterns out with a bandsaw and smooth them carefully to the line with sanding blocks and files. Take care to keep the edges square and make the curves smooth and precise because any inconsistencies will be transferred to the wood parts. With patterns in hand you're ready to begin constructing the piece.

Building the message center—The stock bill, located in the lower right corner of figure 1, gives you all the information you need to cut out the shelves, backs and drawer parts. Rip the piece for the crest rail 2 in. wider than its finished width of 2¾ in. so you'll have some extra stock to attach the crest rail pattern when trimming it with the router (see figure 2).

The dimensions of the stock that's glued up for the case sides are given in figure 2. Center the glueline exactly 7³⁄₁₆ in. from each edge so it will intersect the point where the two arcs meet just above the drawer space on the case sides. Placing the glueline at this

This mahogany message center is a second-year project at the Carpenters' Apprenticeship School in New York City. It's designed to teach techniques, tool use and how to work to a plan.

Fig. 1: Plan and stock bill

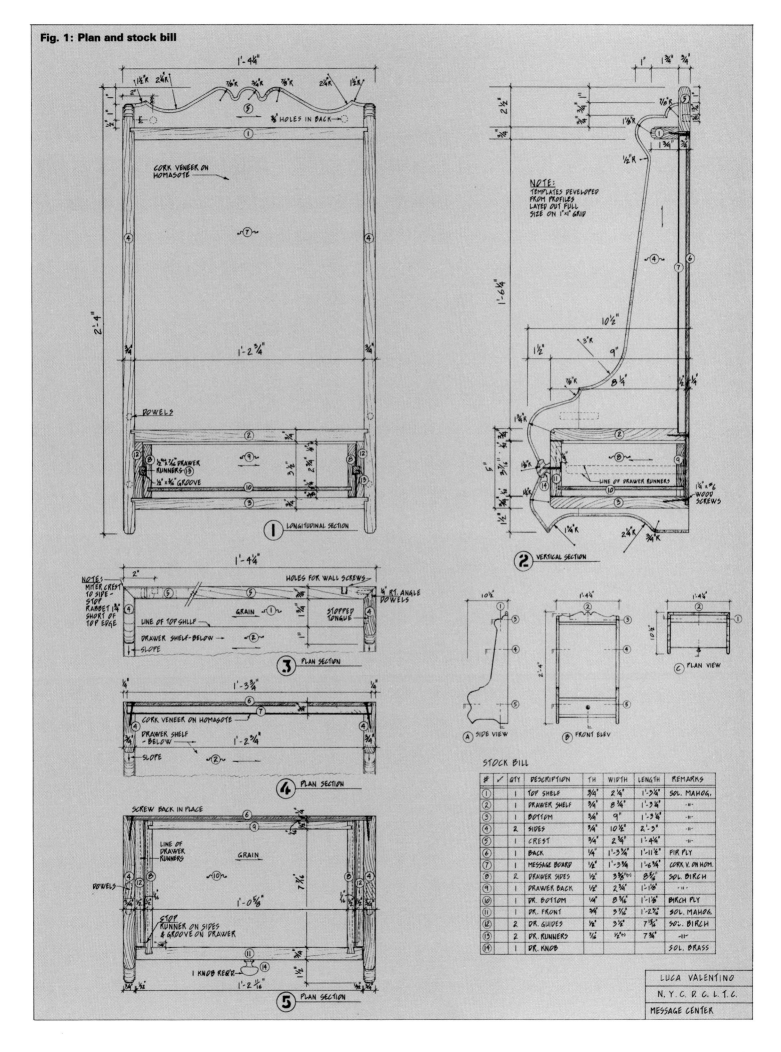

STOCK BILL

#	✓	QTY	DESCRIPTION	TH	WIDTH	LENGTH	REMARKS
①		1	TOP SHELF	3/4"	2 1/4"	1'-3 1/4"	SOL. MAHOG.
②		1	DRAWER SHELF	3/4"	8 3/4"	1'-3 1/4"	-"-
③		1	BOTTOM	3/4"	9"	1'-3 1/8"	-"-
④		2	SIDES	3/4"	10 1/2"	2'-3"	-"-
⑤		1	CREST	3/4"	2 3/4"	1'-4 1/4"	-"-
⑥		1	BACK	1/4"	1'-3 3/4"	1'-11 1/2"	FIR PLY
⑦		1	MESSAGE BOARD	1/2"	1'-3 3/4"	1'-6 3/4"	CORK V. ON HOM.
⑧		2	DRAWER SIDES	1/2"	3 3/8"(±)	8 5/16"	SOL. BIRCH
⑨		1	DRAWER BACK	1/2"	2 3/4"	1'-1 1/8"	-"-
⑩		1	DR. BOTTOM	1/4"	8 3/4"	1'-1 1/8"	BIRCH PLY
⑪		1	DR. FRONT	3/4"	3 1/16"	1'-2 3/4"	SOL. MAHOG.
⑫		2	DR. GUIDES	1/2"	3 1/2"	7 5/16"	SOL. BIRCH
⑬		2	DR. RUNNERS	7/16"	1/2"(±)	7 3/4"	-"-
⑭		1	DR. KNOB				SOL. BRASS

LUCA VALENTINO

N. Y. C. D. C. L. T. C.

MESSAGE CENTER

Fig. 2: Layout for case sides and crest rail

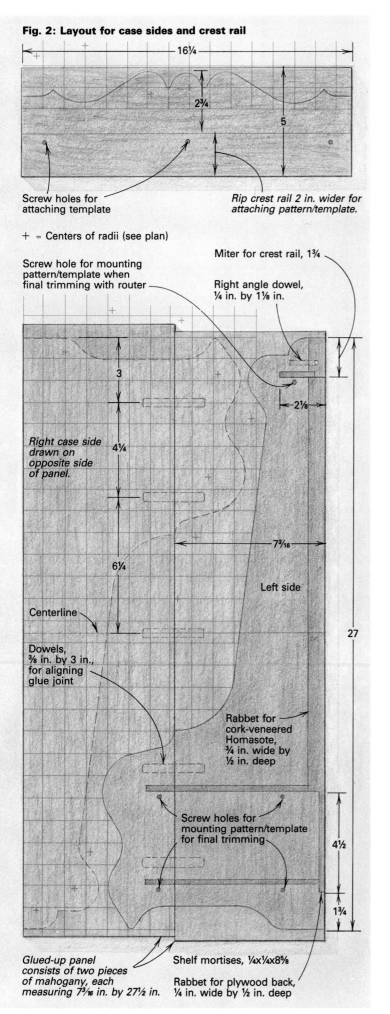

16¼

2¾

5

Screw holes for attaching template

Rip crest rail 2 in. wider for attaching pattern/template.

+ = Centers of radii (see plan)

Screw hole for mounting pattern/template when final trimming with router

Miter for crest rail, 1¾

Right angle dowel, ¼ in. by 1⅛ in.

3

2⅛

Right case side drawn on opposite side of panel.

4¼

7³⁄₁₆

6¼

Left side

27

Centerline

Dowels, ⅜ in. by 3 in., for aligning glue joint

Rabbet for cork-veneered Homasote, ¾ in. wide by ½ in. deep

Screw holes for mounting pattern/template for final trimming

4½

1¾

Glued-up panel consists of two pieces of mahogany, each measuring 7³⁄₁₆ in. by 27½ in.

Shelf mortises, ¼x¼x8⅝

Rabbet for plywood back, ¼ in. wide by ½ in. deep

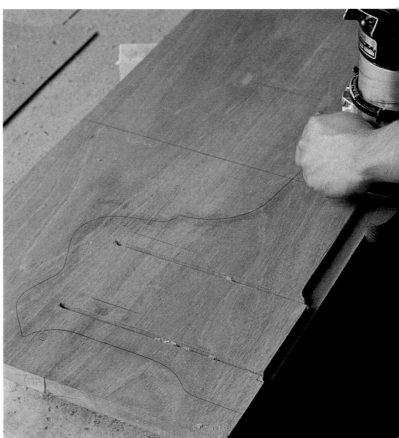

Above: Valentino routs the rabbet for the back with a guide block clamped to the router base. The narrow portion of the back rabbet is for the ¼-in. plywood back that extends top to bottom; the wider portion accommodates the cork-veneered bulletin board. Below: The author cuts the stopped miter on the top of the left case side, stopping the cut when the pencil line on the workpiece aligns with the line on the saw's throat plate. The miter on the right case side was cut using the same setup, but with the side lying flat on the saw table instead of on edge. The holes in the miters, for the right-angle dowels, are drilled before mitering.

Drawing: Vince Babak

point will make the joint virtually invisible on the front edge of the sides. To register the pattern, draw a horizontal centerline on both the pattern and the glued-up stock and align them while holding the pattern's back edge along one edge of the stock. Trace around the pattern once on each side of the stock as shown in figure 2. Don't forget to mark on the stock for the locations of the shelf dadoes.

Rout the shelf dadoes first with a ¼-in. straight bit and a guide fence clamped to the stock. Then, rout the ½-in.-deep back rabbet with a ¾-in.-wide straight bit and a ¾-in.-thick guide block clamped to the router base. The top photo on the facing page shows how the back rabbet steps in from ¼ in. wide, for the plywood back, to ¾ in. wide to accommodate the ½-in.-thick backing board that's framed between the bottom and top shelves and the sides. Rout the ¼-in.-wide rabbet from bottom shelf to top shelf. Leaving the bit set to ½ in. deep, reset the guide block to rout the wider portion of the rabbet. Flip the panel over and cut the dadoes and rabbets on the opposite case side. Square up the rounded ends of the rabbets with a chisel.

After the dadoes and the rabbets are cut, bandsaw out the case sides and the crest rail, leaving them about 1⁄16-in. oversize so you can final trim them with a ¼-in.-dia. flush-trim, ball-bearing-piloted router bit guided by the template. Carefully realign the patterns/templates on the stock and screw them in place. Screw the side template to the inside surface of the case sides, locating the screws ¼ in. below the dadoes so that when the case is assembled the shelves will cover the holes. Now, trim the curves with the flush-trim bit, using a climb or reverse cut to prevent end-grain chip-out. The tight corners that the bit can't reach are cleaned up with a sharp chisel and a mill file after the templates are removed. To rout the decorative profiles on the edges of the sides and crest rail, I use a high-speed steel, ¼-in. roundover bit, the kind with a guide pin as opposed to a bearing (available from Tools on Sale, 216 W. 7th St., St. Paul, Minn. 55102-2599). The guide pin's small diameter fits into the ¼-in.-radius curves in the crest rail, so the profile can be cut without having to work the tight corners with chisels.

In order for the molded profiles of the sides and crest to blend smoothly into one another they must be mitered. To align and strengthen these miter joints, I reinforce each of them with a ¼-in., plastic right-angle dowel, available from Dave Sanders and Co., Inc., 111 Bowery, New York, N.Y. 10002. It may seem troublesome to drill the mating holes in a miter, but it's quite easily done by drilling the holes with a doweling jig before cutting the miters (see the bottom photo on the facing page).

Cutting the stopped 45° miters on the top of the case sides with the tablesaw is a little tricky. One of the case sides is run laying flat on the saw table and the opposite case side is run on its edge. The bottom photo on the facing page shows my tablesaw setup. I screw an auxiliary fence to the saw's rip fence, tilt the blade 45° and raise it until it cuts into the auxiliary fence. I make a test cut on a ¾-in.-thick scrap to be sure the miter intersects the top corner of the test piece. Pencil marks on the fence and throat plate note the beginning point of the cut. I also square a line on the outside face of each case side 1¾ in. down from the top edge and I stop the cut when the line on the side reaches the line on the fence or throat plate. When cutting the miters, the small cutoff may be kicked back, so for safety, turn the saw off before backing either of the pieces off the blade.

The ends of the crest rail are mitered using the miter gauge and the same tablesaw setup. Hold the crest rail's straight edge against the miter gauge face and miter one end; then reverse the miter gauge in the same slot, so that it's in front of the workpiece, and miter the other end. To keep the triangular offcut from kicking back, I push the miter gauge with my left hand and push the offcut clear past the blade with a 2x2x12 backup block in my right hand.

When the curved parts are complete, you can cut the tongues on

the ends of the shelves, rabbet their backs for the backing board where necessary (see figure 1) and rout the decorative bead on their front edges. After dry fitting the shelves to the sides, carefully spread glue in the dadoes and on the tongues and clamp the case together using edge-jointed 2x4s at each shelf to distribute the pressure. Check the case for squareness, and then test-fit and glue the mitered crest rail in place with the right-angle dowels.

Making and fitting the drawer—Drawer construction details are given in figure 1 on p. 45. The sliding dovetails that join the sides to the front are cut with a table-mounted router. First cut the dovetail-shaped dadoes on the inside of the drawer front, and then cut the dovetail tenons on the ends of the drawer sides so they fit into the mortises.

Before gluing up the drawer, rout the stopped grooves for the runners in both the drawer sides and the guide blocks. The guide blocks provide side guides for the drawer by spanning the ½ in. that the sides are setback from the ends of the drawer front. Use a ½-in.-dia. straight bit in a table-mounted router and clamp a stop block to the router table's fence to stop the grooves, ¼ in. from the dovetail shoulder on the sides and 3⁄16 in. from the front of the guide blocks. Be sure to cut all the grooves from the bottom edges of the parts so they line up with each other. Make a single pass to cut the grooves in the drawer sides and then nudge the fence back about 1⁄32 in., indicated in the drawing, and run the guide blocks; this will raise the drawers just a hair to ensure that the sides don't drag on the bottom shelf. Round the front end of the drawer runners to fit the radius of the stopped grooves and glue the runners into the guide block grooves. Now you can glue up the drawer. However, if you're going to stain the drawer front but not the drawer sides, stain it first before gluing the sliding dovetails.

After the glue sets, slide the drawer and the guide block assemblies into place to check their fit. Remove the assemblies and make any necessary adjustments. I only glue the first 2 in. of the guide blocks to the case and then secure their back ends with screws in elongated holes to allow the case sides to expand or contract. Instead of clamps, I use the drawer itself to press the guide blocks against the case sides until the glue sets by wedging Formica shims between the drawer sides and the guide blocks above and below the runners. Then, I remove the drawer and screw in the backs of the guides.

To prepare the piece for finishing, sand it to 150-grit with garnet paper, raise the grain with a wet sponge and sand again to remove the fuzz. A light coat of shellac on the edges of the case sides prevents the endgrain from absorbing too much stain. I use Behlen's dry powdered aniline stain, available from Garrett Wade Co. Inc., 161 Ave. of the Americas, New York, N.Y. 10013. After staining, apply one sealer coat of shellac and two coats of varnish, sanding between coats with 220-grit finishing paper. I rub out the final coat of varnish with mineral oil and a 3M Scotch-Brite pad and top that off with several coats of Butcher's wax, available from most hardware stores, buffed to a soft luster. Although the drawing shows a simple knob for the drawer pull, I chose a polished brass pull (also available from Garrett Wade or from Paxton Hardware Ltd., 7818 Bradshaw Road, Upper Falls, Md. 21156) to add to the style and formality of the piece.

To complete the message center, put the backing board in place and screw the plywood back to the case. Finally, drill two 3⁄8-in.-deep holes in the back of the crest rail so the message center can be hung on flat-head screws anchored securely in the wall. □

Luca Valentino, a graduate of the Carpenters' Apprenticeship School, teaches woodworking classes at the school and is a project manager with Rimi Woodcraft. For more information on the school, write to 140 E. 26th St., New York, N.Y. 10010.

White Cedar Birds
Pocketknife yields fanciful fantails

by Roy Berendsohn

In just seven minutes, Ed Menard carved this intricate, feathered bird from a single block of wet white cedar.

The fantails on Edmond Menard's carved birds are a wonder of low-tech green woodworking. When I first saw one, I assumed he had glued the tiny segments onto a carved bird, but actually the body and tail are whittled from a single block of white cedar, with the speed and precision of a Japanese chef flowering a radish with a few well-placed knife strokes.

Menard's skill transforms a couple of nondescript knives into a complete tool kit, capable of paring out a fanciful white cedar birds every five minutes or so. Since 1976, he estimates that he's carved more than 50,000 birds, making roughly 3,000 to 5,000 of them a year. At a per-bird price of $5 to $7, that's plenty fast enough to make a living.

Menard makes at least a dozen birds a day, but his is hardly the rigorous schedule of a production shop. His customers, primarily tourists, are lured into his driveway off a picturesque area of Route 2 between Plainfield and Marshfield, Vt. by a large carved bird and "bird man" sign placed strategically on his front lawn. Actually, Menard calls himself "Bird Man II," having learned his craft from the original bird man, Chester Nutting.

The two men first met in 1975 when Nutting stopped at Menard's parents' farm to ask directions to a crafts fair. Pausing to talk, Nutting produced a suitcase filled with carved birds. Before Menard's astonished eyes, Nutting—who learned the craft from his grandfather, a New England logger who whiled away his free time by whittling white cedar fans—sat chewing tobacco, whittling out a bird every seven minutes. (Once, he even scooped up a $20 bet for beating that time limit.) Menard was hooked on the spot.

He says the secret to carving the distinctive feather fan is to work the cedar while it's wet. Cedar is ideal for the work—soft, straight-grained and pliable when moist. It exhibits very little tangential or radial shrinkage, so it remains stable as it dries. Menard cuts his cedar in the woods near his home, bucking the 6-in.-dia. trees into 18-in. logs before resorting to some rather unorthodox procedures. He roughs out blanks by feeding whole logs—bark and all—across an old tabletop jointer in a small backyard shed. Next, he saws the cambium layer off the blocks and joints them

into slat 2-in. wide by ⅜-in. thick. Each slat is then crosscut into 8-in.-long blanks from which Menard can carve two birds, beak to beak. He wraps about a dozen or so good blanks in a bread bag and throws them in a chest-freezer in his basement. Carving stock is thawed as it's needed, and scrapwood fires the stove.

Menard begins carving with a Sloyd knife. He first bevels the end of the slat like a gabled roof, and cuts the notches near the end of the tail where the individual feathers will eventually interlock. Next, a shallow, diagonal notch is carved into each side of the slat where the feathers meet the body. Then, the tail feathers (about $\frac{1}{32}$ in. thick) are split out with a small, triangular-shaped Barlow knife pushed into the slats' endgrain. To make room for the blade as the slats start to spread, Menard breaks off a feather near the tail's center, then finishes the tail section. The bird's profile is sawed out on a scroll saw; the bill and breast are shaped with the Barlow blade. After the body is shaped, the wet cedar can be fanned without breaking, and each feather can be tucked into its neighbor (see photo above).

During the winter, the finished birds dry overnight on top of the water heater in Menard's basement; in the summer, the sun does the job. Red, green or purple pushpins pressed into the bird's head become eyes, while a wood burner and torch add wing or tail markings. Larger birds—those with wingspans of 3 in. to 5 in.—are finished with a light coat of shellac. One-inch-wingspan birds, destined to become earrings, are dipped in casein resin. (Personally, I like the birds unfinished. Fresh from the knife, they look crisp and slightly translucent.)

Menard decided long ago that he couldn't work for anyone else. Unlike most woodworkers, who require a substantial investment in machinery and often employ sophisticated marketing, Menard earns his living quietly. Using just a handful of knives and a few ancient machines, he does well selling his wares to the tourists who drop in to see him. I suspect many woodworkers would envy him for that. ☐

Roy Berendsohn is an assistant editor at Fine Woodworking.

In a few deft strokes, Menard pares a point on the blank's end, forms notches that later interlock the feathers and, above, cuts a diagonal notch where the feathers meet the body. Right, the tail feathers are split out by pushing the knife into the end-grain. The cut is stopped at the diagonal notch. A central feather is removed to allow the knife additional room.

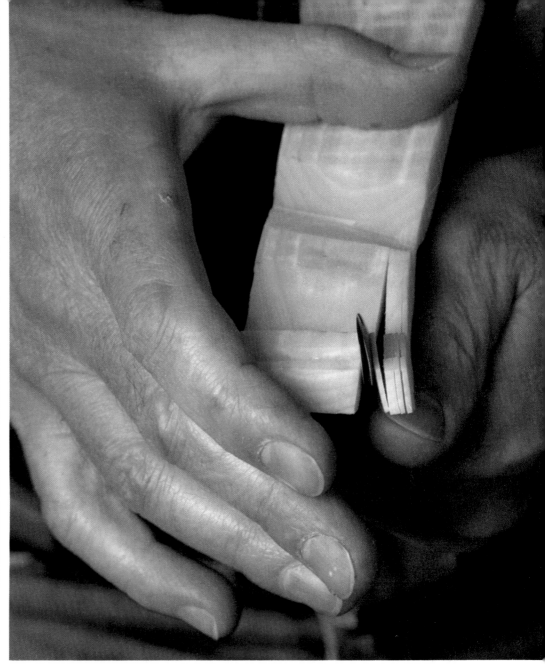

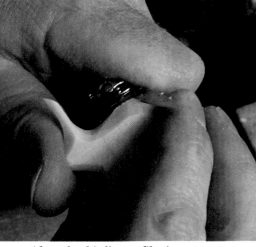

After the bird's profile is cut out on a scroll saw, its breast and bill are pared to final shape with a Barlow knife, above. Menard fans out and interlocks the tail feathers (below), starting with the top feather, which becomes the center feather.

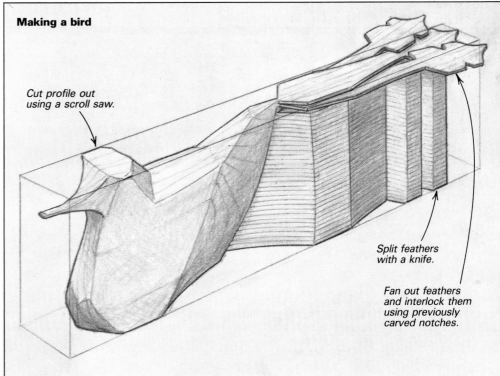

Making a bird

Cut profile out using a scroll saw.

Split feathers with a knife.

Fan out feathers and interlock them using previously carved notches.

Kerbschnitzen
Two-knife Swiss chip carving

by John Hines

It never occurred to me that I could become seriously interested in chip carving—a skill I always associated with primitive folk objects covered with rows of incised squares and triangles repeated in boring symmetry. Then I saw Wayne Barton's work. It was so crisp and lively that it seemed to leap off the table as I walked by his exhibit at a woodworkers' show in San Francisco two years ago.

Like beautiful music, the elements of his carvings flow smoothly without breaks from one segment to the next, often creating stunning curvilinear forms. Even though the pattern of each carving is generally geometrical and symmetrical, the cuts—because they are so perfectly executed—have the boldness of a Picasso stroke. And, like all true artistry, his work gives the impression of effortlessness.

Surprisingly, Barton uses only one short-bladed knife to cut nearly all of his intricate designs, most of which are incised on the lids and sides of jewelry boxes. The designs are based on

series of pyramids, triangles, many of them elongated, and gracefully flowing sweeps. Each facet of the design is created by making two or more converging knife cuts into the wood and popping out a chip. No matter how intricate the design, Barton cuts each wall of the facets with a single stroke. No trial cuts. No clean-up cuts. Just one bold incision to sever the wood fibers cleanly from one end of the facet to the other.

Barton, a professional carver who learned his art in Switzerland, says that the key to mastering chip carving, which he calls *kerbschnitzen* (Swiss for engraving carving), is learning how to hold the knife in an unvarying, cocked-wrist position. This ensures a consistent 65° cutting angle and clean cuts. Then all you have to do is practice until you learn how to make the shallow cuts (seldom more than ⅛-in. deep) meet at precisely the same point at the bottom of each facet.

I was dubious as my classmates and I settled down for five days of instruction at Barton's Park Ridge, Ill., home near Chica-

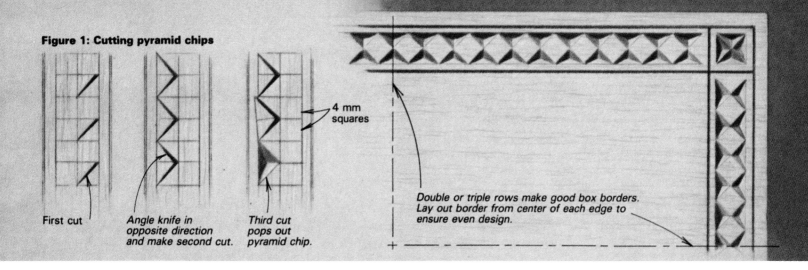

Figure 1: Cutting pyramid chips

First cut

Angle knife in opposite direction and make second cut.

Third cut pops out pyramid chip.

4 mm squares

Double or triple rows make good box borders. Lay out border from center of each edge to ensure even design.

go last summer. The four of us marveled at the carvings in the home—boxes, chair backs, kitchen-cabinet panels—as well as dozens of samples he had carved onto small ½-in.-thick basswood blocks. "You will be able to execute all of these carvings by the end of the week," he said, as he gave each of us several basswood blanks, a cutting knife, and a "stab knife" that is used to impress short, wedge-shaped lines into the wood to enhance some designs. Barton prefers basswood because of its softness, tight, even grain and light color, but you can use just about any wood, although it's difficult to cut woods that are very hard or have very pronounced annular rings.

The two Swiss-style knives Barton uses with his students were specifically designed by Alpine craftsmen for chip carving. The short blades are easy to manipulate, take a keen edge, and resist bending and breaking. The rectangular handles are easier to grasp than the round- or oval-handled models sometimes sold as chip carving knives. Besides the $20 knife set, the only equip-

The sides and lids of Barton's jewelry boxes (facing page), show delicate and complex patterns. Barton cuts the curved pattern with his knife held at a 65° angle to the wood. The key to the kerbschnitzen *is to lock your wrist as shown, so your thumb and fingers guide the cut. Hold your elbow close to your body for better leverage and control. Barton works on his lap and rotates the wood to cut in different directions.*

ment needed is a pencil, a compass, a metric ruler and an eraser.

The first thing you must learn is how to hold the knife, as shown in the photo, below. It'll feel awkward, but be persistent. Wrap your fingers around the handle, with the first joint of your thumb riding on the lower end of the handle near the blade. Cock your wrist out until your thumb is in a fairly straight line with your forearm. With your knife in this position, bend your hand down until your thumb tip, index-finger knuckle and the blade tip form a fairly rigid tripod to support your knife and hand as they move over the work. Seen from the side, the edge of the blade resting on the wood should look like a capital V. To make the same cut on the opposite side of the V, roll the knife about 90° and move your thumb to the top ridge of the blade without changing your wrist position. The hand and knife move as a unit—never try to pull the knife toward your thumb, as you would if you were peeling potatoes. Part of your hand or finger must be touching the work as you cut, and keep your elbow close to your body for better leverage and control. If you want to cut long curves, keep turning the wood as you carve, rather than changing your hand position.

Since you're using only two tools, you can work without a workbench, with its hold-downs and other vises and faults. You can carve just about anywhere, in a comfortable sitting position with the work held in your lap by your non-carving hand. You don't even have to worry about holding the work flat because the position of the hand and knife relative to the work never changes, no matter how many times you shift the work in your lap to find a comfortable position, reach a tight spot or take advantage of the light.

In class we began carving by cutting tiny pyramid chips, probably the most frequently encountered shape in chip carving, as shown in figure 1. "The biggest problem," Barton warned us, "is that unlike chisel carving, once you have committed your blade to the wood, rarely can you alter or cover up a mistake—or a change of heart." You must get each cut right the first time, a tricky operation because the depth of cut varies along the incision. Hold the tip of the knife at the top of the pyramid (the proper 65° cutting angle is guaranteed if you're holding the knife correctly), and stab down to the full depth. Roll the knife to make the same cut from the opposite angle and stab again. Go back to your original knife angle and slice along the triangle to free the chip.

Though getting the correct depth on the first attempt is not easy, it is a skill that comes with practice. As a rule, the wider the chip, the deeper the cut, as shown in figure 2, p. 52. You can see the width of the chip on the pattern you've drawn on the wood. I have found—after cutting quite a few chips—that I now have a pretty reliable feeling for the amount of knife pressure needed

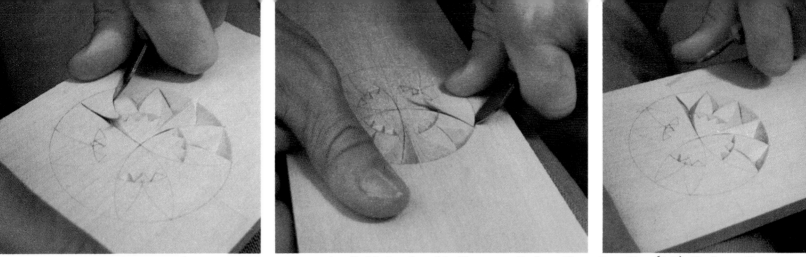

Barton begins his cut at the center of the rosette and pulls his hand and knife as a unit along the pattern line (left). He forces the blade down in a gentle arc to midpoint of the line, then gradually eases it up toward the surface. Then he rotates the piece and cuts along the curved rim (center). A final cut from the rim to the center frees the elongated triangular chip (right).

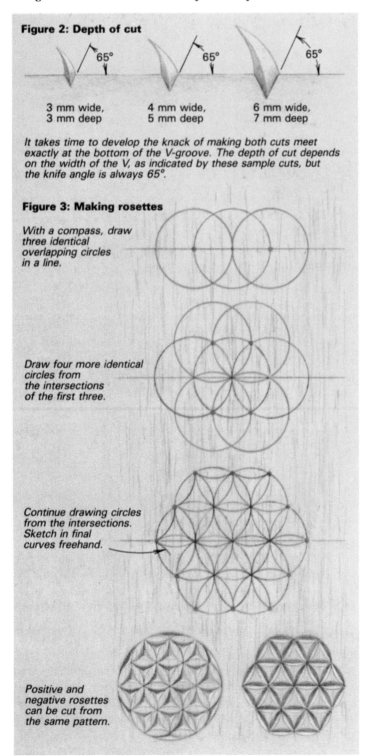

Figure 2: Depth of cut

65°   65°   65°

3 mm wide,   4 mm wide,   6 mm wide,
3 mm deep   5 mm deep   7 mm deep

It takes time to develop the knack of making both cuts meet exactly at the bottom of the V-groove. The depth of cut depends on the width of the V, as indicated by these sample cuts, but the knife angle is always 65°.

Figure 3: Making rosettes

With a compass, draw three identical overlapping circles in a line.

Draw four more identical circles from the intersections of the first three.

Continue drawing circles from the intersections. Sketch in final curves freehand.

Positive and negative rosettes can be cut from the same pattern.

The stab knife's thick edge is ideal for cutting and wedging fibers apart to create decorative indentations.

to achieve the correct depth for various sized chips. If the cuts are too shallow, the chip will not pop out. Then you have to re-enter the incision and try to sever the fibers that were missed the first time. If you don't exactly match the first angle, and you probably won't, you will create a second line on the carved wall which will look like a scar in the finished piece. If you cut too deeply, you create an undercut that robs a work of its crisp look and could weaken the delicate areas.

To remove a crescent, another common design, ease the knife tip below the surface as you pull it along the pattern line. As the blade approaches the other tip of the crescent, reduce the downward pressure and bring the knife tip up so it surfaces precisely at the tip of the crescent. Rotate the piece and cut the wide rim of the crescent. Rotate the piece again and make another cut right next to the first one to free the crescent-shaped chip. If you're cutting a curve with a small radius, you'll have to raise the knife on its tip, leaving a minimum of blade in the wood for a smooth cut. If you want to make a straight trough, cut along the line free-hand rather than try to fit your hand and blade along a straight-edge. You'll cut amazingly straight if you concentrate on the line right in front of the cutting edge. Your hand will follow your eye.

If you do all of your cuts correctly, there is a special reward: the chip springs from the work like a prisoner released. By the end of the week, we novice carvers were beginning to exclaim "Aha!" with increasing frequency, as the chips began to pop out

Sharpening chip carving knives

by Wayne Barton

You'll never be a top-flight carver until you learn to sharpen your knives to a razor edge. If you already have a method that works for you, use it. If not, here's a simple method of getting a perfectly sharp edge at the correct angle on your chip carving knives. Even a brand new knife, which seems sharp, needs this treatment before it is fit to carve with.

The knives I use are the ones principally used by Swiss carvers. Even on large scale work, like ceilings and walls, these short-bladed knives are the tools used, although sometimes a carver may put the blade in a 2-ft. section of a broomstick so he can use his shoulder for leverage. The blade is designed to strike the work at the correct angle when your hand is held in the position described on p. 51, so don't change the blade's shape when you sharpen.

To sharpen the knives, you need two stones, a medium-grade India and a hard, smooth-as-glass honing stone. A hard Arkansas is good. In recent years I've substituted a ceramic block for the hard Arkansas. The block doesn't need to be lubricated with water or oil the way some stones do, so it's great for honing knives wherever you go. I often carve and hone my knives while traveling, if I can get a friend to do the driving.

The stones must be flat. Test them by putting a straightedge across the length and width of the stone. You shouldn't be able to see any light under the straightedge. If the stone isn't flat, replace it or flatten it on a steel plate covered with a little oil and carborundum powder. If you use a stone that isn't flat, you'll round the tip of the knife, changing the cutting angle. You'll also find it easier to maintain a smooth, straight edge if you use a stone that's large enough to sharpen the entire knife edge at once. Unlike many carvers, I never use a leather strop on my knife. It's too easy to use a strop wrong, which will round over the knife edge and tip, decreasing the cutting efficiency. My advice is to stick with the edge you get off the stone.

To sharpen the cutting knife, drop a little oil on your India stone, hold the blade flat on the stone, then raise its back edge about 10°, as shown at right. Don't sharpen at a greater angle or you'll create a thick, obvious bevel that makes the knife drag as you pull it through the wood. Move the knife back and forth on the stone, first one side then the other, using the same pressure and number of strokes on each side. Concentrating the pressure on the heel of the blade helps avoid rounding the tip.

A burr may develop as you sharpen the blade. You can feel it if you run your finger along the flat of the blade, from the back toward the cutting edge. Once you raise a burr along the edge, continue sharpening in the same manner, but use less pressure. Work one side of the knife, then the other, until the burr falls off. If the edge is sharp, it won't reflect any light when you rock the blade slightly under a strong light as you look at the edge from a 45° angle.

Hone your blade on the hard Arkansas just as you sharpened it on the medium stone. Continue until you have a mirror finish that will let the knife slice smoothly through the wood. Be careful to hone each side of the blade equally. You don't want to raise a burr that will drag through the wood, possibly tearing the fibers.

When the blade looks and feels right, cut diagonally across a piece of wood. If the knife drags, check for a burr, a bevel behind the edge, or a dull light-reflecting edge. You can often eliminate the prob- lem with the honing stone, but if you've really been careless, it's best to go back to the India stone. If the knife cuts smoothly, you're ready to start carving.

Once you're knife is sharp, never let the blade get dull. Hone the blade on the hard Arkansas or ceramic block as soon as you feel it dragging and have to use more pressure to make the cut.

The stab knife is sharpened the same way as the cutting knife but at a 30° angle on each side. You want a definite bevel here. The stab knife doesn't cut—its thick edge should indent the wood by wedging the fibers apart. Even though the stab knife isn't used nearly as much as the cutting knife, it does add a nice decorative touch to your work. You'll be surprised at how much you can do with those little indentations. For a start, use your cutting knife to cut a flowing flower stem, then stab around the end of the stem to suggest a billowing flower.   —W.B.

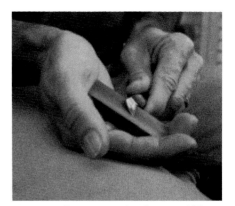

Sharpen the cutting knife at a 10° angle to the stone, as shown above. For a straight, smooth edge, always work on a stone that is large enough to hone the entire blade at once.

of their basswood prisons. Those crisp cuts are too good to hide under a heavy finish, so Barton just sprays his carvings with dull polyurethane after erasing any remaining pattern lines and lightly sanding the surface.

As the week went on, we advanced from borders to grids, then on to challenging and beautiful rosettes. They're easy to lay out with a compass once you get the knack of it, as shown in figure 3, facing page. You can create your own designs, or use the ones in Barton's book. If you develop your own designs, you will probably find that it is much easier to work with chip carving's two-plane perspective than three-dimensional, in-the-round-carving.

We wrapped up the week with a session on free-form carving and lettering. Barton was right. We *could* carve just about any design. But it would take many practice cuts before we could produce first-class work. Like beginning piano students who could plunk out a melody by Mozart, we were not quite ready for Carnegie Hall.

If you like objects with a hand-made look and feel, you'll like chip carving. Machines are often used for in-the-round carving, but *kerbschnitzen* is unique—perhaps the only technique in the woodworker's repertoire that a machine can't duplicate.   □

John Hines is a furniture designer and builder in Weatherford, Texas. Barton's school is Alpine School of Woodcarving, 225 Vine Ave., Park Ridge, Ill. 60068, (312) 692-2822. For more about kerbschnitzen, see Chip Carving Techniques & Patterns, *by Wayne Barton, Sterling Publishing Co., 2 Park Ave., New York, N.Y. 10016, 1984; and* Chip Carving with Wayne Barton, *a video workshop available from The Taunton Press, Box 5506, Newtown, Conn. 06470-5506. Chip-carving knives and ceramic sharpening blocks are available from the Alpine School and several mail-order tool supply houses.*

The simple shape of the author's carved spoon makes it an easy but quite useful beginner's project.

A shaving horse securely and safely holds the blank for rough shaping with a drawknife. When cutting on the pull stroke, the author uses the drawknife with the bevel facing up.

To cut with a push stroke, Greear turns the handles away from his body and cuts with the bevel down. This avoids flipping the draw-knife side to side, a dangerous move with such a long, sharp blade.

When cutting away from the body, be sure the hand holding the knife is behind the blade. Supporting the work with a bench and stop makes this cut easier to control.

When cutting toward the body, use short controlled strokes. To minimize the chance of injury, be sure the thumb is positioned so the handle of the knife hits the base of the thumb before the blade.

Carving Wooden Spoons
Serving up the basics

by Delbert Greear

From *Fine Woodworking* magazine (December 1989) 79:94-96

A spoon is a familiar object, and its simple curves and concave and convex surfaces provide a good introduction to knife cutting and other woodcarving techniques. At its simplest, a spoon is no more than a straight stick with a shallow dish on one end. Such a spoon is easy to carve from a small tree limb or board with just a few tools. More elaborate spoons can also challenge carvers at all levels.

While it's possible to carve an entire spoon with just a regular knife, it's a slow and tedious process, particularly when hollowing out concave areas. I like to work wood while it is still green, splitting a plank of the appropriate size out of a log and roughing it out with a hatchet. I then transfer the work to a shaving horse, as shown in the center photos on the facing page, and use a drawknife for the bulk of the carving.

I enjoy this type of woodworking and heartily recommend it as a welcome break from the sometimes hectic modern world. Others may choose to skip some of the handwork and rough out spoon blanks on a bandsaw before moving to the shaving horse. Either way, after roughing out the shape of the spoon, I hollow the bowl with a gouge, and then refine the spoon with drawknife and knife. Finally, I sand the spoon until it is smooth and pleasant to touch, and then coat it with mineral or vegetable oil or my brew of beeswax and mutton tallow.

Maple and birch are choice woods for spoons of all kinds because they carve easily when green, but set up hard when cured. Many other woods, such as apple, are harder to carve but make good spoons. There is a certain charm to owning a spoon and knowing the parent tree still lives, and orchard prunings make this possible. Spoons and similar small objects can be carved without ever having to cut a tree by using prunings or pieces of the thousands, if not millions, of trees that fall to the chainsaw and bulldozer for no other reason than to get them out of the way of some project or another.

Selecting a good knife – The first necessity for any whittler is a good knife. Opinions on the best knife vary considerably, as do knives and woodcarvers, so you must experiment to find what works for you. A good whittling knife, in my opinion, needs a smooth, contoured handle that doesn't chafe or slip out of your hand. A 2-in. to 3-in. blade is sufficient for most carving. A longer knife is harder to control because the long blade merely moves your hand farther from the cutting action, so you'll need more force to make the cut and put more strain on your hand and wrist. Safety is also a concern; a mistake with a 2-in. blade can cause a serious cut, but a similar mistake with a 6-in. blade can be frightful.

I like to whittle with a fixed-blade Sloyd knife that has a single blade with a slightly rounded end, as shown in the bottom, right photo on the facing page. The upward curve at the end makes the blade more maneuverable, and it is less likely to split the wood than one with a narrow, sharp point. The blade itself doesn't have to be hard steel, but it should be of good quality, and it should hone easily and hold an edge well. Avoid whittling knives with hollow-ground blades because they tend to dive into the wood and don't carve or cut chips as well as a rounded or wedge-shape edge. It takes some luck, or a lot of looking, to find a simple knife that works well and rests comfortably in the hand.

Most of the rough-carving techniques on a small object, such as a simple spoon, should be accomplished with "away" cuts, as shown in the bottom, left photo on the facing page. Shaping the round dish end of the spoon, however, calls for "toward" cuts, as shown in the bottom, right photo on the facing page. Making these cuts can be inherently dangerous, but there are a few rules that, if followed religiously, make these strokes more safe.

When cutting away from your body, hold the stock against a solid piece of wood, such as a tree or stump, and not another area of your body. For cutting toward your body, make controlled muscular movements that have a definite range and stopping point – well short of any flesh. For example, pull the knife with your shoulder and upper arm muscles so your elbow reaches your body before the blade reaches your holding hand. For detail work, pinch the tool toward the thumb of the hand holding the knife so that the knife handle hits the heel of the thumb before the blade does. This also provides good leverage when making short strokes, especially across the grain.

Never depend upon the momentum of the knife to complete a stroke. A knife is not an ax nor should it be used as one, even on a small scale. Pay close attention to the grain of the wood. Slicing into a diving grain binds up the blade and requires the use of excess force that might send the blade skipping along the wood.

Drawknife safety – the shaving horse is generally set up for a pulling stroke with the drawknife, as in the center, left photo on the facing page. To avoid tearing the wood in curved sections of the handle, you'll frequently have to reverse the direction of cut and push with the knife, as in the center, right photo on the facing page. The drawknife is best pulled with the bevel up and pushed with the bevel down, which saves turning the blade from side to side – a dangerous maneuver.

Pulling a sharp drawknife looks a little frightening to the uninitiated, but it is fairly safe if the shaving horse's work surface is long enough and the foot pedal is within easy reach of the operator. The drawing motion is self-limiting – when the biceps are flexed, the arm only goes back so far. The threat of injury does exist, and I urge anyone learning how to use a drawknife and shaving horse to work slowly and carefully.

The main danger in pushing the drawknife is to the fingers. It's easy to nick your fingers when you flip the blade over, especially if the handles are set close to the blade. Actually, the few serious cuts that I have seen or heard about with this tool resulted from dropping it or otherwise mishandling it when the blade was not being used. A secure place to hang or set the drawknife down is, therefore, of importance. Balancing this tool precariously on the stage of a shaving horse is an invitation for trouble.

As with the carving knife, the drawknife is not meant to be driven by momentum, but by steady muscular force. Chopping, prying and jerking are not only bad form, they are also dangerous.

Carving the dish – Once the overall spoon shape is roughed out with a drawknife, you are faced with the problem of hollowing out the dish. Holding a spoon or ladle safely while gouging out the bowl can be difficult on the average shaving horse since it is necessary to carve from many different directions. One solution is to drill a few holes at various places in the worktable and put pegs in them for stops. This keeps the spoon or ladle from twisting when it is clamped sideways. If you are fortunate enough to have a workbench, you may wish to clamp the spoon's handle while it is still rough in order to hollow out the bowl. Other jigs, which can be as simple as a bent nail in a stump, work just as well.

Hollowing the bowl is difficult to do with an ordinary knife, so you will probably want to invest in a gouge or crooked knife, which resembles a regular knife except that the end of the blade is curved upward. I use a gouge that is bent upward along its length as well as across the end of the blade, as shown in the photo on the following page, for roughing out spoons as well as bowls. From long familiarity, I am comfortable with this tool, but if you are new to spoon carving, I suggest that you also give the crooked knife a try. It is perhaps the safer tool for hand-held carving.

Unlike the straight carving knife, curved-edge tools cut more

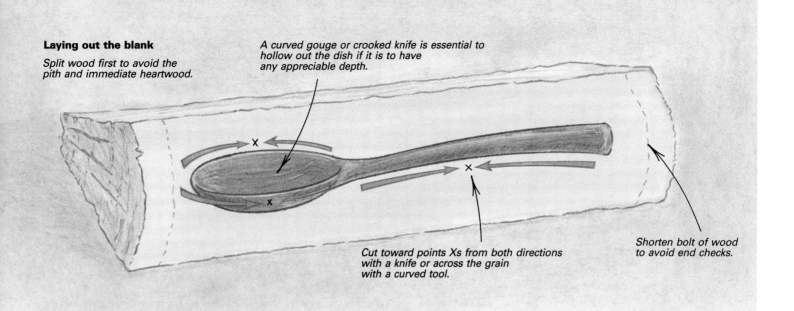

Laying out the blank

Split wood first to avoid the pith and immediate heartwood.

A curved gouge or crooked knife is essential to hollow out the dish if it is to have any appreciable depth.

X X

Cut toward points Xs from both directions with a knife or across the grain with a curved tool.

Shorten bolt of wood to avoid end checks.

Carve out the spoon with a gouge, working from the sides down to the middle. Cut across the grain as much as possible, as cutting with the grain can result in uncontrolled splits that dive into the wood.

smoothly across the grain. Scooping out chips with a gouge parallel to the grain often results in binding and tearing. As the blade exits the wood, it actually cuts against the grain—just as a knife cuts toward a diving grain. Cutting across the long grain, on the other hand, shears the fibers of the wood and lets the blade exit cleanly.

Recurved spoons and fancy ladles—A straight spoon is very handy for stirring and in a pinch it will do for serving and eating as well, although it is a little awkward for these tasks. Some curvature in the handle adds balance to the spoon and a corresponding upsweep in the bowl is handy for scooping food out of a pot or pan. Occasionally you will find a piece of wood that is shaped just right for such a spoon, but this is unusual. To carve recurved spoons, one must learn how to make curved shapes from straight-grain stock.

Newcomers to spoon carving may experience some difficulty with inside curves. You must cut toward the bottom of these curves from both directions, as shown in the drawing above. As with the bowl, if the recurve is sharp and deep, you may want to use the gouge or crooked knife to clean the burr at the bottom of the cut.

Recurved spoons have aesthetic appeal as well as practical value. A fancy soup ladle is a showpiece of the carver's art—and perhaps the epitome of the recurved spoon. Carving a ladle requires time and effort, even after you have achieved skill carving smaller spoons.

Long-lasting spoons—I scrape and sandpaper my spoons until they are smooth and free of splinters. After they are dry, I heat them and rub in a homemade finish of beeswax and mutton tallow, which is melted together in equal proportions, to penetrate and seal the wood. Mineral oil and some vegetable oils also make good finishes, as do commercial finishes especially formulated for woodenware.

Wooden bowls and utensils occasionally receive some bad press as being dangerous to your health. Although wooden chopping blocks seem to be the principal culprits as documented sources of food poisoning, wooden spoons, platters and bowls are generally banned from eating establishments, probably because they eventually crack and these cracks can harbor old food and thus breed bacteria. One way to avoid this is to make a spoon thin. A thin spoon dries quickly and has little time to mildew and sour, and the wood is also more flexible to accommodate expansion and contraction without cracking. Personally, I don't believe that smooth, well-sealed and well-cared-for woodenware is dangerous in the home kitchen. A nicely made wooden spoon or ladle is often easier to clean than a metal one with rivets and seams that can harbor food particles.

A wooden spoon that goes through regular cycles of wet and dry will not be protected from cracking unless it is well designed. The trick is to balance the forces in the wood, while still maintaining the needed strength. Avoiding the pith of the log, as shown above, and carving thin bowls are important here. A living tree is in a state of dynamic tension with itself and with the forces around it, such as wind and gravity. A piece of green wood inherits a share of this tension and other stresses develop as the wood dries. In a well-designed carving (of hollowware especially), woodcarvers can release much of this tension while conserving and emphasizing the natural strength of the wood. Although scientific principles are involved (see *Understanding Wood* by R. Bruce Hoadley, The Taunton Press, 1980), this process remains an art that can only be learned through experience.

Salad spoons—Salad spoons offer woodcarvers more chances to exercise their artistic muse. Salad spoons are best carved and used in sets. Traditionally one piece of the set is a spoon and the other a fork, or rather a sort of "spoon-fork." Carve the spoons with broad handles to give them balance, an easy-to-grip end and a place for decoration. I enjoy carving salad spoons to match a serving bowl, and these sets seem to be popular items for sale. I generally stick to symmetrical shapes, but don't hesitate to use your artistic skills here, as decorative salad spoons can make even a modest dining table seem rich. ☐

Delbert Greear is a woodworker in Helen, Ga.

Drawing: Roland Wolf

Making Snowshoes
Cold-bending the Indian way

by Henri
Vaillancourt

Red paint adds a decorative, personal touch to the lacings of these finely woven snowshoes. The mesh keeps the shoe from sinking into soft snow, but the Indians' sophisticated interlocking design makes this practical device beautiful as well.

For centuries, North American Indians have been using woodbending techniques to turn native hardwoods into snowshoes, canoes and other tools they need for survival. Their nomadic life meant they had to shape and bend wood quickly, without any elaborate steaming, sawing or jigs, and the cold-bending method they devised is as useful today as their snowshoes and canoes are.

The snowshoes are, in fact, one of the Indians' most brilliant inventions, and making a pair is a good way to learn about harvesting and bending green wood. I've always been fascinated by the self-sufficiency of the Indians in the harsh environment of Canada and the northeastern United States. Unfortunately, as youths abandon the ways of their parents, the old skills are in danger of dying out. During the past eight years, I've spent considerable time with various Canadian tribes, learning and recording some traditional snowshoe-making techniques. Here I'll describe the methods used by the Attikamek Indians in central Quebec, who still make a traditional snowshoe with a flat, somewhat angular toe, along with the type of harness once widely used in the northeastern United States and adjacent Canada. Even today winter travel for these people is not a frivolous sport but a rugged necessity—without snowshoes, the Indians would be unable to travel through deep snow to get food or firewood.

The Attikameks' snowshoe is one of the most versatile. It tracks well in open country and is maneuverable in rough or brushy areas. The broad, somewhat square front end gives the shoe a good grip on steep slopes. Since each pair is handmade by eye, no two pairs are exactly alike. Each maker shapes the front and crossbars and weaves the shoe to suit his own personality and tastes. The pair shown above, for example, has a more rounded front and is much larger than the pair shown on p. 60.

To make the snowshows, the Indians cut down a live tree and then repeatedly split it into riven sections larger than the components of the finished shoes. Using an ax, the maker hews the riven sections into rectangular staves, which he shaves smooth. To make the pieces easier to bend, he whittles the major bending points to thin them, then flexes the stave against his foot or knee until it's pliable enough to be bent and shaped freehand.

The Indians have a choice of four hardwoods that can be split, shaped and bent while green to make frames. Because of its strength and durability, yellow birch is preferred; the softer white birch is the next best. I've found, however, that my local New England birches are brittle and hard to bend. Black ash bends well but wears out quickly, especially in wet or crusty snow. Maple is a durable alternative, but it's difficult to work. White ash, which doesn't grow in Attikamek country, is common in the U.S. Northeast and makes good snowshoes, as does hickory.

The most workable trees are in the 6-in. to 12-in. diameter range. Look for a tree that's straight-grained, fast-growing and free from knots. Remember, you'll be splitting the wood, not sawing it, and the straighter the grain, the better the tree will split and the more unbroken long fibers it will have. A good indication of straight grain is the straightness of the fissures or vertical grooves in the bark of some trees. You can also strip off a length of bark to expose the grain. Fast-growers usually display bushy tops and horizontal or drooping branches. These trees have wider growth rings and a higher percentage of fibers to low-density earlywood vessels, so they're stronger than slow-growers. The Indians often chop out a chip from the tree's base to check the growth rings: rings about $\frac{1}{8}$ in. apart mean that the wood will be easy to cold-bend; closer rings indicate that it will be more brittle and harder to bend.

After you fell the tree, cut an 8-ft. log from the butt end. Split the log in two with wooden wedges, mallets and an ax, then into quarters, eighths or sixteenths, depending on the size of the trunk. You should end up with pieces about 2 in. wide on the bark side. Hew and shave these pieces into rectangular staves, 1 in. by ¾ in., as in figure 1. The Indians hew the staves with an ax or a chainsaw, as shown on the facing page. They use a crooked knife for smoothing, but you might be more comfortable with a drawknife, spokeshave or plane. Dress the staves evenly along their length to ensure symmetrical bending. Following the grain closely, so as not to cut across the long fibers, will minimize fracturing during bending. As no tree is perfectly straight, the dressed stave usually waves or twists, but this unevenness disappears when the snowshoe is given its final form.

To make shoes for an average-size man, cut the staves about

7½ ft. long (figure 2A). Make a pencil mark 6 in. from each end of the stave where the ends will come together to form the tail—the 6-in. length allows an inch or so to be trimmed off the finished, assembled tail. Make another mark halfway between the two tail marks for the center of the toe. Now draw two more lines 2 in. on either side of this center mark to set the width of the square toe and the placement of the front bends. You should also draw another mark on each side of the stave halfway between the centerline and the tail marks, where a temporary brace will be set while the bent frames dry.

To make it easier to bend the square toe, take a knife and shave the inside face of the stave, the pith side, for about 8 in. on either side of the centerline. The finished thickness should be about ⅜ in. to ½ in. Also shave the stave on either side of the tail marks, but this time on the outside (bark side), as the bend here will be in the opposite direction.

Rather than steaming or boiling the green wood to limber it, you repeatedly bend the stock against your foot or knee. Do the tail sections first. Put your foot near the tail mark, on the bark side of the stave, and flex the stave gently back and forth enough to limber the wood, so it can be bent into the tail shape. You may have to shift your foot several times to produce a smooth curve. Depending on the wood and the skill of the maker, the limbering process can take from 30 seconds or less to several minutes. You'll find that the wood will largely spring back to its original shape when you release it, but that's all right. Limbering bends the stave more than necessary for the finished frame, to make it easier to pull the frame into its final shape.

When you've limbered both tails, bend the sides in the same way, but this time put your knee on the pith side. Bend the stave for 9 in. or 10 in. either side of the brace marks. Flex the stave slightly before moving your knee up or down the stave—too much bending while keeping the pressure in only one position would result in irregular, angular curves. If, in spite of all precautions, the curves are uneven, you can shave the straight sections again to make them more flexible and then rebend them. Like the tails, the sides should be somewhat overbent.

To bend the toe, place your knee at one of the marks on either side of the centerline. Flex the stave back and forth a number of times until you form a sharp bend at that point. Bend the other side of the toe the same way. Splintering often occurs during this process, but the stave is thick enough for you to trim off any slivers after the frame has dried. You could also bind the splinters in place with thread to prevent deeper cracking.

To bend the stave into its final form, place your foot on the flat part of the toe section and pull the two ends of the stave upward until you can insert a stick, or spreader, approximately 14 in. long at the halfway marks (the exact length of this stick depends on the shape desired). Next bend the two sides around this stick and bring the ends together to form a tail. Match the pencil marks indicating the start of the tail and tie the ends securely with twine. Now check if the frame is symmetrical. If it looks uneven, use your knee on the inside or outside of the frame and bend the stave until the curves look right. Bend a second frame to match the first, and tie the pair together with twine to keep them from warping as they dry.

The Indian method of cold-bending takes a fair amount of skill, so those unwilling to practice would be better off using a bending form. Make one from 1-in. boards or plywood cut to the shape of the inside of the snowshoe frame and mounted on a wooden backing somewhat larger than the form. Even though the Indians bend wood cold, I would advise beginners to use hot

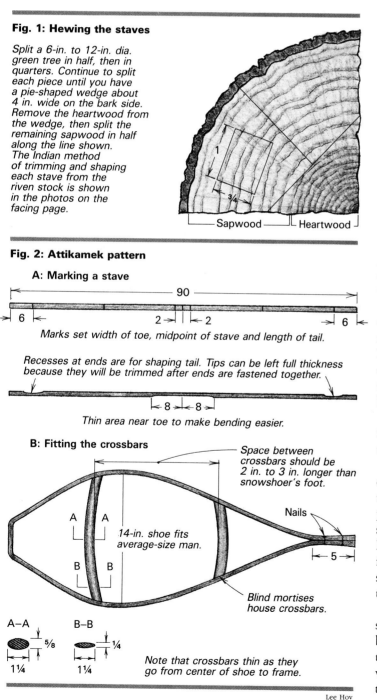

Fig. 1: Hewing the staves

Split a 6-in. to 12-in. dia. green tree in half, then in quarters. Continue to split each piece until you have a pie-shaped wedge about 4 in. wide on the bark side. Remove the heartwood from the wedge, then split the remaining sapwood in half along the line shown. The Indian method of trimming and shaping each stave from the riven stock is shown in the photos on the facing page.

Sapwood — Heartwood

Fig. 2: Attikamek pattern

A: Marking a stave

|← 90 →|

|← 6 →| |← 2 →| |← 2 →| |← 6 →|

Marks set width of toe, midpoint of stave and length of tail.

Recesses at ends are for shaping tail. Tips can be left full thickness because they will be trimmed after ends are fastened together.

|← 8 →|← 8 →|

Thin area near toe to make bending easier.

B: Fitting the crossbars

Space between crossbars should be 2 in. to 3 in. longer than snowshoer's foot.

A   A

14-in. shoe fits average-size man.

Nails

B   B

|← 5 →|

Blind mortises house crossbars.

A–A ⅝ 1¼

B–B ¼ 1¼

Note that crossbars thin as they go from center of shoe to frame.

Lee Hov

From *Fine Woodworking* magazine (November 1984) 49:77-80

Sweat, not steam, is the key to this low-tech method of bending green wood. An Indian needs only a knife, an ax and his body. After splitting a stave out of a live tree, Moise Flamand, an Attikamek from Quebec, hews it with his ax (top left). Then, using his hand as a vise, he shaves the piece with a crooked knife (above). Stepping on the end of the stave, he flexes the piece until it's limber enough to bend (bottom left). To make the sharper front bends, he shaves the area thinner, then uses his knee as a fulcrum for bending the wood (below).

Black-and-white photos: Henri Vaillancourt

A temporary horizontal spreader establishes the characteristic snowshoe shape as the ends of the staves are pulled together. Twine holds the tails together until the green frame has dried.

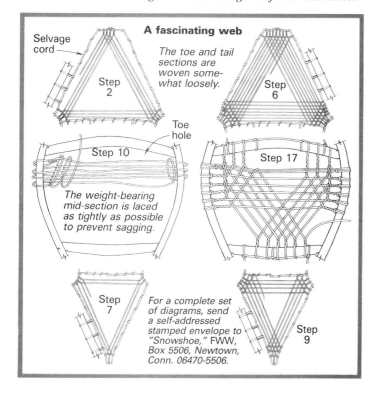

A fascinating web

Selvage cord

The toe and tail sections are woven somewhat loosely.

Step 2

Step 6

Toe hole

Step 10

Step 17

The weight-bearing mid-section is laced as tightly as possible to prevent sagging.

Step 7

For a complete set of diagrams, send a self-addressed stamped envelope to "Snowshoe," FWW, Box 5506, Newtown, Conn. 06470-5506.

Step 9

water for the entire bending process—it will make the wood more pliable and easier to handle. Either stand the stave in a pot of boiling water, or hold it over the pot and give the section to be bent a liberal dousing with a ladle for a minute or two. You could also douse the stave with hot water as you wrap it around the form. Then hold it in place with wooden blocks nailed to the backing. First nail a block to hold the toe section, and then simultaneously bend both sides of the stave around the form and fasten them with more blocks. Finally, force the tails together and hold them in place with additional blocks.

After the bent frames have dried for several days, clinch-nail the tail with two nails (any type of nail will do). Next cut the blind mortises for the two crossbars as shown in figure 2B. The two Attikamek crossbars are oval in section and bowed—toward the front and toward the back, respectively. Shaved from the same wood as the staves, they're about 1¼ in. wide and ⅝ in. thick at the midsection, tapering to ¼ in. at the tenons, which have no shoulders. The distance between the bars should be several inches greater than the length of the user's foot.

Next drill the frame for a rawhide or twine selvage cord, which will anchor the weaving in the toe and tail sections. Bore these holes (from 1/16 in. to ⅛ in. in diameter and spaced ⅛ in. to ¼ in. apart) in pairs through the frame from the outside. Place the first pair one above the other about 1½ in. from the ends of the crossbars, and successive pairs on 1½-in. to 2-in. centers. To countersink the cord and protect it from wear, chisel a ⅛-in. deep groove between the holes on the outside edge of the frame. Pass the cord through each pair of holes and knot it on the inside before carrying it to the next pair. You should also loop and run the selvage around the crossbars.

Once the selvage cord is attached, the shoe is ready for weaving. The Attikamek still cut lacings for snowshoes from raw moose or deer hides, but you could substitute untanned cow or calf skin. For those who don't wish to work skins, woven nylon cord from the hardware store is a fair substitute. The ⅛-in. dia. cord is good for both the midsection and the end weave.

The Indians usually leave their snowshoes unfinished, but if you wish, you could give the pair a coat of good spar varnish after you complete the lacing. Some makers, especially those who often travel on wet snow, also varnish the lacings.

To make a harness, the Indians pass a pliable leather strap through the weave near the toe hole of the center section and fasten it around their foot. This harness holds the ball of the foot down, but leaves the heel free to lift. The leather strapping used in commercial harnesses is too stiff for this style harness. Very soft leather is needed, but if you can't get it, you can substitute ¾-in. lampwicking or cotton clothesline.

For snowshoeing, Indians ordinarily wear soft moose or caribou skin moccasins over several pairs of wool socks or liners of wool blanketing or felt. The heelless moccasins don't abrade the lacings, and I find that they let me "feel" the snowshoes and harness. You can readily sense if the harness is poorly adjusted, and how the snowshoe is behaving in relation to your foot. This lets you adjust your stride and balance in subtle ways that are difficult to explain but quickly learned. □

Henri Vaillancourt lives in Greenville, N.H., and is an authority on the traditional crafts of the Northern Woodland Indians. His book, Making the Attikamek Snowshoe, *is available from The Trust for American Cultures and Crafts, Box 142, Greenville, N.H. 03048. The Trust also makes video tapes on Indian technology, including snowshoe-making.*

Klompen
Shoes from trees

by Anne Siegel

Bob Siegel makes wooden shoes from green Aspen chunks with tools like this spoon auger used to hollow out each shoe. The shoes are wedged in a notch cut into his walnut-log workbench. The flat end of the bench is a cutting board for rough shaping the shoes with an ax. When not in use, the rest of his tools hang from pegs in the front of the bench.

About 15 years ago my father, obligingly following my mother into another Wisconsin antiques store, spotted something interesting and emerged with an armful of oddly shaped tools. A full-time insurance agent and weekend woodworker, he never dreamed that he was carrying the remnants of the dying European craft of wooden shoe making.

In 1912 there were about 4,000 carvers in the Netherlands who each year produced about six million pairs of inexpensive, durable shoes for the farmers, fishermen and other workers. Each carver made about five pairs per day—splitting each one out of a log with a froe, then shaping the exterior with an ax and long knife and hollowing the inside with a spoon-shaped auger. The Netherlands now produces about three million pairs per year, most of them for tourists, but today they're turned out by duplicating lathes and boring machines following models handcarved by the few remaining craftsmen.

The Dutch call their wooden shoes *klompen* after the "klomp, klomp" sound they make on cobblestone streets. In France they're called *sabots*. Workers protesting the 19th-century mechanical wonders that were putting them out of work, threw their *sabots* into the whirring machines at several factories. They didn't derail the Industrial Age but they created the word sabotage.

As his collection of old tools grew, my father, Bob Siegel Jr., (everyone calls him Sieg) became interested in the history and carving of these shoes. Sieg decided to learn how to use the tools so he could demonstrate the craft. He began in the early 70s by observing a master *klompenmaker* in Orange City, Iowa, and another in Holland, Mich. Later he spent three weeks in the Netherlands, where he studied with 12 *klompenmakers*.

Each man had his own methods of carving, and sometimes different tools, but the result was always the same—a shoe that fit the foot. The skill of the craft is not so much in using the tools or in the unique shape of the finished product, but in having the shape of the foot in mind and carving it by eye quickly and efficiently. The carvers found that the only way to master the art of carving a foot shape inside a block of wood was to carve a lot of shoes.

Aspen is the best shoe wood, although willow and beech can also be used. The wood should be lightweight, split and carve easily, resist checking and not discolor with age. Since the wood is always worked green, carvers would often move right out to the forest, cut down a tree and turn the whole thing into piles of shoes—a mature aspen yields about 75 pairs. Dry wood is harder to cut and tends to split when the shoe is hollowed out. The carved wet wood doesn't usually check when it dries, perhaps because the carving, from start to finish, takes less than two hours and the thin sides dry simultaneously inside and out.

Sieg works on a walnut-log workbench, trimmed underneath until it weighs about 70 pounds—light enough to carry, but still heavy enough to be stable. Instead of a vise, he's cut a deep, wide notch into one end of the bench top where he can wedge a pair of shoes while hollowing them. The top stands on three splayed legs secured from underneath with wedges. Removable pegs in the front and sides of the bench hold his tools—a mallet for securing wedges, a metric ruler, a rasp for enlarging the instep and a wooden bit brace to bore tiny holes in the sides to string the shoes together.

Klompen are carved in pairs, so the carver can concentrate on making the shoes the same size and give them the proper left-foot, right-foot contours. The carver needs three measurements—

From *Fine Woodworking* magazine (September 1985) 54:55-57

the length of the person's foot; the length of the log section to be crosscut (20% longer than the foot gives you enough wood for a strong toe and heel) and the inside length of the shoe, which is generally a little greater than the footlength.

To carve a pair for a one-year-old child, for example, you need a 6-in. blank. Cross cut the log to length, then split it into quarters with a froe and maul. Sieg then uses a side ax, a one-hand version of the hewing ax, to smooth two adjacent surfaces at right angles to each other. These flat sides will be the side and the sole of the shoe. Then he chops the remaining sides until he has roughed out the shoe exterior to within a ¼-in. of its final contours. It takes about 10 minutes to chop out a pair.

Next, he refines the exterior shape with a block knife, a long blade with a handle at one end and a little curlicue at the other. The curlicue end fits loosely into a screw eye at one end of the bench, so the knife can be used like a paper cutter for straight cuts and rotated slightly in the screw eye to do a curved cut (photo 3, facing page). The long blade gives the knife powerful leverage and enough control to shave a pair of *klompen* to a nearly finished stage in about 20 minutes. It's important to accurately shape the exterior so that when the *klompen* are hollowed out to fit the foot, the top and side walls will be only about ⅜ in. thick.

The rough shoe is now wedged into the bench notch. With a spoon auger, Sieg bores a hole near the heel by pressing down hard on the shaft, while simultaneously twirling the handle. If you hold the auger handle with your right hand, you'd twist it clockwise; lefthanders go counterclockwise. You control the cut by holding the lower shaft with your other hand. The first wood section removed will look like a button. On large *klompen*, Sieg bores a second hole, just in front of the shoe's high crown (roughly equivalent to the top of the tongue on a leather shoe), then breaks out the wood between the holes. He spoons out the rest of the heel area, just as you would scoop ice cream from a bucket.

Working with his spoon auger, Sieg bores a hole from the heel to the toe, slightly longer than the person's foot, then enlarges the opening, scooping circular curls of wood from the lower half of the *klompen* until the walls are the right thickness and the arch is properly contoured. He can hollow out a pair of *klompen* in about 30 minutes.

Sieg releases the nearly completed shoes from the bench and trims them with the block knife. Finally, the inside front half of each shoe is smoothed with a long chisel that's hooked at the end and the outside is scraped smoooth with a metal scraper or a piece of glass. Sometimes the shoes are left unfinished, sometimes they are painted. In some European areas where the low-cost wooden shoes are considered poor people's fare, a Sunday pair might be painted black and outfitted with glued on laces and eyelets until they looked like real leather shoes. Sieg decorates many of his with carved tulips, hearts and windmills.

Sieg now demonstrates *klompen*-carving at trade shows, festivals and other events around the country and sells full-sized shoes for adults, who buy them for the same reasons that European workers do—*klompen* worn with thick socks are warm in winter; with thin socks they are cool in summer. They're good safety shoes and easy to slip on and off. They also keep your feet dry when working in the garden or another damp area, and, if you get tired of wearing them, they make unique mantle pieces. □

Anne Siegel is editor of Oregon Magazine *in Portland Ore. Bob Siegel lives in Mequon, Wisc.*

A froe and mallet split the shoe blank out of the green log (1). A 10-in. diameter log yields four blanks. Sieg uses a side ax to square the sole and one side, then begins shaping the shoe (2). The ax is beveled only on the side away from the cut, making it an efficient planing and carving tool. After bracing the shoe with his bench and thigh (3), he refines the shoe shape with the lever-like block knife that pivots in a screw eye attached to the bench. The leverage of the long block knife makes it good for heavy crossgrain paring (4).

Sieg wedges the shoes to the bench, which he braces with his legs (5), then bores a hole in the heel with a T-handled spoon auger. After boring two holes, he uses the auger like a pry bar to break out large chunks of waste from between the two holes (6). After clearing the heel, Sieg uses the spoon auger like an ice cream scoop to enlarge the opening and shape it to fit the foot (7). Large curls of wood are removed from the top (8), until the wall reaches proper thickness and from the bottom until the arch is properly contoured for support and comfort.

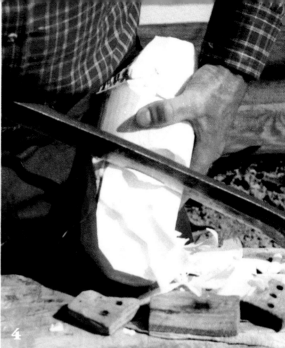

To hollow the toe, Sieg turns the auger with his right hand while guiding the shaft with his left (9 and 10). The block knife creates a ready-to-wear finish (11).

Carving Incised Letters

Just a few tools do the job

by Roger Holmes

I first saw Frank Cushwa carve a sign at the Bridgewater Fair, a cattle-and-cotton candy fest up the road from us in rural Connecticut. With a single skew chisel and a couple of gouges, Cushwa incised eight or so 2-in.-high letters in a piece of pine, a nameplate for someone's vacation home. Layout and carving took all of about 20 minutes. It was a handsome sign. Though sketched freehand, the letters were nicely formed and spaced, and the carving was crisp. Until then, I had thought letter carving required complicated layout and a trunkful of carving tools. Cushwa made it look easy—well, accessible at least—so I decided to look him up and find out more.

Cushwa and his wife, Rhonda, run their business, Kent Carved Signs, out of a building just behind an old railroad station in the center of Kent, Conn. While Frank carves at a waist-high, lectern-like bench, Rhonda tends the phone, the order book and the computer. It's clear from a glance at the 15 or 20 signs displayed around the showroom that carving is only part of the job. Most are painted pine or poplar, though some are polyurethaned butternut or walnut. After carving, letters are either painted to contrast with background colors, or gilded with 23K gold leaf. Gold leaf is popular for commercial signs—doctors' and lawyers' offices, bakeries, shops. Gold, according to Cushwa, reflects light as well as status and makes a letter stand out like nothing else. It is also expensive: 2-in.-high letters, for example, cost $5 apiece painted, $8 each gilded.

Cushwa is a self-taught carver. After receiving his master's degree in music performance on the clarinet, he decided against music as a career—he liked the playing, but hated the hustling required to make it pay. In 1979, a chance encounter with a sign carver demonstrating his work in a shopping mall planted the seed of his new career. A carver in Amherst, Mass., told him a bit about tools and techniques; type books provided a short course in lettering. Experiment and practice did the rest.

Cushwa's technique is straightforward and involves using carving tools rather like knives, pushing or pulling them to make slicing instead of chopping cuts. The technique is similar to chip carving, in that several angled cuts pop a chip of triangular cross section out of the wood to create an element of a letter. Straight cuts are made with a skew chisel that is as large as practical for the letter size. Curves are roughed out with a skew, then the outside, concave curves are finished with one or two gouges, the inside, convex curves with the skew. Almost all the cutting is done from just four hand postions, shown in photos **2**, **3**, **4** and **7**. Cushwa has built up the shafts of some of his tools with duct tape to

Frank Cushwa carves a sign (top) with only a skew chisel and a few gouges. His waist-high bench, its surface about 2½ ft. on a side, allows him to move around large signs. Cushwa lays out letters freehand (bottom), using a plastic rule for straight lines. Spaces between letters should be roughly equal in area.

From *Fine Woodworking* magazine (July 1986) 59:48-51

Three basic hand positions are shown here as Cushwa sets in and makes two vertical straight cuts for an I. Some trimming with the skew completes the letter.

make the pencil-grip he frequently employs more comfortable.

The beauty of the method is most evident in the curved gouge cuts. With the waste cleared by the skew, the gouge needs only to establish its own bearing surface as it slices down at the beginning of the cut. Then, pushed or pulled according to grain direction, it cuts a fair curve across the wood, guided by the rubbing of its bevel on the surface just cut and, minimally, by hand and eye. This flowing movement is essential to the technique, whether the cut is straight or curved. In some cuts, the hands, wrists and tool may be rigid, the upper arms and body moving them as a unit across the wood. In others, the fingers and wrists combine to pivot the cutting edge in an arc.

As economical as Cushwa's method is, it's hard work, and hard on the body. A run of some 300 signs carved over a twelve day period at the New England States Exposition last year induced a painful case of tendonitis in his right elbow. To lessen the strain, Cushwa has been experimenting with other carving styles, as well as the use of a router to clear waste prior to hand cutting.

Though a simple sign may require only a skew and two gouges to carve, Cushwa's tool collection is much larger than that. To accommodate letters of varying size, his skews range in width from ⅜ in. to 1¼ in. Gouges are similar widths, the sweeps mostly #5, #6 or #7, and include a few in a fishtail pattern. Punctuation—periods, commas and so on—require narrower, tighter-radius gouges.

Cushwa prefers thin tools, which slice through the wood with less effort. To reduce drag on the skews further, he extends the sharpening bevels back about ½ in. from the cutting edge. He doesn't grind the bevels, but works them over a series of oilstones—medium and fine India, then hard Arkansas. Three increasingly fine grits of buffing compound on a wheel, followed by stropping with leather, bring the tool to a mirror polish, which also lessens friction. He works a small, second bevel at a slightly higher angle on the hard Arkansas stone, then rounds the tip minutely and the skew is ready to carve. Gouge bevels are also lengthened, though not quite as much—most of the

6

To avoid cutting against the grain on a diagonal cut (above), reverse the skew and push it away from you. Cushwa uses the hand position at right to make the top cut of a horizontal letter stroke.

wood is removed first by a skew, so drag isn't as important. Corners are slightly rounded to keep them from catching during a cut. Once he prepares a tool with stones and buffing, Cushwa can carve pine with it for days with only frequent touch-ups on the hard Arkansas stone.

Cushwa's skews are extremely sharp but fragile because of the long bevel. A surprising amount of flexing occurs on curved cuts (Cushwa likens the varying flexibility among skews to that found in clarinet reeds), and you must be constantly aware of the stress on the tool. Rounding the tip, Cushwa discovered a couple years back, helps keep it from snapping off on curves, and saves much tedious sharpening time.

Regardless of how well it's carved, a sign is only as good as the form and layout of its letters. Cushwa has a good eye and what penmanship teachers used to call a good "hand." He keeps a copy of the Lettraset catalog of transfer type close at hand for reference, and studies other type books from time to time. (These books are available at most art supply stores or libraries.) Most of Cushwa's signs employ letters based on the Caslon face, an austere, distinguished face consisting of straight lines and simple arcs. Serifs, small tails ending the strokes that form the letter, add a simple touch of grace.

Cushwa rules layout lines on the board, then draws the letters with a 6B pencil (**1**). A short plastic ruler aids him with the straight lines, but curves are all freehanded. The letter shapes are roughly, but fluidly indicated; Cushwa defines the final shape while carving. Spacing is important and more difficult to alter once carving has begun. After establishing the center of a line by measurement, he spaces the letters and words by eye, trying to make the spaces between the letters in a word roughly equal in area. Cushwa will erase three, four or more times until a layout looks right—he says he spends more money on erasers than he does on tools.

Lettering freehand mirrors the carving style—the movements are much the same for both, so the two tasks are complementary. If you're uncomfortable with freehand lettering, you can trace letters, shrinking or enlarging them if needed with an overhead projector. Blue, black or white carbon paper works for transferring the tracings, depending on the color of the groundwork.

After layout, Cushwa fixes the board securely to the carving bench with as little obstruction as possible. Small signs are held by two commercially made aluminum bar clamps called Back-to-Back Bench Clamps, which clamp to the benchtop and the work (available from Woodcraft Supply Corp., 41 Atlantic Ave., P.O. Box 4000, Woburn, Mass. 01888). C-clamps hold large signs. Carving begins by making cuts with a skew along the base and height

lines; Cushwa calls these stop cuts (**2**). Make them deep in the center and shallow at both ends, which form the points of the serifs. Two vertical cuts complete an I, the simplest letter (**3, 4**). Each cut begins and ends at the points of the serifs, curving with a twist of the wrist into or out of the straight cut. The hands and tool are rigid for the straight cuts, pulled by the upper arms and shoulders. In these and virtually all other cuts, the heel of the right hand rests on the work (as for holding a pencil) and steadies the cut. Likewise, all cuts are made holding the tool at an angle between 30° and 40° to the wood. Cushwa says precise angles and the depth of the cuts are less critical than the width of the letter's strokes. Nevertheless, his cuts are of a fairly uniform angle, resulting in the narrow strokes being shallower than the wider strokes.

After clearing the chip, clean the juncture of the two cuts and the serifs. Trim as needed to even the surfaces and straighten lines (**5**). Remember, this is freehand carving; each letter need

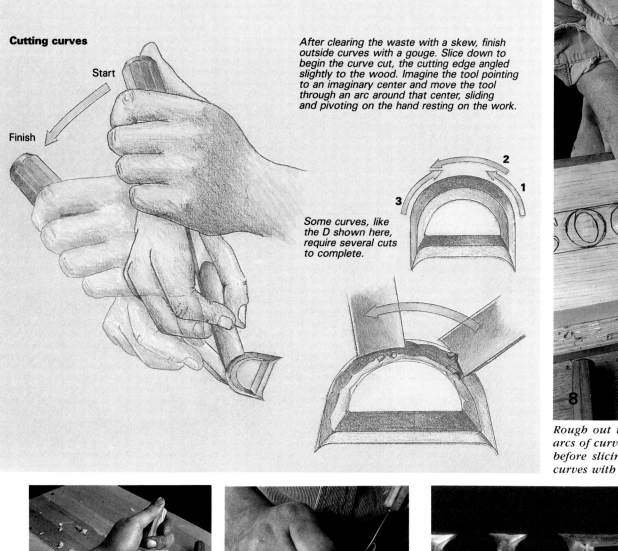

Cutting curves

Start

Finish

After clearing the waste with a skew, finish outside curves with a gouge. Slice down to begin the curve cut, the cutting edge angled slightly to the wood. Imagine the tool pointing to an imaginary center and move the tool through an arc around that center, sliding and pivoting on the hand resting on the work.

Some curves, like the D shown here, require several cuts to complete.

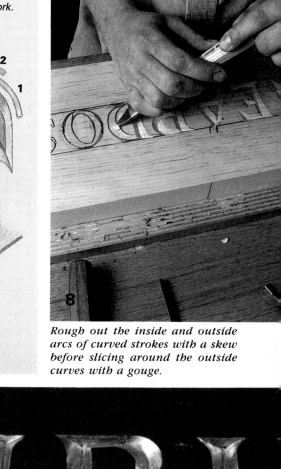

Rough out the inside and outside arcs of curved strokes with a skew before slicing around the outside curves with a gouge.

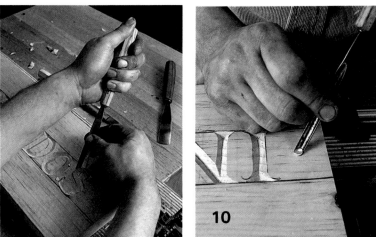

Tight curves are cut with a narrower gouge and a pivoting motion (left). A 360° pivot around a tight radius makes a period (right).

Gold leaf against a painted background brings out the full character of incised letters.

not be uniform or perfect to create a pleasing sign.

Diagonal cuts are made much like vertical cuts—hands and tool moved as a unit by the upper arms and shoulders. In photo **6**, Cushwa has reversed the skew and is pushing it away from his body in order to cut with the grain. Horizontal cuts are complicated only by the tendency of the tool to follow the grain. Top and bottom stop cuts for an E are just like those for an I, only stretched out between the points of the serifs at each end. After cutting the letter's vertical stroke, make vertical stop cuts at the ends of the letter's three horizontal strokes, then make the remaining horizontal cuts (**7**). The horizontal strokes are narrower than the vertical one and are, therefore, shallower, widening and deepening into the serifs.

Cushwa roughs out curved letter strokes with a skew, shifting hand positions and reversing tool direction as the grain dictates to cut both the inside and outside curves of the stroke (**8**). A

gouge of as large a sweep as is comfortable finishes the outside curve, as shown in the drawing. Think of the tool as pointing to the center of an imaginary cone forming the outside curve. Slice into the wood and rotate the tool through an arc around that center to make the cut. While the upper arms and shoulders move the hands and tool laterally, the tool is also pivoted, the right hand serving as fulcrum. Large curves may require several cuts to complete. Finish inside curves with a skew.

Small-radius curves are cut much like large ones. Rough them out with a skew. Pay particular attention to grain direction on an S. The gouge cut may be almost entirely pivoted (**9**). A period is the tightest radius curve—twirling the tool almost on a point pops out a tiny plug (**10**). Photo **11** shows how nicely gilded letters stand out on a painted background. □

———————————

Roger Holmes is an associate editor of Fine Woodworking.

Turned Pens and Pencils

A *retractable ballpoint*

by Richard Elderton

After my second ballpoint pen broke in half, I noticed the flimsy plastic joint between the metal top and the plastic bottom. The thin plastic joint doomed the pen to a short life. To avoid this fate, I decided to clothe my two naked Parker refills with suits of wood.

The design is simple and functional—a wooden cap and barrel, shaped on the lathe and bored out for the refill and the trigger mechanism that advances the pen point for writing. The cap slides onto a sleeve turned on the barrel, and the two pieces are held together by a pin in the cap, which twists and locks in an L-shaped groove routed in the barrel. So far, I've resisted suggestions to add inlays or other adornment, partly out of laziness and partly to retain the basic quality of the rosewood and other exotics I use.

The first step is to rip blanks about ¾-in. square for barrels, ⅜-in. square for triggers and ³⁄₁₆-in. square for pins, then crosscut the cap and barrel blanks as shown in the drawing, or to fit your refill, plus an extra ³⁄₁₆ in. I don't cut off the trigger and pin blanks until after these tiny pieces are shaped.

Turning techniques—I use a 3-jaw chuck for the turning and boring operations. By inserting the blank deeply into the chuck and gripping it tightly, I can do all the boring and end-grain shaping without the piece vibrating or whipping. First, I turn the ¾-in. blanks to cylinders that can be gripped in the 3-jaw chuck without being damaged. After chucking each cylinder in the 3-jaw, I square both ends with a skew chisel.

The cap and barrel must be bored in stages. I mount a Jacobs chuck in the tailstock to advance different-diameter bits into the spinning cylinders. To hollow the cap, I begin with a ⅜-in. brad-point bit to bore the main hole to about ½ in. from the top of the piece, then complete the bore with a ⁷⁄₃₂-in. sleeve drill. The sleeve drill, which centers the second hole in the first, is made

Tired of plastic pens breaking, the author made a two-piece rosewood housing for his ballpoint refills. The tiny trigger on the top makes the pen retractable. A boxwood pin fit into the top locks into a groove in the barrel to hold the pieces together.

with a drill rod and twist drill. I bore a deep axial hole in the center of the drill rod, again using the 3-jaw and Jacobs chucks, and epoxy in the twist drill. The barrel is hollowed in the same way as the cap, but this time I bore with a ¼-in. brad-point bit, followed by a ⁷⁄₆₄-in. sleeve drill.

I rechuck the barrel with about 1¾ in. of the open end protruding from the jaws and turn down a shaft, ⅜ in. dia. and 1⅛ in. long. This shaft slides into the hole bored in the cap, which I deburr by sanding with 220-grit paper rolled into a cylinder. Then I gently push the cap onto the slightly oversize rotating barrel just enough for the burnishing action to indicate high spots to be removed with light skew cuts. Once the cap goes halfway on under power, test fittings are done with the lathe stopped, and the surfaces are sanded with 320-grit paper until everything fits.

To avoid breaking the barrel when it's shaped, a short section of ¼-in.-dia. rod is inserted in the sleeve before the piece is clamped in the 3-jaw. A ball-bearing tailstock center is also snugged up into the small hole at the end of the barrel to steady and center it precisely as I turn the shape with a roughing gouge and skew. The next step is to mount the cap on a ⅜-in.-dia. rod. A piece of rubber tubing wrapped around the cap end prevents slippage in the jaws. Again, a live center provides end pressure for stability. Shape the cap, then try it on the barrel and adjust the pieces as needed. Do final sanding with the grain while the lathe is stopped.

A spring about ⅝ in. long makes the pen retractable. If you can't find a ³⁄₃₂-in. OD spring, you can make one by wrapping 0.014-in.-dia. piano wire tightly around a piece of ⁷⁄₆₄-in. drill rod clamped in a vise. Remove the spring from the rod and stretch it until it has about 14 turns per inch, then cut it to size. Once the spring is made, I can put it on the refill, assemble the parts I've made so far and calculate the dimensions of the trigger mechanism in the cap.

Calculating part sizes—The math here may seem a nuisance, but it avoids the wasted time and frustration of trial-and-error methods. To begin the calculation, I insert the depth gauge of a vernier caliper through the hole in the cap and use it like a trigger to depress the refill until it protrudes the correct amount from the barrel. I record this reading to the nearest ¹⁄₃₂ in., then proceed as shown in figure 3.

The oversized, square trigger stock can now be mounted in the 3-jaw, with just enough for one trigger protruding. I turn the whole section to ⁵⁄₁₆ in. dia., then cut the steps shown, taking care to make the length of each step correct. The ⁷⁄₃₂-in.-dia. section is

Photos this page: Michele Russell Slavinsky

crucial—if it's too slack, the trigger will slip; too tight will make it difficult to retract the refill.

After parting off the trigger from the square blank, I remount it with the chuck gripping the 7/32-in. section and turn a rounded point. I'm now ready to put the trigger in the pen and test the mechanism. If it doesn't work, I recheck the dimensions and adjust as needed.

Routing grooves—I used to hand-carve the twist lock, but the simple router jig shown at right simplifies the process greatly. First, I drill a 5/64-in. hole about 3/16 in. from the open end of the cap, perpendicular to the pen's long axis. I like to recess the hole with an 1/8-in. counterbore to make a flat-bottomed socket for the pinhead. I made my counterbore from 1/8-in. rod, just as I did the sleeve drill, but filed in the tiny teeth before epoxying in the 5/64-in. pilot. The next step is to mount the 3/16-in.-square stock in the chuck with about 1 in. protruding. I turn it down to 1/8 in. dia., then reduce the diameter of the first 1/8 in. to create a square shoulder and 5/64-in.-dia. shaft. A small 1/4-in. skew made from an old screwdriver or drill rod works well here. After test fitting the pin, I adjust its length to fit the thickness of the cap, form the rounded head and part the piece off. The pin must protrude about 3/64 in. into the cavity to lock into the routed groove.

To cut the groove, I take out the pin, assemble the cap and barrel, then rotate the pieces until there's a good grain pattern

Cutting the groove for the locking pin is simple with this router arrangement. The pen barrel is pushed onto a guide rod, which fits snugly inside the barrel, as the bit cuts the groove. Twisting the barrel creates the final skewed section of the groove.

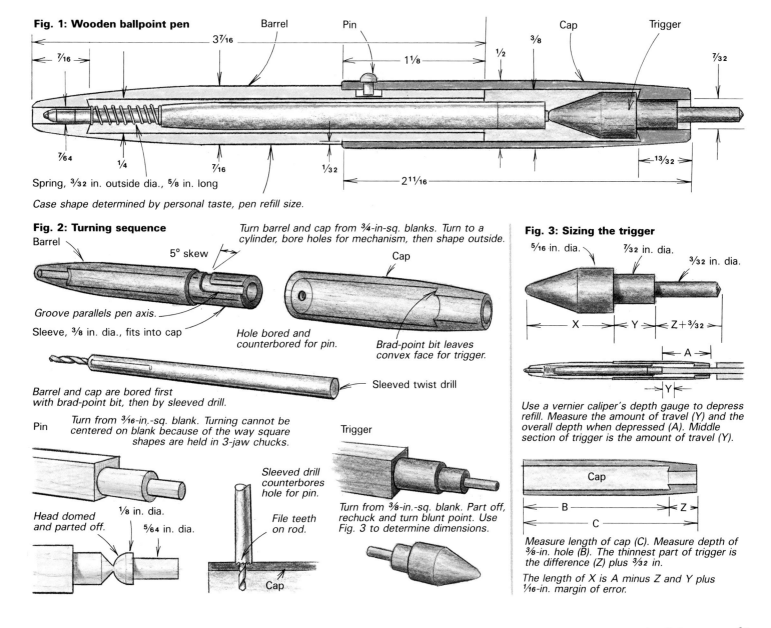

Fig. 1: Wooden ballpoint pen

Barrel Pin Cap Trigger

3 7/16

7/16   3/8   1/2   7/32

1 1/8

7/64   1/4   7/16   1/32   13/32

Spring, 3/32 in. outside dia., 5/8 in. long

2 11/16

Case shape determined by personal taste, pen refill size.

Fig. 2: Turning sequence

Barrel

Turn barrel and cap from 3/4-in.-sq. blanks. Turn to a cylinder, bore holes for mechanism, then shape outside.

Cap

5° skew

Groove parallels pen axis.

Sleeve, 3/8 in. dia., fits into cap

Hole bored and counterbored for pin.

Brad-point bit leaves convex face for trigger.

Sleeved twist drill

Barrel and cap are bored first with brad-point bit, then by sleeved drill.

Pin

Turn from 3/16-in.-sq. blank. Turning cannot be centered on blank because of the way square shapes are held in 3-jaw chucks.

Trigger

Sleeved drill counterbores hole for pin.

Head domed and parted off.

1/8 in. dia.

5/64 in. dia.

File teeth on rod.

Cap

Turn from 3/8-in.-sq. blank. Part off, rechuck and turn blunt point. Use Fig. 3 to determine dimensions.

Fig. 3: Sizing the trigger

5/16 in. dia.   7/32 in. dia.   3/32 in. dia.

X   Y   Z + 3/32

A

Y

Use a vernier caliper's depth gauge to depress refill. Measure the amount of travel (Y) and the overall depth when depressed (A). Middle section of trigger is the amount of travel (Y).

Cap

B   Z

C

Measure length of cap (C). Measure depth of 3/8-in. hole (B). The thinnest part of trigger is the difference (Z) plus 3/32 in.

The length of X is A minus Z and Y plus 1/16-in. margin of error.

down the length of the pen. After marking the hole location with a pencil dot, I remove the cap and sketch a pair of lines about $\frac{3}{32}$ in. apart and flank the dot at a 5° angle, skewing away from the joint. After drawing a line parallel to the axis from the top of the skewed lines to the top of the barrel, I switch on the router, mount the barrel on the rod as shown and push the barrel forward, cutting down to the skewed lines. At the skew, I twist the barrel and push it to follow the angle. My $\frac{5}{64}$-in.-dia. router bit is ground from a $\frac{1}{4}$-in. drill rod; I set the depth of cut with a feeler gauge inserted between the mounting rod and bit. After refitting

the pin and filing it down so it doesn't bottom out in the groove, I secure it with a spot of white glue. I finish the pen with wax or shellac after the glue dries.

After wrestling with making the pen, you may be disappointed to discover that few people will see beyond the pen's pleasant shape and glistening finish to realize it is actually made of wood. Perhaps my wife has a case when she says the pens need a little embellishment. ☐

Richard Elderton is a cabinetmaker in Hawkley, England.

A mechanical pencil

by Earl C. Kimball and Cynthia A. Kimball

We enjoy the clarity of line produced by 0.5mm mechanical pencils, but dislike the plastic models sold in art and department stores. Wooden pencils feel better in the hand, so we decided to fit the self-contained lead cartridge of a mechanical pencil into an all-wood housing.

Turned wooden casings let you customize mechanical pencils to your hand and show off your turning skills. The pen, above, is turned from walnut and maple.

Any good hardwood can be used for the casing. We usually begin with a walnut, ebony, mahogany or maple blank, bore a hole lengthwise through the center, then slide the blank on a mandrel that can be mounted in a Jacobs chuck and turned on the lathe. We prefer Pentel 0.5mm and Pilot 0.5mm pencils, but other brands might work; adapt the measurements shown in the drawing to fit your pencil. The first step is to remove the innards from the plastic, usually by unscrewing the tapered tip from the lead cartridge.

The original plastic sleeve becomes a rough model for determining the size and shape of the wooden case. For our pencils, we started out with a $\frac{3}{4}$-in.-square hardwood block, about 2 in. longer than the desired pencil. The excess length is used to hold the blank on the mandrel and will be discarded after turning. We make sure our original blocks are square in section, then draw diagonal lines from corner to corner. We drill through this mark with a $\frac{7}{32}$-in., brad-point drill, which isn't deflected by slanting grain as much as a high-speed steel bit. I use the horizontal boring feature on my Shopsmith Mark V multipurpose machine to drill the blanks. You could also clamp the blank upright in a vise or against a high fence on a drill-press table. To bore through the 6-in. to 8-in. blanks, we generally drill in from one end with an extra-long bit. If you can't find long bits, you can drill in from both ends with regular-length bits. It's fine to have a hole at each end, because the top hole will be plugged with the eraser.

The pencil point must be reinforced so that pressure from writing won't split the wood. We use soft aluminum tubing (available from model airplane stores) with a $\frac{7}{32}$-in. OD as a sleeve. Bore out the inside diameter to accept the lead cartridge. The tube should be inserted about $\frac{3}{32}$ in. into the blank, then epoxied in place before being cut off about $\frac{1}{8}$ in. longer than the wood blank.

Our turning mandrel is a custom-shaped, mild-steel mandrel with shoulders to fit the inner shape of the pencil. It can be turned on the lathe or mounted in a drill chuck and filed to shape as it is rotated. We epoxy the block to the rod at both ends to prevent spinning, so it's not necessary to make a tight-fitting mandrel.

The blank is mounted on the lathe by fitting the mandrel at the pencil's top into a Jacobs chuck and the other end into a drilled wooden plug in the tailstock. Turn to any desired shape. Note the pocket clips (salvaged from old felt-tipped pens) fit in shallow rabbets turned on the pencils. After sanding the pencils, we finish with tung oil. Finally, we carefully cut the pencil from the block with a skew. We saw through the excess tubing with a jewelers' saw, then remove the mandrel. If the reinforcing ring isn't securely fastened, we reglue before inserting the pencil mechanism. ☐

Earl C. Kimball is a forester in McCall, Ida. His daughter, Cynthia Kimball, is a graduate student at the University of Idaho at Moscow.

Fig. 4: Turning a wooden pen

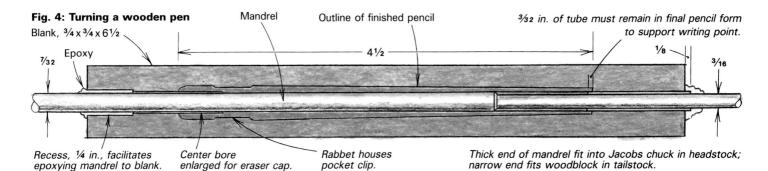

Mandrel · Outline of finished pencil · $\frac{3}{32}$ in. of tube must remain in final pencil form to support writing point.

Blank, $\frac{3}{4}$ x $\frac{3}{4}$ x $6\frac{1}{2}$

$\frac{7}{32}$ · Epoxy · 4$\frac{1}{2}$ · $\frac{1}{8}$ · $\frac{3}{16}$

Recess, $\frac{1}{4}$ in., facilitates epoxying mandrel to blank. · *Center bore enlarged for eraser cap.* · *Rabbet houses pocket clip.* · *Thick end of mandrel fit into Jacobs chuck in headstock; narrow end fits woodblock in tailstock.*

Photo: Michele Russell Slavinsky

Turning Boxes

A *perfect fit for lids and inlays*

by Kip Christensen

A challenge for even experienced turners, an inlaid box requires patience in preparing and drying the stock, precision in fitting the lid and inlays and artistry in shaping the form. The largest of these, only 3½ in. in diameter, is Macassar ebony with Indian ebony and spalted maple inlays; the smallest has inlays of tagua nut and spalted maple; the third is rosewood topped with holly and tulip.

The feel of a properly fitted lid on a turned box provides a fascination that some people find almost addictive. When the lid is lifted with a gentle twist, there's a touch of vacuum resistance, and as the lid is removed, the box catches a small breath of air. When the lid is replaced, the box vents a soft sigh of relief.

I was introduced to turned boxes seven or eight years ago. After trying to make one, I realized there was more to it than meets the eye: Both technical and aesthetic challenges must be met for a box to be successful. I've made boxes with shapes that looked nice but were unacceptable because the lid was not comfortable to grasp or easy to remove. A perfect grain match where the lid meets the base is another element of a quality box.

And then there's the fit between the lid and the base. There's a very fine distinction between a fit that is too tight, too loose or just right. The nature of wood complicates the matter of obtaining, and in particular, maintaining a perfect fit. Even the slightest expansion or contraction in the wood can be detected in the fit, resulting in a loose-tight-loose-tight feel as the lid is rotated. A box that is flawless in every other aspect but lacks that just-so fit is always somewhat of a disappointment. Wood movement, due to seasonal changes in the atmosphere, cannot be completely eliminated, but it can be significantly reduced by rough-turning the box to its basic shape and then patiently controlling the drying of the wood. After having made a few hundred turned boxes, I still find the process challenging and fun, and the end result rewarding.

The addition of an inlay to the top of a turned box can highlight a unique piece of wood or other material. I have experimented with inlays of metal, plastic, scrimshawed bone, tagua nut, stone and wood. The inlay, which is actually an insert, is a circular wafer about ³⁄₁₆ in. thick fitted and glued into a recess in the top of the box. Figure 1 on page 72 shows a cross section of a box with two concentric inlays. However, the addition of an inlay is not always an improvement; it may even detract if the box is made from an exceptional piece of wood.

Making a turned, inlaid box can be broken down into three separate processes: preparing the box blank, preparing the inlay and finally, turning the box. The procedure may seem long and cumbersome, but in reality, each step (with the exception of drying the blank) can be accomplished rather quickly. Once you're comfortable with the process, the challenge comes in improving the efficiency of your cuts and reducing production time while still maintaining the fine distinctions that result in a quality box.

Preparing the box blank—Hardwoods with tight, close grain are most appropriate for turned boxes, because they turn more cleanly and generally present fewer wood-movement problems than ring-porous woods. The direction of the grain should run parallel to the lathe bed to make any wood movement less critical to the fit of the lid. Box blanks can be made from quartered log sections or from precut turning squares. If beginning with a log, I saw a bolt 12 in. to 15 in. long, quarter it with a chainsaw and remove the bark and sapwood. Sapwood is attractive in some species, but I generally remove it completely, because it's typically less stable than heartwood and therefore more susceptible to movement that may undermine the fit of the lid. When a 3-in.- to 4-in.-thick piece of wood is hollowed out, stresses are relieved and movement occurs, even with dry wood. So, whether beginning with green or dry wood, I rough-turn the box blanks inside and out, then set them aside to stabilize.

Begin by mounting a 3-in. to 4-in. turning square between centers, and with a large gouge, turn a cylinder of equal diameter its full length, then turn its ends clean and square with its sides. A cylinder 12 in. to 15 in. long will yield four to six box blanks. I lay out for the lids and bases by cutting ¼-in.-deep kerfs with a special narrow parting tool. I made the tool, shown in figure 2 at right, by grinding a ¼-in. by ¼-in. steel bar so it will cut a kerf less than ¹⁄₁₆ in. wide. Removing a minimum of wood here preserves the best possible grain match between the box and the lid. Mark the cylinder across the kerf lines with a magic marker to indicate pairs of lids and bases. Remove the cylinder from the lathe, and using the narrow kerfs to guide the bandsaw blade, saw it into lid and base blanks (see the photo this page).

To remove the bulk of the wood from the interior of the blanks, mount the bottom of the base blank on a waste block and faceplate or in a three-jaw chuck. If you're turning green wood, leave some extra thickness at the blank's base and screw a faceplate to the bottom, because the green wood will not glue well to a waste block. Hollow out the center, keeping in mind the desired shape of the box and leaving the wall approximately ½ in. thick. Hollow out the inside of the lid in the same manner. Now, take the parts into the house and lay them on their sides to allow air access to all surfaces. Allow three to six weeks if you begin with dry wood and 16 to 20 weeks for green wood. During the first three weeks, watch the blanks closely for initial surface checking. I've found that if I place the blanks in a double paper sack, it reduces checking by slowing down and evening out the drying process of the hollow blanks. When the moisture in the blanks has reached equilibrium with the new environment, they are ready to be finish-turned. You can measure this to some extent by weighing the pieces periodically. When they stop losing weight, they are at equilibrium.

Preparing the inlays—The recess in the lid must be sized to accept the inlay, so the inlay must be turned before you work on the box. First, bandsaw the inlay stock, which you've selected for exceptional color or figure, into ³⁄₁₆-in.- to ¼-in.-thick wafers. The round or square wafers should be large enough so that when they're turned true, they'll yield the desired diameters. To mount an inlay wafer on the lathe, remove any accessories from the spindle and place double-faced tape on the end of the arbor shaft. Sand the bottom side of the inlay flat on a belt or disc sander, and center the sanded side of the wafer against the tape. Slide the tailstock up to the wafer and adjust the tailstock center so it exerts light pressure against the center of the wafer. Turn the inlay round, taking care to leave a 90° angle between the edge and the sanded bottom. Remove the inlay from the lathe and set it aside.

Turning the box—To mount the base during the turning process, I prefer a center-screw faceplate and waste block. I use a three-jaw chuck to hold the lid for turning, but you could also use another faceplate and waste block.

First, mount a 2-in.-thick waste block on the faceplate and turn it round and its face flat. Make the waste block's diameter about ⅛ in. larger than the diameter of the base blank you'll be turning. This makes it easy to center the blank by eye when gluing it to the waste block. The 2-in. thickness of the block holds the box far enough away from the faceplate to allow access for shaping the bottom. Sand the bottom of the box blank flat and glue it to the waste block. With a ⅜-in. spindle gouge, turn the blank just enough to bring it into round inside and out. To turn the lip that will receive the lid, I use a modified parting tool, as shown in the top photo on the next page, but a skew or normal parting tool will also work. I've designed this tool (see figure 2 this page) to cut

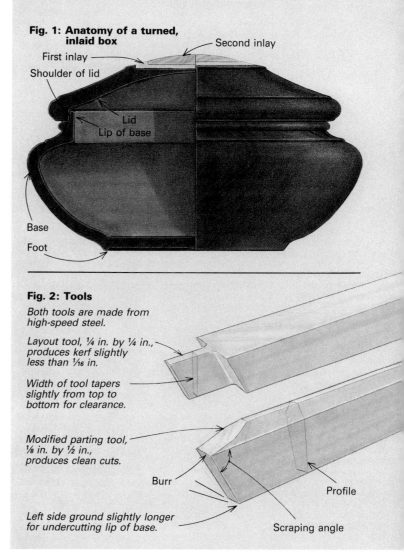

Fig. 1: Anatomy of a turned, inlaid box

First inlay — Second inlay
Shoulder of lid
Lid
Lip of base
Base
Foot

Fig. 2: Tools

Both tools are made from high-speed steel.

Layout tool, ¼ in. by ¼ in., produces kerf slightly less than ¹⁄₁₆ in.

Width of tool tapers slightly from top to bottom for clearance.

Modified parting tool, ⅛ in. by ½ in., produces clean cuts.

Burr

Profile

Left side ground slightly longer for undercutting lip of base.

Scraping angle

Christensen bandsaws the rough-turned cylinder into base and lid blanks. Thin kerfs, made with his narrow parting tool, are used to lay out the sections and guide the bandsaw blade. Marks across the kerfs identify lid and base sets and register the grain match.

From *Fine Woodworking* magazine (March 1989) 75:72-74

With a modified parting tool, the author turns a lip on the base to receive the lid. The base is glued to the waste block, which is mounted on a center-screw faceplate. The 2-in.-thick block holds the work away from the faceplate to allow access for tools to shape the bottom of the box.

A shallow recess for a second inlay is cut into the first with a modified parting tool. The interiors of both the base and lid are turned to completion, and the lid is pressed onto the base to mount the inlays and shape the exterior of the box.

with a true scraping angle, which gives a much cleaner cut than the blunt angle on standard parting tools. (This tool is now available from Craft Supplies USA, 1287 E. 1120 S., Provo, Utah 84601.) Make the lip's sides parallel to the lathe bed or slightly undercut and about 1/8 in. to 3/16 in. long. The shorter the lip, the better the grain match between the lid and base. Now I use a gouge to shape the outside, then make the finish cuts on the inside with freshly sharpened scrapers, leaving the walls about 3/16 in. to 1/4 in. thick. Don't sand the base until after the lid is turned to fit it, because heat from sanding can cause the base's shape to temporarily distort.

Remove the box and faceplate from the lathe and attach the three-jaw chuck. Mount the lid blank in the chuck, with the inside surface exposed, so you can fit the lid to the lip on the base. If you don't have a three-jaw chuck, mount the faceplate and waste block that's attached to the lid on the lathe. True the inside face of the lid and make a couple of concentric pencil lines on the lid's face, approximately the diameter of the base's lip. Hold the base up to the lid and use the concentric lines to visually determine where to cut the recess to mate with the lip on the base. Turn the recess to a depth matching or slightly exceeding the length of the lip on the base, with a diameter about 1/16 in. smaller than the lip. To fine-tune this fit, turn a small chamfer on the shoulder you just created

on the lid. Try the base to the lid. When the base's lip fits inside the chamfer, you know you're close, and you can see just how much more needs to be removed for a perfect fit. Every small cut on one side of the circle is simultaneously coming off the other side, so proceed cautiously. When you make the final sizing cuts on the sides of the recess, they must be parallel to the lathe bed, not tapered in or out. The fit should be snug but not forced. Now finish shaping the inside of the lid, but remember, you'll be inserting an inlay in its top, so don't dish it out too much. The final cut should be as clean as possible to avoid excess sanding, so make sure your tools are sharp, and take a light cut. To avoid heating up and distorting the lid, use light pressure while sanding; if you feel the sandpaper warming up, take a break and let the work cool down.

Finishing–The finish can now be applied to the inside of the lid. If a finish with a strong odor is used on the inside, the odor will likely become a permanent characteristic of the box. To avoid this, I use a light coat of mineral oil topped with a coat of odorless paste wax. Then, I remove the lid from the chuck and the chuck from the lathe. If you are using a faceplate, just part the lid off the waste block. Remount the faceplate and the base on the lathe, and press the lid onto the lip of the base with the grain lined up.

The recess for the inlay is cut at this time, before the final shaping of the lid. True the top of the lid with a gouge or a scraper, then working from the center out with a parting tool, cut a recess about 1/8 in. deep and the diameter of the inlay. Here again, I prefer my modified parting tool, and I use the concentric lines and the chamfer on the shoulder of the recess as I did when fitting the lid to the base. The bottom of the recess should be flat, and the sides should be parallel with the lathe bed. If glue is applied to the full bottom surface of the inlay, it may pull the lid out of shape as it dries. So, apply yellow glue only to the inlay's edge and the outer edge of its bottom, and tap it into the recess with a mallet. If a double inlay is desired, simply cut a slightly shallower recess into the first inlay, as shown in the bottom photo this page, and insert an inlay wafer with a smaller diameter. The inlays should fit so tightly that you don't need to wait for the glue to dry before cutting the recess for the second inlay.

With inlays in place, turn the total exterior shape of the box so the form flows continuously from top to bottom. When the shaping is completed, take the lid off and sand and apply finish to the inside of the base. Then, replace the lid and sand and finish the outside of the entire box. Because I turn tiny beads and sharply defined lines, I take special care to preserve them while sanding. I cut the sandpaper into 1/4-in. strips so I can sand right up to the smallest beads without rounding them over. I sand the inside of my boxes to 400 or 600 grit and the outsides to 600 grit or 1,000 grit. On the exterior of most of my boxes, I use Super Rapid Pad by Mohawk Finishing Products, Inc., Route 30N, Amsterdam, N.Y. 12010. This is an extremely fast-drying finish that provides a good gloss without excessive buildup.

The box is completed now except for the bottom. Separate the base from the waste block with a parting tool. To hold the base on the lathe while turning the bottom, cut a shoulder on the waste block to fit the inside diameter of the base lip. If the fit isn't tight enough, use masking tape to build up the diameter of the shoulder for a pressure fit. Then shape, sand and apply finish to the bottom. I usually turn a small foot to add a touch of detail to the bottom (see figure 1, page 72). Take the base off the lathe, gently press the lid onto the base, and admire your latest creation. A well-made box will feel nice in the hand and provide an attractive haven for anything from paper clips to diamond rings. □

Kip Christensen is a woodturner and assistant professor of industrial education at Brigham Young University in Provo, Utah.

Bricklaid Bowls

*Turning large bowls
with glued-up parts*

by Robert Sterba

The more woodturners I meet, the more I realize that most of us didn't start out as turners. We all got hooked somehow. I once made cabinets, built-ins and some furniture. My mistake was building a spindle lathe. From the beginning, I discovered a new awareness of shape—the most important and, often, most overlooked element in any three-dimensional object. Turning is a marvelous exercise in shape. Subtle variations in line can completely change the tone of a piece. You can get an idea of what I mean by taking a few same-size blocks and seeing how many different shapes you can cut. Variations on a theme like this are my favorite pastime.

If, four years ago, someone had said, "Son, you could spend the rest of your life turning and exploring round shapes," I might have choked. I certainly would have laughed, but here I am. The interplay of line and shape is really what my work is all about. For me, when a woodworker can bring color, grain and texture to enhance—almost caress—a shape, craft is well on its way to becoming art.

Since shape is my main concern, I don't find wood and woodworking tools all that fascinating. You may wonder why I even use wood, since its figure is hidden beneath layers of colored lacquer. I've never believed that *tools* and *how* you produce an object are as important as the object itself. And, I reject those who proclaim, "Oh, look at that beautiful piece of wood!" as a way to avoid thinking and to excuse ugly designs. All that, to borrow a phrase from California woodworker Garry Knox Bennett, is "tech-no-wienie" woodworking—it's boring and it's time to grow out of it.

I like wood because it's immediate. I don't have to bake it, fire it or melt it. Wood is a material, just as clay is dirt and glass is sand. About seven years ago, I watched a friend, Scott Taylor, turn a maple dish, apply spray-can black lacquer, then polish it with rottenstone. The result was a low-tech, high-tech finish that didn't rely on expensive, highly figured wood. I had stumbled on a way to search for the perfect shape, and there would be no grain to get in the way.

My typical bowl has more than 100 small pieces of wood laminated into a bowl shape as large as three feet in diameter. The technique dates back to at least the 18th century, when it was used to prepare oval tabletops for gilding. Patternmakers also use these so-called bricklaid laminations to construct large shapes that resist warping when they absorb or give up moisture with the changing seasons. After I laminate the rough bowl, I mount the blank on a lathe and turn it to refine the form. I don't

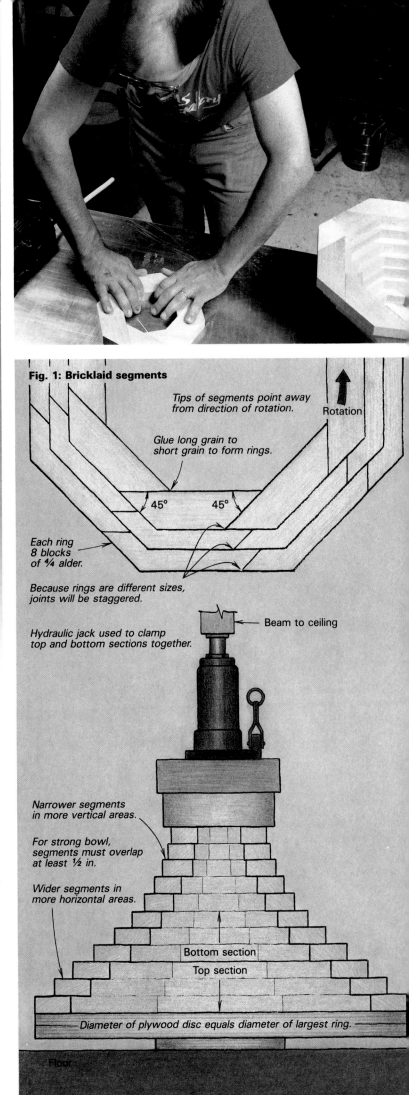

The glistening lacquer finish on the author's 24-in.-dia. bowl makes it hard to believe there's wood beneath the 24 coats of finish. For him, wood as a material isn't as important as shape and color. To make a bowl blank, right, he glues together small wooden segments to form rings, which are laminated together.

use solid baulks of wood because I live in New Mexico, where 36-in.-dia. trees are pretty scarce. And, the few problems I've experienced with lacquer fracturing have been across the grain, so lamination techniques let me design that flaw out of the piece.

My basic materials are alder and medium-density fiberboard (MDF). Fiberboard is wonderful stuff. It's denser and finer-grained than industrial flakeboard, and can be turned with high-speed steel or carbide tools. I like alder because it's available, already milled, from a local hardwood distributor. All I have to do is saw the planks apart and glue the pieces together, using one of the construction techniques shown in figures 1 and 3. The simplest method is to glue small blocks together to make one larger block. Staved constructions resemble coopered barrels. It's an easy way to construct hollow, straight or tapered cylinders. Segmented, stacked laminations involve assembling many small blocks of wood, with 45° angles cut on both ends, into increasingly larger rings which are, in turn, laminated together to form a hollow bowl shape.

Segmented, stacked laminations are very stable and strong. I start by ripping 4/4 alder into 1¼-in.- to 2½-in.-wide strips, in ¼-in. increments. This sticking is then carefully surfaced and jointed. For accuracy, I cut the 45° bevels on the ends of each segment with a motorized miter box or chop saw. Eight blocks are needed for each ring (figure 1). These are glued together, endgrain to long grain, to form a ring. I usually use hot-melt glue to hold the segments together, but make sure the glue is hot enough to flow evenly and that it hardens to a good bond. An alternative method would be to join the segments together with yellow glue, clamping the pairs tightly with pinch dogs (available from Woodcraft Supply and Garrett Wade) and letting them dry on a flat surface. Handplane the surfaces, as needed, to ensure a good joint between rings.

The rings are assembled in increasingly larger diameters. The more vertical the shape, the narrower the segments. The more horizontal the shape, the wider the segments. As with the staved cylinders, I make full-size drawings to work out the measurements. I like to make sure the rings overlap at least ½ in., as shown in figure 1, when I glue them together. The rings are

Drawings: Lee Hov

Fig. 1: Bricklaid segments

Tips of segments point away from direction of rotation.

Rotation

Glue long grain to short grain to form rings.

45° 45°

Each ring 8 blocks of 4/4 alder.

Because rings are different sizes, joints will be staggered.

Hydraulic jack used to clamp top and bottom sections together.

Beam to ceiling

Narrower segments in more vertical areas.

For strong bowl, segments must overlap at least ½ in.

Wider segments in more horizontal areas.

Bottom section

Top section

Diameter of plywood disc equals diameter of largest ring.

Floor

Clamps set across each 45° joint secure the rings to each other and to a plywood faceplate. A shop-built cradle supports the rings and attached faceplate during glue-up.

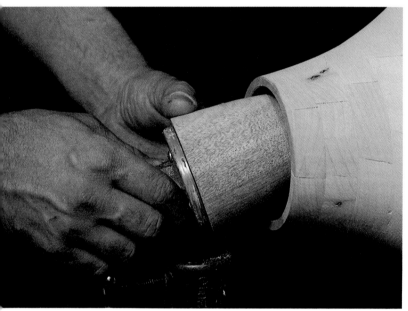

A faceplate screwed to a 3-in.-long tapered plug is glued into the bottom of the turning before the bowl is finish-turned.

quite fragile. The endgrain/long-grain joint is not, at this time, very strong, although it becomes stronger when the rings are bonded together because I rotate the rings slightly to stagger the joints. I dry assemble all the rings to make sure the form is right and everything fits. Direction is important in assembling the rings. Be certain that the rings are laid up in the same direction, so that the outside point of each facet points *away* from a counterclockwise rotation, if your lathe rotates in that direction.

Begin building the turning by gluing and screwing together plywood or MDF discs to make a 1½-in.-thick disc equal to the diameter of the largest ring. My turnings are 18 in. to 36 in. in diameter and 12 in. to 18 in. deep, so the backing disc must be strong. Bandsaw the disc somewhat round and mount it on your lathe. Start slowly and flatten the disc. (The pedestal lathe I use has a 1½-in.-dia. headstock shaft. I consider this the minimum size for this work.) Dismount the disc and lay the largest ring on it. Glue and clamp it in place. I spread yellow glue on one face, then clamp the pieces together as shown in the top photo, above. After about 20 minutes, remove the clamps and add another ring. A combination of 3- and 4-in. C-clamps and Jorgenson quick clamps works well. Clamp over each joint, being careful to keep the rings centered. An

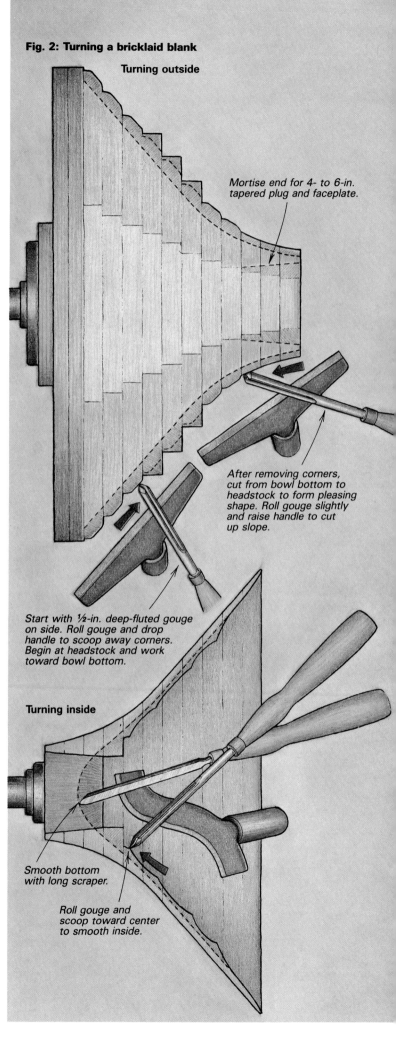

Fig. 2: Turning a bricklaid blank

Turning outside

Mortise end for 4- to 6-in. tapered plug and faceplate.

After removing corners, cut from bowl bottom to headstock to form pleasing shape. Roll gouge slightly and raise handle to cut up slope.

Start with ½-in. deep-fluted gouge on side. Roll gouge and drop handle to scoop away corners. Begin at headstock and work toward bowl bottom.

Turning inside

Smooth bottom with long scraper.

Roll gouge and scoop toward center to smooth inside.

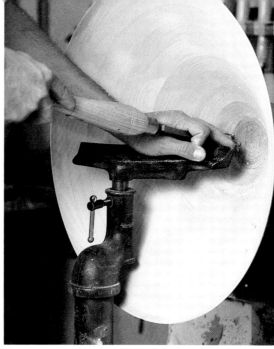

Sterba uses the shoulder of a deep-fluted gouge to shear the ridges from the lamination, left, and to shape the inside of the bowl. The bowl bottom is carefully finished with light scraper cuts, above.

Caution

A large bricklaid bowl blank is a rather imposing mass of wood and glue. Even though I have never had a blank shatter or tear loose from the lathe's faceplate, it could certainly happen. I don't think you can be too cautious. You should always start your lathe slowly, about 400 RPM to 600 RPM, and stand back. I let these things spin for a while before I get too close. If the bowl's going to come apart, I'd just as soon not be around. I also wear heavy leather gloves and a face shield when I'm roughing out.

off-center assembly will vibrate dangerously on the lathe.

While the glue is setting on the larger rings, I assemble the narrower-diameter rings to form the smaller part of the bowl. I glue the top and the bottom together using a one-ton hydraulic jack bearing against a post and a beam in my ceiling for pressure. I let the assembly dry for a day or two before turning, then screw on a 6-in. faceplate with #14 hex-head sheet-metal screws, which have impressive holding power.

Turn the outside first, beginning at the end nearest the faceplate. Knock off all the edges with a ½-in. deep-fluted gouge. The open flute should face away from the headstock. Work your gouge almost horizontally, lowering the handle as needed to keep the cutting edge slightly above center. The cut resembles a dip-and-scoop motion. Hit it wrong and it sounds like a kettledrum vibrating. Take it easy, go slow and get the feel of the piece. It flows and so should you. After knocking off the corners, cut from the narrow end toward the headstock. Correct the shape to create a pleasant form. Here, cut with the flute facing the headstock and raise the tool handle as you cut up the slope. Don't forget that you have limited wall thickness. When you're satisfied with the shape, mortise the bottom for a tapered plug and begin

to part off the disc. Turn the plug, endgrain up-and-down, and seat it in the mortise with an even spread of glue. After the glue sets, remove the faceplate and turn the bottom flat.

The next day, mount a 3-in. to 4-in. faceplate on the plug with 2-in. to 3-in. lag screws. Mount the plug end on the lathe, remove the faceplate on the other end and cut off the disc. It will crash down and take off rolling, so watch out. True up the outside of the turning, as close to round and balanced as possible, with a deep-fluted gouge. Now you can begin shaping the inside of the bowl with a deep-fluted gouge, as shown above, left. Most of the cutting is done with the gouge's long shoulder. The flute should face the center of the bowl. As you cut, roll the gouge and scoop toward the center until you smooth the walls to the shape you want. Careful work with a scraper held slightly below the center of the turning, as shown above, right, is often needed near the bottom, where it can be difficult to maneuver the gouge.

If this bricklaid procedure seems too intimidating, you might try a simpler lamination for your first bowl. Cut several blocks slightly larger than the bowl you want, and make sure the stock is flat. Generally, a couple of passes through the planer or jointer will do it. I spread a thin layer of Titebond glue with plastic auto-

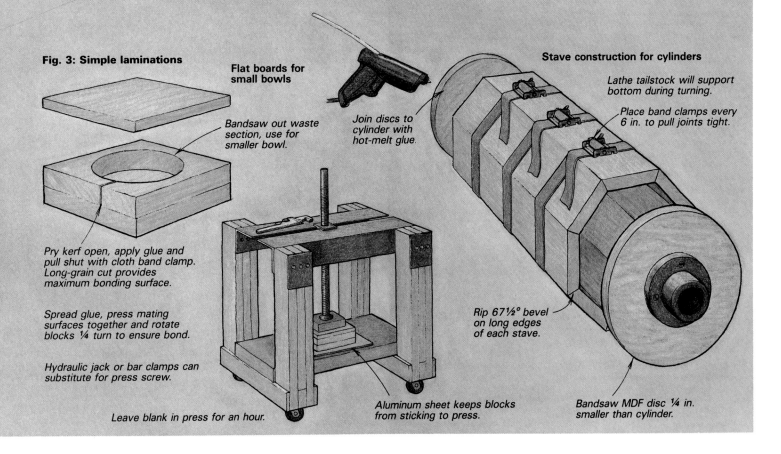

Fig. 3: Simple laminations

Flat boards for small bowls

Bandsaw out waste section, use for smaller bowl.

Join discs to cylinder with hot-melt glue.

Stave construction for cylinders

Lathe tailstock will support bottom during turning.

Place band clamps every 6 in. to pull joints tight.

Pry kerf open, apply glue and pull shut with cloth band clamp. Long-grain cut provides maximum bonding surface.

Spread glue, press mating surfaces together and rotate blocks ¼ turn to ensure bond.

Hydraulic jack or bar clamps can substitute for press screw.

Rip 67½° bevel on long edges of each stave.

Leave blank in press for an hour.

Aluminum sheet keeps blocks from sticking to press.

Bandsaw MDF disc ¼ in. smaller than cylinder.

The stave-built cylinder is mounted on the lathe with a faceplate screwed to one MDF disc. The tailstock is snugged against a disc on the other end, then the piece is turned like a large spindle.

body putty paddles onto one or two sides of the mating pieces, depending on my mood. After pushing the blocks together, I twist them about ¼ turn to spread the glue and ensure good adhesion. This somewhat messy mass of glue and wood is placed in a press and screwed down tight for an hour. My press is very simple—basically, it's two pieces of heavy angle iron and a 1-in. veneer-press screw. You could use a hydraulic jack and a wooden frame.

To save wood and time, I often bandsaw the center from the middle or from the top of the piece (see figure 3); I later make this cutout the base for another turning. Bandsaw with the grain for maximum long-grain gluing surface. Force the kerf open with a screwdriver and inject glue into it. My favorite glue injector is a hog or horse syringe from the local vet supplier. Dull the point before using. Although it isn't necessary, you can insert veneer to help fill the kerf before snugging it up with a band clamp—an inexpensive

hardware store band clamp works well. Once the cloth band becomes stiff with glue, I leave it in a can of water overnight and wash it out the next day. Another tip is to do your gluing on an aluminum sheet. Dry glue won't stick and wet glue washes off.

Stave construction uses less wood, and also helps control the across-the-grain movement. Most of my staved constructions have eight segments. This calls for a 67½° bevel cut on each long edge of the stave. To figure out the angles and widths of segments, I always draw a full-size plan of the top view of the cylinder. The method is described in *Tage Frid Teaches Wood-working: Shaping, Veneering, Finishing* (The Taunton Press, 1981). First, square and surface the staves and cut them to size. Set your tablesaw blade to cut the 67½° bevel, and rip the bevel on both long edges (figure 3). Stand the eight pieces up and apply glue to both edges of every other piece. Place band clamps over the cylinder, every 6 in. or so, and dog them down. If the angles are not precisely right, the shape is somewhat self-correcting. Remove the clamps after the glue has set, but let the glue cure overnight before turning.

To turn the piece, bandsaw two discs from MDF, ¼ in. smaller than the intended final circumference. Place a disc on one end, and run a bead of hot-melt glue around it. Let the glue cool, then do the other end. Mount a faceplate and chuck it up, supporting the end with your tailstock as shown at left. After you turn the piece, pop off the discs with a putty knife or screwdriver. I rabbet the cylinder ends to receive a top and bottom, using a straight bit in a router and a standard V-shaped edge guide. For a cone shape, you could use the tapered staves discussed on the facing page.

My finishing procedures are basically the same for all my turnings. I sand from 100 grit to 180 grit, using a power-sanding disc. Then I apply three coats of catalyzed polyester primer, and set the form aside to stabilize for two to three weeks. Next, I sand the primed shape to 320 grit, removing the dust with a tack cloth. My primary finish is nitrocellulose lacquer (available from Sherwin Williams Co., 101 Prospect Ave., Cleveland, Ohio 44115, and its local distributors). Before spraying, the finishing room is cleaned,

Tapered staves on the tablesaw

by F. B. Woestemeyer

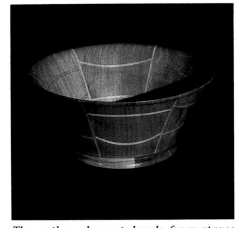

The author glues up bowls from staves tapered on the tablesaw. Angled blocks set the miter gauge and blade angle.

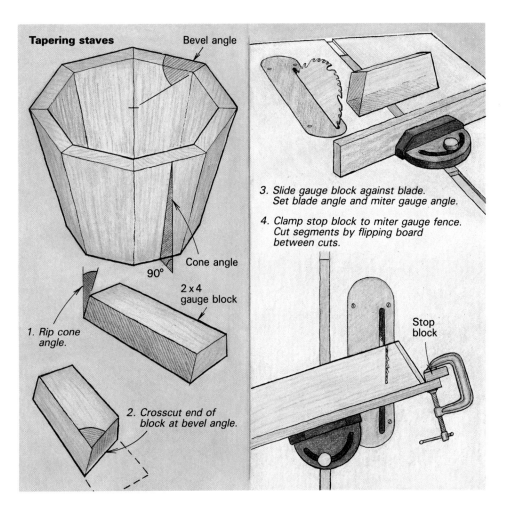

Tapering staves

Bevel angle

Cone angle

90°

2 x 4 gauge block

1. Rip cone angle.

2. Crosscut end of block at bevel angle.

3. Slide gauge block against blade. Set blade angle and miter gauge angle.

4. Clamp stop block to miter gauge fence. Cut segments by flipping board between cuts.

Stop block

My tablesaw method for cutting tapered staves makes quick work of a task that can be very tedious. And, the speed of the method doesn't cost you anything in accuracy. The key to this technique is a master gauge block made from a scrap of 2x4—it preserves the setting angles for the sawblade and miter gauge.

To make the gauge, first tilt the sawblade to the desired cone angle of each segment and rip one edge of the gauge block to this angle, as shown in the sketch. Return the blade to vertical and set the saw's miter gauge to the segment bevel angle. The bevel angle (B) can be calculated from the number of sides on the turning blank (N) with the following formula:

$$B = 90 - (180/N)$$

For example, where there are eight staves the bevel angle is 67.5°.

With the miter gauge set to the bevel angle, trim the end off the gauge block, as shown. Be aware that minor inaccuracies in the cone angle will simply flare the blank a little more or a little less. But inaccuracies in the bevel angle are more critical because they will result in gaps in the segment joints. Through trial and error, you may wish to recut and adjust the bevel angle until the resulting segment joints are perfect.

To set up the saw, first place the gauge block against the blade and tilt the blade flat against the end of the block. Then, leaving the block in position against the blade, set the miter gauge by matching the back edge of the block.

To cut the segments, first prepare a stock board whose width equals the height of the segments. After setting the saw as described above, clamp a stop to the miter gauge fence so all segments will be the same size. For the first cut, lop off the waste end of the stock board. Flip the stock board over, push it against the stop block and make the second cut. This second cut will form the second edge of segment one and the first edge of segment two. Flip the stock for each successive cut. Even-numbered segments get their wide edges from one edge of the stock; odd-numbered segments from the other. If the stock is lighter on one side (or if you have laminated with contrasting woods), then the odd segments will be different from the evens. You may wish to use only odd segments for one glue-up and only evens for another.

Once made, a gauge block is good for all glue-ups of the same number of faces and cone angle. It takes only a few moments to set the blade and miter gauge to the angles of the block again for a later project. □

F.B. Woestemeyer is a woodworker in West Chester, Penn.

then cleaned again. The bowls, still attached to their faceplates, are screwed onto threaded wooden rods for spraying. The turning shown began with eight coats of red lacquer. After 48 hours, I sanded the lacquer with 600 grit and polished with pumice before applying eight more coats of lacquer. After 72 hours, I sanded again to 600 grit, polished with pumice and rottenstone, then applied four light coats of dyed, almost-transparent lacquer. After these coats dried, I applied two coats of clear lacquer containing a pale platinum pearl, then two clear coats. When the lacquer dried, I sanded to 1,000 grit and polished with rottenstone. The turning was finally highlighted with sterling silver leaves, then glazed and polished to protect it from the environment. Finally, the faceplate was removed and the bottom covered with veneer.

By combining these methods of construction—cutting away, adding and subtracting—you open a whole new world of woodturning. Go slowly, have fun, and don't forget to consider the movement of the wood. □

Robert Sterba is a sculptural woodturner and lacquer artist in Albuquerque, N.M.

Segmented Turning

Swirling patterns by cutting and reassembling a single board

by Michael Shuler

I've always been fascinated with turned forms, even before I knew what a lathe was. When I was 14 years old, I made miniatures on a makeshift lathe from birch dowels. A pocketknife was my only tool, but I was turning wood, and that was all that mattered. Later, in high school, I turned candlesticks, then chair legs, lamps and other creations, searching for a way to make the lathe a tool for artistic expression. Then one winter, sick in bed with a cold, I read some back issues of a woodworking magazine a friend had given me and discovered the work of turning greats like Frank Knox and Ed Moulthrop, as well as the wealth of different things the lathe could do, including segmented turning.

Segmented work and the design possibilities it offered met my needs for artistic expression, but most segmented vessels tended toward strong contrasts, with some makers using half a dozen or more different woods in a single piece to achieve a colorful effect. I wanted to see what could be done by segmenting a single kind of wood in a bowl. After experimenting with different geometric patterns and methods of gluing up segments, I discovered a way to create a striking look in a turned vessel that didn't require the use of several colored woods to achieve pattern and contrast.

I start with a single board, take it apart, reorganize the figure and put it back together in the form of a bowl. The pattern that's formed by the grain of the reassembled board flows almost continuously through the bowl from top to bottom. The segments grow proportionally smaller, all the way from the rim down to the base. Inside the bowl, the wedge-shape segments meet at their points, forming a radial geometric pattern. The combination of the decreasing size of segments and the grain of the wood makes looking into some of these bowls feel like you're someplace in the sky looking down at a hurricane or looking into the iris of an eye. Before going through the specific steps involved in making bowls like the ones pictured above, I'll generally discuss how this segmentation method works and how the designs develop.

Segmentation strategy—When finished, one of the large bowls looks as if it's been tediously glued up from hundreds of separate pieces, but these pieces aren't cut and glued up individually. The process revolves around the cutting of thinly tapered wedges that are glued up into discs: a large one for the body of the bowl and a smaller one for the base. For the larger disc, wedges are first glued up into two half discs, which are bandsawn apart into concentric half rings. Then the matching pairs of half rings are glued together; these rings are stacked atop the base disc and glued into a cone-shape bowl blank. The vessel is then turned to final form and finished.

Photo this page: Michele Russell Slavinsky; all other photos: Susan Helgeson

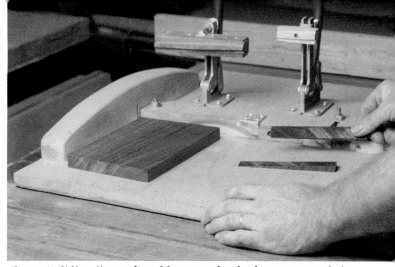

Wedges are the bowl's basic building blocks and provide an economical way to glue up the large number of pieces needed for a complex segmented pattern. Although any number of wedges may be used for the body and base discs, I've settled on 104, because it results in segments that are about ⅜ in. wide on the outer rim of a 12-in. bowl, an arrangement pleasing to my eyes. Also, 104 is evenly divisible by many other numbers: 52, 26, 13, 8. Divisibility isn't important for your first bowl, but it allows me to divide the rings into sections and play with the order of wedges in these sections to get special grain effects and contrasts. I typically use figured woods or exotics, but even plain-grained woods become attractive when segmented by this method.

Cutting the wedges—The first step is to cut a board into the two kinds of wedges needed for each bowl. The wedges that make up the large disc for the body are crosscut, so the figure of the side grain shows on the bowl's sides. The wedges for the base disc are ripcut, because these must taper to a pinpoint and converge at the center of the bowl. It's practically impossible to cut these fine points across the grain.

If you start with a board that's ¾x5⅜x60 in., you can produce a large and a small bowl at the same time. The disc glued up from the crosscut wedges yields the body of a 12-in.-dia. bowl and part of a 4½-in.-dia. bowl. Two base discs must be made from ripcut wedges—one for each bowl. Mark a line on one side of the board, to help later in orienting the wedges in the large disc. Crosscut the 5-ft. length to get two 18-in. lengths for the body, four 2½-in.-long crosscut strips for the base of the larger bowl and two 1½-in.-long strips for the base of the smaller bowl.

To cut the wedges, I built a special sliding taper jig that rides in the tablesaw's miter-gauge slots. The jig has two stations: one for crosscut wedges and the other for ripcut wedges. An adjustable fence and two stops reference the stock for the acute-angle cuts. Two DeStaCo quick-action clamps (one for each wedge-cutting station) clamp the board directly over the blade to ensure that the board is perfectly flat and doesn't budge during the cut (see the photo at the top of this page). These clamps are available from Woodcraft Supply, 41 Atlantic Ave., Box 4000, Woburn, Mass. 01888; (800) 225-1153. An 80-tooth, triple-chip-grind (TCG) carbide blade leaves a smooth surface on each wedge that's ready for gluing. The sawblade passes through a block fastened to each clamp, which helps keep splintering on top of the cut to a minimum.

Before cutting begins, carefully adjust the position of the stops and fence so the crosscut station will yield 5⅜-in.-long crosscut wedges that have a .062-in. taper. This means that for the large bowl, the body wedges taper from .37 in. on the fat end to .037 on the skinny end. Because the ripcut station uses the same fence, the wedges for the base have the same taper as the body wedges. However, a spacer screwed to the fence makes it possible for the blade to take thinner cuts: The 2½-in.-long ripcut wedges are .15 in. on the fat end, tapering to a sharp point at the other end. Check the wedges with a micrometer to verify the measurements and tweak the fence's final position accordingly. Also, make sure the sawblade is dead square to the jig. These steps are necessary if wedges are to glue up into a disc without gaps in any of its 104 seams.

Cut the crosscut wedges first, placing the end of the board against the fence and clamping it down. After cutting off a wedge, slide the jig back, well away from the blade, before unclamping and removing the wedge. Flip the board edge for edge before each successive cut, and arrange the wedges on a separate table in a circle, with the same side up as they came off the saw. I usually count the number cut and mark the halfway point of the disc with a strip of paper. When all 104 wedges are cut, set the dry-assembled disc aside.

Above: A sliding jig on the tablesaw makes both crosscut and rip-cut wedges—the basic building blocks for the author's segmented bowls. Two quick-action clamps hold the stock securely during cutting to help maintain the high accuracy required for flawless glue-ups. Below: The wedges for the small disc, which makes the base of the bowl, are glued up using a band clamp, like the ones used in plumbing. While the base wedges are assembled in random order, the body wedges are left dry-assembled in the order they came off the board (seen here in the background) before glue-up.

Cut the ripcut wedges for the base the same way as described above, only using the second station on the sliding jig. These wedges don't have to be as carefully ordered and oriented as the ones for the body, so I just cut them off and collect the 104 I need in a coffee can. The base for the small bowl only needs 20 wedges, because it's much smaller; these are cut as described earlier, only using another sliding taper jig made specifically for this operation set to cut at 18°.

Gluing up the discs—Instead of trying to glue up all the wedges for a bowl in one step, glue up a small disc for the base, then glue up two half discs for the body. The disc for the base is glued up in a band clamp, like the hose clamps sold in hardware stores for plumbing or exhaust systems (see the photo above). Buttering one side of each ripcut wedge liberally with yellow glue, assemble them in the clamp in a random order, aligning the points in the center as you go. The points pretty much align themselves, but you'll have to squish the wedges around occasionally to get the points to meet perfectly in the center. When all 104 wedges are in place, tighten the clamp with a box wrench until the joints are snug. Be warned that this glue-up is hectic: You only have five or 10 minutes before the glue sets, and you won't know how the disc

Above: The wedges for the body of the bowl are glued into half discs in a special clamping jig made by the author. The steel clamping strap is tightened with a wrench to close the joints between all the wedges. Right: With the table set to 45°, half rings are bandsawn from the half discs following concentric lines scribed on earlier with a large pair of dividers. Below: After matching pairs of half rings are glued together, the seven largest rings are stacked to form the bowl body. The pattern of segmentation is changed by rotating the rings in relation to each other.

Above: The ring layers of the bowl are glued up, two at a time, in a press welded up from rectangular steel tubing. Here, the author tightens the press screw, which bears on a waste block glued to the bowl's base disc. Right: With the lathe rotating at 1,200 RPM, the author turns the outside of his segmented bowl to final shape. When the walls approach 1/8 in. to 1/16 in. thickness, he supports the rim of the bowl with three fingers, to keep the cut from chattering.

will come out until after the glue-up. Any small error in wedge angle is multiplied 104 times, so the wedges need to be extremely accurate to form a perfect disc. But don't be discouraged if your discs don't come out perfectly: Keep an extra length of bowl stock on hand, in case you need to make another base.

I glue the half discs using a clamping jig I made from a ⅛-in. by 1-in. steel strap with a short section of threaded rod welded to each end. The rods are slipped through holes in a 1x2x15-in. rectangular steel tube that's slotted to allow clearance for the ends of the strap (see the top, left photo on the facing page). The gluing operation is simple, but it must be done quickly before the glue sets up. One side of each wedge is buttered as before and placed in the clamping jig in the same order and orientation as it was dry-assembled. When all 52 wedges are in the jig, the strap is tightened by torquing nuts on the threaded rods with a box wrench. Two small steel plates are bolted to either side of the half disc through the hole in the middle, to keep the center area flat during tightening. Snug up the strap a little, bolt on the plate and then finish tightening the strap. Considerable force will be needed to get the joints between all the wedges tight. Again, this is a hectic process, but it shouldn't take more than five minutes from start to finish.

Wait a couple of days for the glue to cure, and then carefully break the discs out of their steel clamps by tapping the edges of the straps with a hammer. Waxing the steel ahead of time helps keep the glue from sticking. Face off the base discs on a three-jaw chuck on the lathe, making both sides flat and true. Flatten both sides of the two half discs using a ¾-in. straight bit in a router-rail jig. The jig supports the router a fixed distance above a table that holds the half disc in place. It takes many passes with the router to surface the half disc, sliding the router both sideways and front to back on the rails, but the jig brings the thickness of the two halves to within .003 in. of each other. Flatten one side of each disc, then the other, removing about ¹⁄₁₆ in. of material per side to wind up with a final thickness of about ⅝ in. An overarm router or abrasive planer can also do the surfacing, provided both half discs are made uniform in thickness.

Next, lay the two half discs on a scrap of plywood so they form a circle, and match up the grain so the wedges are in the same continous order as they came off the saw. Tape the outer edges to the plywood so the discs can't shift, and drive a finish nail into the plywood at the middle of the disc so the end of the nail sticks up about ½ in. Now place the point of a divider in the dimple in the nail's head and scribe a series of concentric circles on the discs that are ⅝ in. apart (the same distance apart as the thickness of the disc). Starting with the largest circle just at the outer rim, you should be able to scribe nine or 10 circles. Remove the half discs from the plywood and take them to the bandsaw. With the bandsaw table set to 45°, saw each half disc into a series of half rings, following the scribed lines. Next, true up the ends of each half ring on the disc sander—just a touch—until they are clean of glue and square.

Glue the two halves of each ring together by taping them down to a flat surface and using the tape to keep the mating edges pressed together. A slab of Corian works well as a gluing surface, but any really flat surface that glue doesn't stick to will suffice. Once the rings have dried, do a little touch-up sanding to remove any glue squeeze-out and to ensure ring flatness. For this, I use another slab of Corian on which I mount four sheets of 60-grit, closed-coat, silicone-carbide paper. With a light touch, I move each disc back and forth on the sandpaper, occasionally rotating it.

Gluing up the rings—All the rings from the large disc, except the smallest one, are stacked on top of the 5-in. base disc to form the body of the large bowl. But before the base disc is ready, it needs to have a ring cut off its outer edge for the smaller bowl. Take the faced-off disc, and with a pair of dividers, score about a 3½-in.-dia. mark on one side. Remount the disc on the three-jaw chuck, and with a narrow parting tool held at 45° to the face of the disc, make a plunge cut at the line and pop out the base of the large bowl. The ring that's left over, combined with the smallest ring from the large disc and the extra, small base disc make up the small bowl.

Back to the large bowl: As you stack the rings into a cone, you'll notice the seam on each ring where the grain in the first wedge meets the grain in the 104th wedge. By rotating each ring slightly and staggering the seam a half a segment between layers, like rows of bricks in a wall, the segments become more visually individual and the bowl's grain pattern is accentuated. To de-emphasize the seam and to get a bowl with an even grain pattern all the way around, start with a board that has grain that's similar at both ends.

To glue up the large bowl, I glue the layers of rings two at a time, using a special press frame I made by mounting a square-threaded screw in a frame welded from the same rectangular steel tubing used for the half-disc clamping jig. First, glue the base disc to a thick waste block, clamping the assembly in the press as shown in the lower, left photo on the facing page. Glue on the layers of rings two at a time, truing the face of the outermost ring after each glue-up. Do this by mounting the waste block on a screw center chucked in the lathe, taking a very light cut. Truing overcomes cumulative errors in the flatness of the rings and keeps the glue joints between layers perfect. The small bowl is glued up one layer at a time, truing faces for flatness between layers.

Turning the bowl—All that remains is to turn the bowl to final shape on the lathe. Remount the assembled bowl to the screw center and rough-turn the outside profile first. Then turn the inside to final shape and return to the outside for the final turning. I like my bowls to be featherlight, so I typically turn the walls down to ⅛ in. to ¹⁄₁₆ in. thick. When the walls start to get really thin, I turn with my left hand's thumb (I'm right-handed), guiding the tool while three fingers ride on the outside of the rotating bowl, steadying the rim. Cloth tape on my fingers protects them from friction burns. About 1,200 RPM is a good speed for doing the final turning.

Because there are so many gluelines in these segmented bowls, turning them tends to dull the edges of most lathe tools quickly. I used to turn with a gouge designed by Jerry Glaser made from A-11 steel, but now I find his micro-grain, carbide-tipped gouge tools to be superior (available from Glaser Engineering Co. Inc., 1661 E. 28th St., Signal Hill, Calif. 90806; 213-426-1722). To prevent turner's elbow (a turner's version of tennis elbow), Glaser recommends weighting the hollow handle of lathe turning tools with about 10 oz. of #9 lead bird shot, which helps absorb arm-fatiguing vibrations.

Sand the outside and inside of each bowl down to 320-grit paper, with the bowl on the lathe. Then, French polish the bowl by applying thin coats of shellac while the bowl's still on the lathe (not spinning). When the finish dries, reverse the bowl on the lathe to turn the foot. I mount the bowl on a special chuck consisting of a rounded cone that bears against the inside while a collar presses against the bowl's outside. The collar has three bolts around it that screw into a faceplate that mounts on the lathe. The bowl can be adjusted in this collar, to be accurately recentered within .005 in., something I verify with a dial indicator. To complete the bowl, part the waste block from the bottom and turn and finish the foot. □

Mike Shuler is a woodturner in Santa Cruz, Calif.

Making a Mosaic Bracelet

A laminated helix from colored veneers

by Richard Schneider

The helical structure of the DNA molecule gave me an idea for a bracelet. From a flitch of rosewood veneer, I cut sixteen matched pieces, 3 in. square. I drilled a hole in the middle of each, stacked them on a pin and rotated each square slightly as I glued them together. The bracelet I turned from the helical stack had a spiral grain pattern, but it wasn't very striking. Later, Terry Ryan, one of my apprentices, suggested making the squares from some multicolored veneer laminates I was using in my work. The problems of getting from the idea to the finished product were not all that easy to conquer, but the resulting bracelet was one of the most startling pieces of laminated woodworking we had ever seen.

In this article, I will describe how I make a helical-mosaic bracelet. Once you understand the helical-mosaic concept, the possibilities for variation are endless. The concept can be ap-

plied to turnings in any number of ways.

Most women can wear a bracelet with an inside diameter between 2¼ in. and 2⅝ in., with 2⅞₁₆ in. about average. The outside diameter should be ⅜ in. larger, which will leave a wall thickness of ³⁄₁₆ in. For a more delicate bracelet, reduce the wall thickness to ⁵⁄₃₂ in. I don't recommend making them thinner than that.

Making the bracelet blank—The striped squares that are stacked up to form the helix are resawn from a glued-up block of hardwood laminates and dyed veneers, as shown in the drawing on the facing page. One-quarter-in.-thick hardwood laminates make an attractive pattern, but any thickness from ¹⁄₁₆ in. to ½ in. will work, and each will produce different effects. Even thickness is important—if the laminates taper, you will have problems. I resaw the laminates slightly thicker than I want,

From *Fine Woodworking* magazine (November 1986) 61:80-83

then sand them to thickness on an abrasive surfacer.

To build the block, I stack up several varieties of hardwood laminates, generally alternating between light- and dark-colored woods. Then I slip colored veneers in between the laminates. The number of laminates isn't important, but the height of the stack must be greater than the outside diameter of the bracelet you want to make. An average-size bracelet needs a 3¼-in. to 3⅜-in. stack.

Any thin epoxy can be used to glue up the block. I use Resin #1000 and Hardener A-95 (or AB-91 for longer pot life) made by R.B.C. Industries, 25 Holden St., Providence, R.I. 02908. I wipe oily hardwoods with rubber-cement solvent or acetone. After the solvent dries, I wipe epoxy on each piece with a bondo scraper or a discarded credit card. I've found that epoxy sets up more quickly if left in a container so, to extend the pot life, I flow the mixed epoxy out onto a piece of coated paper (freezer paper would work) and scrape it up with my applicator.

After completely surrounding the laminate stack with wax paper, I clamp the stack with C-clamps. If the pieces slide too much, I use clamps across the edges to keep the block square.

After jointing the block square and trimming the ends, I mark off and drill the ½-in.-dia. holes needed for the dowel pin in the bracelet-gluing operation, as shown in the drawing. The laminated block is now ready for resawing.

Resawing—Because the slices need to be so thin, the resawing process is one of the most difficult tasks in making the bracelet. You will not get satisfactory results unless the table is square to the blade and the blade is tracking properly. I use a ¼-in. 14-tooth raker blade, .025 in. thick (manufactured by L.S. Starrett Co., Athol, Mass. 01331), and the fence setup shown in the drawing at right.

To set up, I place the wooden fence against my saw's adjustable metal rip fence and adjust both fences for a test cut slightly thicker than .032 in. Then I lock down the adjustable fence.

To minimize tearout at the bottom edge of the cut, I cover the bandsaw table with Masonite. Once I've locked the adjustable fence, I remove the wooden fence and saw part way through the Masonite, guiding it against the metal fence and stopping when the sheet covers the table. I then replace the wooden fence.

With a large piece of walnut or oak, I run a series of test cuts to check the setup for thickness and parallel. Using business cards as shims between the fences, I can move the wooden fence until I get a cut of .032 in., plus or minus .005 in., for the full length of the cut, at which point I clamp the wooden fence securely to the table. This process will take forever and at some point you will just settle for the best you can do. Once set, resaw the entire block without changing the setup or making adjustments.

As I make the first pass through the saw, I note which side of the block is up. I'll call this up side "odd" and the bottom side "even." After the first cut, I put the odd side of the block against the jointer fence and joint the face I've just cut. I make the second cut with the even side up. Then, the even side goes against the jointer fence and my third cut will again have the odd side up. Flipping the block like this cancels out any minute errors in the bandsaw or jointer being out of square.

Proceed to cut the block into slices, moving the block slowly and evenly, never stopping in the middle of a cut, and always applying a constant pressure against the fence. As the slices come off the saw, it's very important to lay them on top of each other and keep them in the order they came off the block. Continue sawing until you have cut at least 25 slices.

Cut the stack of slices into four decks, as shown in the drawing below. Each deck of tiles will make one bracelet. It is very important to keep the tiles in order, so I place a rubber band around each deck until it is time to glue up the bracelets.

Gluing up the blank—I've found that the bracelets are much more elegant if a solid piece of hardwood—ebony, rosewood or cocobolo—is glued to both sides of the deck to form the edges of the bracelet. The edge pieces should be ⅛ in. to 3⁄16 in. thick and surface sanded on both sides. If the deck is glued up without these pieces, the edges of the bracelet will be the striped laminate itself.

Make a glue-up board, as shown in the drawing on p. 86, long enough that one end can be clamped to your bench. Drill a ½-in. hole three-fourths of the way through the board 2½ in. from one

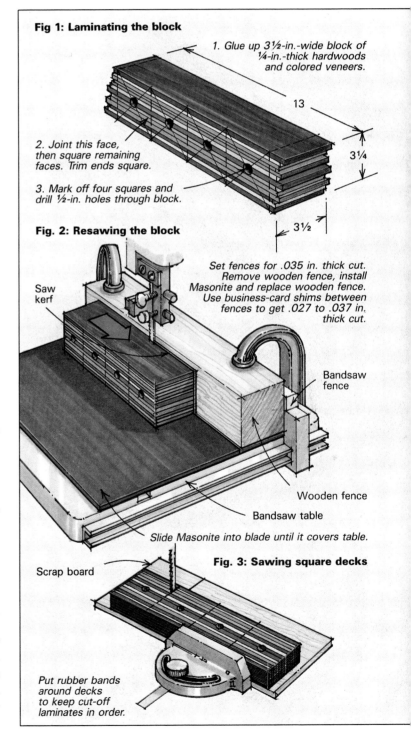

Fig 1: Laminating the block

1. Glue up 3½-in.-wide block of ¼-in.-thick hardwoods and colored veneers.

2. Joint this face, then square remaining faces. Trim ends square.

3. Mark off four squares and drill ½-in. holes through block.

13

3¼

3½

Fig. 2: Resawing the block

Saw kerf

Set fences for .035 in. thick cut. Remove wooden fence, install Masonite and replace wooden fence. Use business-card shims between fences to get .027 to .037 in. thick cut.

Bandsaw fence

Wooden fence

Bandsaw table

Slide Masonite into blade until it covers table.

Fig. 3: Sawing square decks

Scrap board

Put rubber bands around decks to keep cut-off laminates in order.

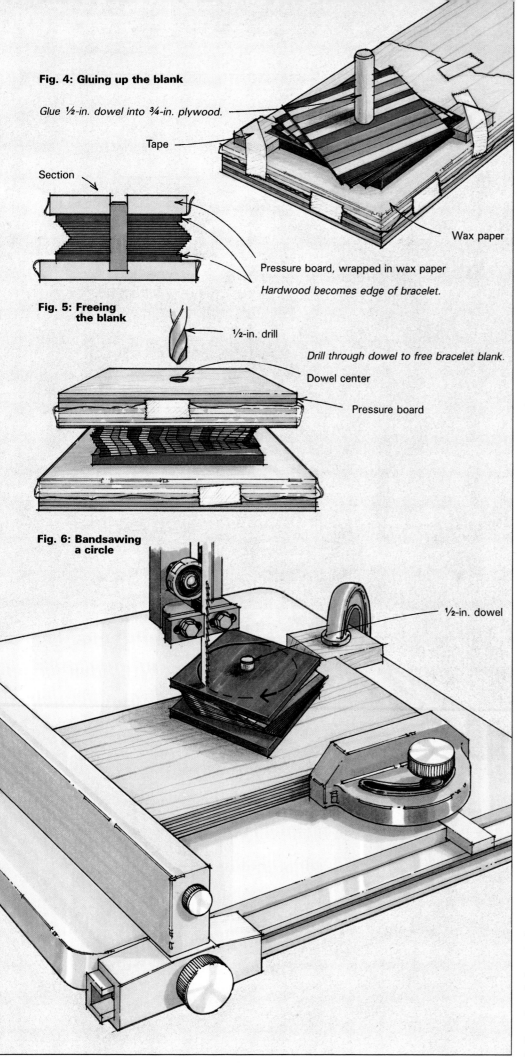

Fig. 4: Gluing up the blank

Glue ½-in. dowel into ¾-in. plywood.

Tape

Section

Wax paper

Pressure board, wrapped in wax paper

Hardwood becomes edge of bracelet.

Fig. 5: Freeing the blank

½-in. drill

Drill through dowel to free bracelet blank.

Dowel center

Pressure board

Fig. 6: Bandsawing a circle

½-in. dowel

Schneider forms a chevron pattern by rotating the colored tiles on a ½-in. dowel (top). When the design is right, he caps the deck with a hardwood edge piece and a pressure board before applying clamps (center). For turning, the bracelet is mounted on a mandrel in a 3-jaw chuck. To cut the inside, the parting tool (drawing, facing page) is plunged straight into the face of the bracelet (bottom).

end on centerline. Glue in a ½-in. wooden dowel long enough to pass through the bracelet deck and edge pieces and protrude about ¾ in. into a pressure board, as shown. The pressure board is just a piece of plywood about the size of the bracelet deck—a little larger won't hurt—with a ½-in. hole all the way through the center. I bevel the top of the dowel pin to facilitate sliding the tiles on. Before gluing, I cover the glue board and the pressure board with wax paper.

Now you're ready to design and glue the bracelet all at once. I recommend that you wear rubber gloves and that you have good ventilation. First, spread a thin coat of runny epoxy on the inside surface of one of the edge pieces, and slide it down over the pin. Next, take the first laminate tile from the deck, wipe epoxy on both surfaces, and slide it down on the pin and set it on the edge piece so that the laminate lines fall in the direction of the grain of the edge piece. Repeat this process with each tile until the entire deck has been glued and placed on the pin.

Rotating the pieces determines the design. How you do this is completely up to you, but I recommend that you make the simple chevron design the first few times.

To make the chevron, rotate each piece by the same amount until you have reached halfway plus one (assuming you are starting with an odd number of tiles in the deck), then reverse the rotation and return to the starting point. Each piece may be rotated ⅟₁₆ in. or ³⁄₁₆ in., or you can even vary the amount, gradually increasing the rotation with each piece. A good way to get the feel is to do a number of dry runs trying different rotations.

When you are satisfied with the design, cap it with the other edge piece and the pressure board. I like to align the top and bottom edge pieces so the grain runs in the same direction. Install a very large C-clamp directly over the dowel hole with the screw beneath the board to combat the torque problem. Apply pressure very slowly—the whole business wants to spin on the pin and destroy your design. If the epoxy is too thick it will be impossible to clamp the bracelet without ruining the pattern.

Once the large clamp is tightened successfully, place four smaller C-clamps on the four corners of the pressure block as close to the middle clamp as possible, tightening them little by little as you would tighten the lug nuts on a car wheel.

The next day, remove the clamps and clamp the glue board to the drill-press table. Drill a ½-in. hole right through the dowel and into the glue board, allowing the blank to come free. Next, bandsaw the blank round, as shown in the drawing at left, leaving as much material as possible. The bracelet is now ready for turning.

Turning the bracelet—I turn bracelets on an old 6-in. Craftsman metal lathe which I run at 836 RPM—dropping to 532 RPM for final sanding. Although I've never tried it, I can't see why you shouldn't be able to turn these bracelets on a wood lathe.

Before you can turn the bracelet you have to get hold of it somehow. I do that by mounting it on a mandrel made of ½-in. stainless steel threaded rod 4 in. to 5 in. long, with a washer and nut on each side, as shown in the photo at left, which I grip in a 3-jaw chuck. If the bracelet doesn't fit tightly on the mandrel, I wrap a piece of paper or masking tape on the threaded area of the rod.

First, I turn the outside diameter of the bracelet. Then, I face off the edge piece until it is the thickness I want. I then chuck up the other end of the mandrel and face off the other edge piece to the same thickness.

At this point, I cut a 45° bevel on the edges, then sand the bracelet right to finish while it is still solid. Reversing the rotation, I usually sand from 120 grit through 400 grit. I finish sand

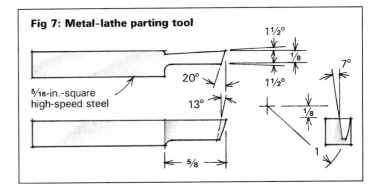

Fig 7: Metal-lathe parting tool

with a 3M product called Wetordry Tri-M-ite 15-micron polishing paper (available from The Luthier's Mercantile, P.O. Box 774, 412 Moore Ave., Healdsburg, Calif. 95448). This polishing paper seems to burnish the surface, causing it to glisten.

Once the bracelet has been sanded, it can be parted off. I made the parting tool, shown in the drawing above, from a ⁵⁄₁₆-in.-square high-speed steel tool bit blank (available from Campbell Tools Co., 2100 Selma Road, Springfield, Ohio 45505). It is a fragile bit and must be kept sharp and installed in the tool holder properly or it will break off, usually ruining the bracelet in the process.

Install the parting tool in the tool holder so that the length of the tool is parallel to the mandrel and the tool point is at the height of the mandrel's center. Move the cross slide away from center until the tool is aimed to cut the inside diameter. Wind the longitudinal slide to plunge the tool straight into the face of the bracelet, stopping when you've cut halfway through the bracelet. Then back out and without changing the setting of the cross slide, chuck up the other end of the mandrel and repeat the process from the other side. When the cuts meet, the bracelet will fall free. Stop the lathe immediately to avoid damage from the chuck jaws.

If the mandrel is the slightest bit crooked, the two cuts will not meet perfectly and there will be a ridge on the inside of the bracelet. This ridge can be sanded off using a sanding spindle on the drill press.

When the inside is smooth, I chuck it up again with just the tips of the 3-jaw chuck's jaws applying pressure outward from the inside of the bracelet. Tape on the jaws protects the bracelet. I sand the inside that projects beyond the jaws with sandpaper wrapped around a dowel. Then I turn the bracelet around, and sand from the other side.

Before finishing, I flatten the edges of the bracelet on a piece of 400-grit paper taped to a smooth surface and then repeat with the Tri-M-ite polishing paper.

I finish my bracelets by wiping on a coat of ZAR Satin Wipe-On Tung Oil Finish (manufactured by United Gilsonite Laboratories, Scranton, Pa. 18501). I allow it to stand a few minutes, then wipe it off with a lintless cloth. I then hang the bracelet on a dowel to dry for 24 hours. When dry, I wipe it down with a paper towel or cloth and return it to the lathe, spin on a second coat, and wipe it off immediately. I turn it around, coat the other side and return it to the dowel to dry. A final sanding with Tri-M-ite and a coat of Johnson's Paste Wax applied on the lathe, finishes the job. □

Richard Schneider, of Sequim, Wash., has been building classical guitars professionally for 23 years. He began making wood jewelry in 1973.

Carved Bowls

Texture enriches the basic shape

by Alan Stirt

I began carving the outside of my turned bowls about ten years ago after seeing fluted Chinese porcelain bowls. Once I started carving textures, I found all sorts of possibilities. At first, I carved wide flutes like the ones on the big bowl shown below, but later I began experimenting with other textures. The fine-line pattern on the shallow bowl, for instance, was inspired by photos of African masks. Carving the bowls makes them somewhat evocative of the porcelains and masks that inspired them, and the process allows me to create bowls ranging from those with a fragile, delicate quality to others that stress strength and movement.

I originally cut flutes by pressing my bowls against abrasive drum sanders of various diameters mounted in my lathe's Jacobs chuck. I liked the finished pieces, but hated the technique and the dust so much that I switched to a carving gouge. The carved flutes weren't as precise as sanded ones, but they had a wonderful texture and a pleasingly irregular look. To give my sore arms a break, I later bought an electrically powered Rakuda flexible-shaft carver with interchangeable bits (available for about $200 from Woodline, The Japan Woodworker, 1731 Clement St., Alameda, Calif. 94501). I powered the shaft with a ⅛-HP, 3450-RPM motor equipped with an on/off foot switch. The tool's reciprocating gouge is easily guided by hand. Less pressure is needed than when using regular carving tools, but the same techniques apply. The Rakuda makes clean cuts.

The basic techniques for carving fluted bowls are the same for both green and dry wood, but I prefer green wood—it's easier to carve and is readily available near my home in northern Vermont. By taking advantage of the drying power of a microwave oven and a heat gun, I can start with a green-wood block in the morning and end up with a carved, dry-enough-to-be-stable bowl in the afternoon.

I begin by roughing out the green blank so the bowl approximates the shape I want, leaving the walls ¾ in. to 1 in. thick. I like bowls with finished walls about ¼ in. to ⅜ in. thick, so my roughing out leaves plenty of stock to compensate for any warping that might occur when I zap the piece in the microwave. In designing the bowls, I also leave the areas to be carved about ⅛ in. to 3/16 in. thicker than the rest of the bowl; the exact amount of extra thickness depends on the length and depth of the flutes I have in mind. I often carve flutes from the bottom of the bowl to the rim, but if just a section of the bowl will be fluted, I create a

Stirt carved the flutes and other textures on his turned bowls with an electric reciprocating gouge. Large flutes were inspired by Chinese porcelain; fine-line patterns by African masks.

visual boundary for the carving by cutting a cove or by changing the angle of the wall.

After screwing a faceplate to the rim side of the bowl, I shape the outside with ½-in. and ⅜-in. high-speed-steel, deep-fluted bowl gouges with their sides ground back and their noses relatively blunt. The long side edges can remove a lot of material quickly, and the blunt nose is good for following sharp concave curves—especially on the inside of bowls. The roughing cuts are made mostly with the sides of the tool, with the bevel rubbing. When I shape the outside of a bowl, the gouge's flute faces away from me and the cutting is done with the left side of the cutting edge, moving from the foot to the rim (the wood cuts more easily this way, as compared to cutting from the rim to the foot). On the inside of the bowl, I cut from the rim toward the center— again with the gouge's flute facing away from me, but cutting now with the right side of the tool's cutting edge.

I've successfully microwave-dried roughed-out 15-in.-dia. bowls, but the process works best for bowls 10 in. in diameter or less. Drying time depends upon the mass, species, moisture content and grain structure of the bowl, so I can't give any exact "recipes." However, there are some general principles that work for me. For example, I do all my drying on a defrost cycle—usually a couple of ten-minute treatments are enough. I never get the bowls too hot to hold in my hand, and I use a turntable stand (built-in on some microwaves or available as an accessory in department stores) to rotate the bowls and ensure even heating. I haven't had much luck microwaving bowls with a moisture content greater than 20-25%, so I let roughed-out bowls that are really wet air dry for a while before I microwave them. If the bowl is too wet, endgrain checking and honeycombing below the surface of the wood are likely to occur.

After microwaving the blank, I remount the bowl on the lathe with a three-jaw chuck (or, with a faceplate and double-face tape) and finish turning it. I employ the same techniques used for roughing out, but take very light cuts to produce the cleanest and smoothest surface possible. On the outside, I sand the areas that won't be carved—sandpaper grit is hard on carving tools. I sand the inside with a foam-backed abrasive disc chucked in an electric drill. If I skip the microwave and go directly from green blank to finished bowl, I usually don't have any problems sanding the outside, but the interior walls may be wet enough to gum up the sandpaper. I get around this by directing a heat gun into the inside of the spinning bowl for a few minutes until the surface is dry enough to be sanded. Salad bowls are then finished with food-safe Livos Kaldet Resin and Oil finish (available from Woodpecker's Tools, Inc., 614 Agua Fria St., Santa Fe, N.M. 87501). Decorative bowls and platters are finished with tung oil.

At this stage, the bowls are ready to be fluted. To draw guidelines for the flutes, I center the bowl on a plywood layout grid with 48 equally spaced lines radiating from a center point. (There's nothing magical about having 48 radius lines, by the way—it was simply the number of indexing points on the lathe where I drew my first layout disc. After experimenting with other numbers, I decided I liked the look of 48 flutes best.) I also draw a number of concentric circles from the same center point to help align the bowl on the grid. Then, I center the bowl by eye, rim side down, over the circle that most closely matches the circumference of the bowl and mark the 48 points on the rim before remounting the bowl on the lathe.

To draw guidelines for straight flutes, I substitute my tool's regular tool rest with the wooden guide shown in the top left photo on p. 90. I made the guide by bandsawing a slight curve on the flat piece of scrap; so far, it's fit every bowl I've turned. One end

Top: The author shapes the outside of bowls from foot to rim with ½-in. and ⅜-in. deep-fluted bowl gouges. The tool's flute faces away from him as the left side of the tool shaves the green wood. Above: The right side of the cutting tool cuts the inside of the bowl.

of the guide is screwed to a post that fits into the lathe's tool-rest holder. The flat surface of the guide keeps the pencil horizontal and locates its writing point at the exact center of the spindle. This ensures that the flutes will be perpendicular to the faceplate—if they're off a little, they just don't look right. Using the points on the rim as starting points, I slide the pencil along the rest of the area to be carved to indicate the flutes.

I use basically the same procedure to make a bowl with spiral flutes, only the scrapwood guide is used to transfer the points on the rim to the bottom of the area to be fluted. The result is 48 evenly spaced points on both borders of the carving area. To draw the spiral flutes, I just connect offset dots with a straight,

A wooden straightedge on a post fit into the lathe's tool-rest support, above, lays out the lines for flutes. Stirt then carves the flutes with a Rakuda reciprocating gouge, right. The jig shown holding the bowl is constructed from scrapwood, and is large enough to fit bowls of all sizes. The backing board is adjusted to hold the bowl at a comfortable work height. For a smooth flute, Stirt makes several light passes, cutting from the base to the rim, below.

flexible plastic ruler. I usually skip two or three dots, but you can use any offset that looks good. I've also carved some flutes marked out with a flexible, *curved* piece of plastic. There are many possibilities, so don't hesitate to experiment.

The jig shown for carving the bowl is very simple—a backing board, a plywood base, a shelf to rest the bowl on and a 1-in. by 1½-in. hardwood cleat fastened to the base board with ½-in. threaded rods and wing nuts (see large photo, above). Set the backing board to a height that's comfortable for carving. Lean the base board against a workbench, rest the bowl on the shelf and clamp it in place with the cleat by tightening the wing nuts. I carve from the foot toward the rim, as shown. With the power carver, you just push the gouge into the wood and the blade will begin to cut. The reciprocating action is so slight that you barely notice the back-and-forth motion, although the noise can get a little irritating at times. Usually, I increase the depth of cut slightly as I move up the bowl. Most flutes take about three or four passes with a shallow gouge. The width of the blade generally sets the width of the flute. For a bowl

like the one shown here, I use a 24mm gouge with a #7 or #8 sweep; 16mm and 30mm blades with #7 and #8 sweeps are also handy. After carving the uppermost segment of the bowl, I loosen the wing nuts, rotate the bowl and bring another section to the top.

As you progress around the bowl, the grain orientation constantly changes from endgrain to side grain, then back to endgrain again. Adjust your carving for each flute: the wilder the grain or harder the wood, the slower the movement and lighter the cut. With a little practice, it's relatively easy to judge how fast and deep to carve. If you don't have a power carver, you can hand-carve with a ½-in. to 1¼-in. #7 carving gouge. I recommend that you push the tool by hand, rather than use a mallet and risk cracking the turning.

If you want to try some other textures, substitute a ½-in., 60° V-groove parting tool for the gouge. You can also carve several fine lines by eye between the layout lines on the side of the bowl, experiment with various cross-hatching effects or even carve along the bowl's rim. To carve the rims of bowls, I make a layout guide like the one shown in the top right photo. I cut a

To carve the handles and feet of this mahogany salad bowl, Boyce followed faceplate turning with gouge work, revealing delicate sections turned into the bowl's sides and bottom.

Carved handles and feet

by Dale Boyce

Sometimes, the shapes that come directly off the lathe are just a little too round for me, so I've been experimenting with sawing apart or carving my turnings, exposing section profiles that would otherwise be hidden. To add interest to this otherwise featureless round salad bowl, for example, I carved three feet into the bowl's base and shaped a pair of handles from a rib turned around the bowl's circumference.

Here's the basic turning sequence I used to create the bowl. With the blank screwed to a faceplate, I first turned the bottom profile. The center of the bottom should be kept as flat as possible so that the faceplate can be attached to it for remounting the bowl on the lathe.

Next, I wasted the bowl's inside and turned the outside profile and the rib for the handles. To do so, I first glued a scrapwood disc to the bowl's now-flattened bottom. I inserted a piece of newspaper in the glue joint so the disc and bowl could later be separated. An alternative to the paper joint is to use Dexter-Hysol hot-melt glue, applied with the company's 3010 gun (glue and gun are both available from Dexter-Hysol Corporation, 164 Folly Mill Road, Seabrook, N.H. 03874). When the bowl has been turned, the hot-melt glue can be parted with a heat gun, and the bowl's bottom can be cleaned up with a scraper and mineral spirits (a solvent for the glue).

Once the disc is glued down, carefully center and screw the faceplate, then remount the bowl on the lathe.

After turning the outside and inside profiles and the rib, I laid out the handles while the bowl was still on the lathe. For strength, the long grain of the bowl should run into the handles. With the rib turned thin, carving the handles and wasting the unwanted portion of the rib was easy with a ¾-in., No. 3 carving gouge. Before laying out and carving the elliptical cutouts that form the bowl's three feet, I removed the disc by tapping a wide chisel, bevel facing the disc, into the paper joint. Sanding and a coat of walnut oil (which can be purchased in health-food stores and specialty food shops) completed the bowl. □

Dale Boyce is an architectural woodworker and turner. He lives in Portland, Me.

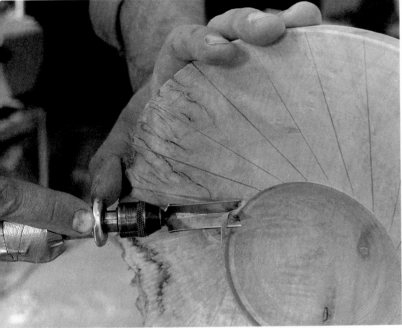

To lay out the rim design, Stirt bandsaws a piece of scrap to fit the rim, rotates a straightedge from it until he likes the angle (top), then glues the pieces together. The fixture is then moved around the bowl to mark the lines. Above, the thin lines along the rim of a cherry bowl are cut with a ½-in., 60° V-groove parting tool.

curve in a scrap of wood so it fits snugly against the rim, then play with the angle of the lines by rotating a straight piece of scrap jutting out from the curved piece. When the angle looks right, I Super Glue the two pieces together, then move the guide around the rim and pencil in guidelines at intervals that look right. Next, I carve the lines with the bowl on the lathe.

Once you're done carving, finish the carved areas with the same oil applied to the rest of the bowl previously. I set green-wood bowls aside for a week or so, just to make sure everything is dry and stable. Dry bowls sit for a day or two until the oil sets up.

Finally, the bowls are remounted on the lathe and rotated at the slowest speed—about 200 RPM on my lathe. I oil and wet-sand everything (except the carving) with 400-grit wet-or-dry sandpaper. To remove any rough spots on the flutes, rub them lightly (particularly the ones on the side grain) with grocery-store-variety Scotch-Brite pads. The ridges left by the carving tool remain. □

Alan Stirt is a professional woodturner in Enosburg Falls, Vt.

Pepper Mills and Saltshakers

A seasoned approach to multiples

by Sven Hanson

The tops of this saltshaker and pepper-mill set feature the author's 'theme stripe,' a layer of padauk between layers of walnut. This stripe adds a decorative touch and identifies the set as one item in his line of kitchen accessories.

Making multiples, instead of one-of-a-kind pieces, is like converting your old stereo to play digital compact discs. The highs are higher; the lows are lower. The clinkers are as painful as a child's first violin lesson, while the winners feature the sounds of contented craftsmen, appreciative words from customers and the crisp sound of currency as it's tucked into the cash box. Even if money isn't your object, wouldn't it be great to make 20 Christmas gifts in the time it normally takes to make just a few? Or wouldn't it be great to increase the potential of your tools, while improving your accuracy through the use of well-designed jigs?

My goal in making these salt-and-pepper sets was to make money, so my first consideration was the economics of the project. A few years of selling small salt-and-pepper sets for $29.99 at craft fairs proved to me that people would pay a premium price for quality kitchen accessories. I thought I could get $49 for a taller set that included a pepper mill. A visit to some local shopkeepers with a sample set supported this assumption. But the real proof came when I sold 24 sets at a craft fair at the $49 price. Forty-nine dollars seems like an easy price to meet, but…that's the retail price. To make money, I have to produce a set for $25. The grinder mechanism and the #6 XXXX cork, together cost $4 per set. The wood costs about $3. That leaves $18 for labor and overhead, so to make a profit, I have to produce more than one set per hour. To get this kind of efficiency, there are some things you should do before you ever touch the wood.

Organizing—A full-scale drawing will let you finalize your design and help you visualize and organize each step of the process. If you make notes at this planning stage and add to them as you work, you won't have to resolve problems when you do your

second run, weeks or months later. Think through the order of procedures; each operation will affect future ones. For example, on this project, the salt escape holes are drilled *after* the finish is applied to avoid filling the holes with oil and steel wool while finishing. Also, the dowel stems that join the tops to the bases are glued in and drilled after most of the other drilling so they won't get in the way during the roundover operation and make sanding and finishing more difficult.

An important piece in the puzzle of organizing your procedures is the designing of jigs to execute repetitive processes with precision. For this project, my jigs are very simple: I use one jig for sawing, three different jigs for drilling and some special boards for holding parts while finishing.

For crosscutting and ripping, I use a sliding-cradle jig on my tablesaw. On the back fence, I mark the lengths for the various pieces with a drafting triangle and a fine-line mechanical pencil for maximum accuracy. I clamp a stop block at these lines when making multiple cuts, but if one or two extra cuts need to be made after the initial run, I just slide the piece up to the line and cut. I always make a couple extra of each part to test setups or to replace damaged or defective parts.

Most of the drilling is done on the drill press using the L-shaped jig shown on the facing page to locate and support the wooden blanks. On a run of 18 salt-and-pepper sets, I will drill more than 100 holes with this jig, so I make sure the upright supports are square to the base and each other.

The second drilling jig is simply a piece of ¾-in. plywood roughly the same size as the drill-press table. The jig is clamped to the table, and a 1-in.-dia. hole, ⅝ in. deep, is bored near its center. The stems of the pepper-mill tops are placed in this hole

Photo: Michele Russell Slavinsky; drawings: Roland Wolf

so they are automatically centered under the chuck when drilling for the grinder shaft.

The third drilling jig is a piece of ¼-in.-thick aluminum plate, 2⅛ in. sq., which fits over top of the saltshaker as a guide for drilling the salt escape holes (see figure 1).

To hold the pieces during finishing, I adapt the ¾-in.-thick plywood trays that I use to hold and carry the parts between tools during the machining processes. For the tops, I drill a grid of ¾-in. holes, 2½ in. apart, an even number in both directions, and tap a 1½-in.-long dowel into each hole. For the bodies, I drill ⅜-in. holes and drive pine sticks, ⅜ in. by ⅜ in., 7 in. long, into them. I drop 1-in.-long pieces of 1¼-in. dowel with a ⅝-in. hole drilled in the center over these sticks. These dowel "donuts" fit into the hole in the bottoms of the bodies and keep the bodies off the board during finishing. Because these shakers and mills are used in the kitchen, they should be neat and clean, even on the bottom.

Cutting and drilling—After I've planned my procedures, designed my jigs and determined how much wood I'm going to need (an 8-ft. 2x6 will make 18 sets), I head to the lumber store to get the cleanest 8/4 walnut I can find. Forget scraps from the floor, you'll do better getting the best of the best.

Back at the shop, I begin by laminating blanks for the tops. I use what I call my "theme stripe": a layer of padauk between two layers of walnut. The theme stripe works two ways for me. Since I make a line of kitchen items, shoppers can put together an ensemble of pieces. And, items made of very different shades of walnut, or even of different woods, clearly bear a family resemblance. Center the stripe and glue up seven 12-in.-long and 2-in.-sq. blocks. This will give you four extra tops in case anything goes wrong later. While my laminations are drying, I begin cutting the bodies to length with my sliding-cradle jig on the tablesaw.

I do all my ripping and crosscutting on the tablesaw with a 24-tooth Freud rip blade. With a sharp blade and a slow, steady feed, I get as many cuts to the inch and as clean a cut as with a crosscut blade, and I don't have to change blades. By taking great pains to see that all my sawcuts are extremely smooth, I get by with only one step on the belt sander (150 grit). This saves a good deal of time at one of the most tedious parts of the job and reduces the chances of missing a side while sanding, only to have it show up like a sore thumb after the first coat of finish is applied.

After I've crosscut enough stock to make 36 bodies (18 sets), I rip them as wide as the stock is thick (my original stock was 1¾ in. thick) by placing the endgrain of the pieces against the fence of the sliding-cradle jig and butting them to a stop block clamped to the fence. Here's where the sharp rip blade and the steady jig create perfectly sized, easily sanded pieces. I move them off the jig onto plywood trays, keeping them in pairs. The careful placement of the pieces before and during an operation ensures that each piece gets completed in its proper turn.

By this time, the blanks I laminated for the tops are ready to work. I scrape off the glue, lightly joint one side and lightly surface the other on the tablesaw. Leave the pieces slightly larger than the thickness of your original stock or they'll end up small after they're routed and sanded. The mark for crosscutting the cuboid tops is the same one used for ripping the bottoms to width. Before I leave the tablesaw, I cut the lengths of 1-in. dowel for the stems. Mark 1 in. on the tablesaw jig and cut 36 pieces. Caution! Don't use a stop block, or you'll be asking for a kickback. I use an ice pick to keep the 1-in. cutoff from flying away, and when the dowel gets short, I start a new one.

After the tops and bodies have been cut to size, I carry them over to the drill press on the plywood trays. I clamp my drilling jig to the drill-press table and start with the largest hole. Figure 2 on the next page shows the steps for drilling. Keep the bodies in pairs and replace them in the same position on the tray, but turned, so you can tell at a glance that each operation has been completed.

Routing and sanding—Next, I round the edges on a router table with a ¼-in. roundover bit. I do the tops first, pushing them only halfway through, then turning them and completing the cut by feeding from the opposite corner. All 12 edges are done in this way so the bit can't tear out the corner at the end of a cut. Roundover the edges of the bodies in the same way, leaving the bottom four edges square to provide a stable base. I do the short edges at the top first and then the long edges. I try to push fast enough not to burn and slow enough not to tear out. The routing is one of the most tedious jobs, and if you don't do it in an orderly fashion, you'll miss edges. I actually count out loud, like musicians count: one, two, three, four; two, two, three, four; and so on. Once a groove is established, I let my mind relax. I just keep an eye on my fingertips and take short breaks as necessary to relieve the "highway hypnosis."

Now we're in the middle of the ocean of work. One noisy, dusty, boring job is behind us, one ahead of us: sanding. I smooth the flat surfaces first on a 6-in. by 48-in. Shopsmith stationary belt sander with a brand new 150-grit belt. To get the most from my

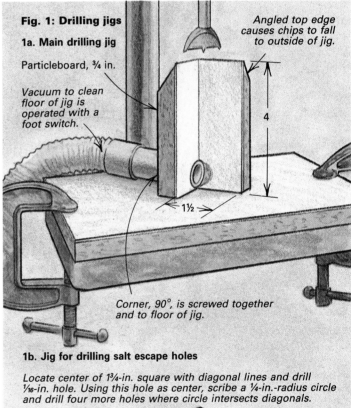

Fig. 1: Drilling jigs

1a. Main drilling jig

Particleboard, ¾ in.

Vacuum to clean floor of jig is operated with a foot switch.

Angled top edge causes chips to fall to outside of jig.

4

1½

Corner, 90°, is screwed together and to floor of jig.

1b. Jig for drilling salt escape holes

Locate center of 1¾-in. square with diagonal lines and drill ¹⁄₁₆-in. hole. Using this hole as center, scribe a ¼-in.-radius circle and drill four more holes where circle intersects diagonals.

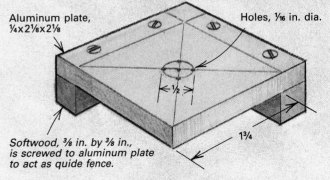

Aluminum plate, ¼x2⅛x2⅛

Holes, ¹⁄₁₆ in. dia.

½

Softwood, ⅜ in. by ⅜ in., is screwed to aluminum plate to act as guide fence.

1¾

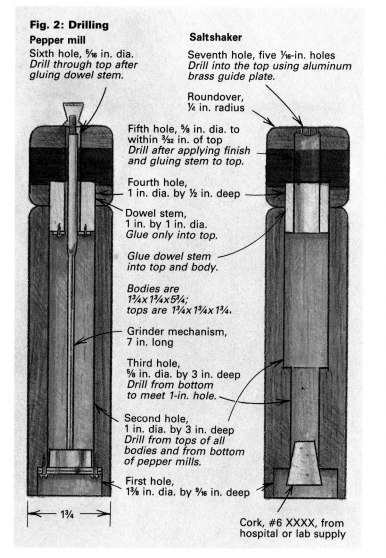

Fig. 2: Drilling

Pepper mill

Sixth hole, ⁵⁄₁₆ in. dia.
Drill through top after gluing dowel stem.

Saltshaker

Seventh hole, five ¹⁄₁₆-in. holes
Drill into the top using aluminum brass guide plate.

Roundover,
¼ in. radius

Fifth hole, ⅝ in. dia. to
within ³⁄₃₂ in. of top
*Drill after applying finish
and gluing stem to top.*

Fourth hole,
1 in. dia. by ½ in. deep

Dowel stem,
1 in. by 1 in. dia.
Glue only into top.

Glue dowel stem
into top and body.

Bodies are
1¾x1¾x5¾;
tops are 1¾x1¾x1¾.

Grinder mechanism,
7 in. long

Third hole,
⅝ in. dia. by 3 in. deep
*Drill from bottom
to meet 1-in. hole.*

Second hole,
1 in. dia. by 3 in. deep
*Drill from tops of all
bodies and from bottom
of pepper mills.*

First hole,
1⅜ in. dia. by ⁹⁄₁₆ in. deep

|← 1¾ →|

Cork, #6 XXXX, from
hospital or lab supply

belts, I use a rubber belt cleaner often. I sand the flat surfaces first on all 72 pieces, then the roundovers, long edges first, and then the endgrain. Just like in the routing, I develop a pattern and count as I go. Each edge gets three swipes: the first is pressed hard, the second medium and the last pass is light. This way, when I switch to the 220-grit orbital sanding, the scratches are relatively shallow and only the corners need much work. Before the orbital sanding, I wipe each part with a wet sponge. This not only raises the grain to allow the sandpaper to do its job more easily, but later on, when the salt-and-pepper sets are used in the kitchen, they'll be far less likely to water-spot. I load four sheets of paper at a time on the orbital sander and slice them off one at a time with a thin ruler as they wear out.

After the final sanding, I use a narrow foam brush to apply Armor-All (available at most auto-parts stores) over the padauk to preserve its red-orange color. Twenty-four hours later, the raised grain is smoothed with steel wool. (Even after the water treatment, the grain will raise a little.) At this point, I convert the plywood trays to hold the parts for finishing.

Finishing and final drilling—My clients seem to prefer a thick, glossy finish, so I apply a light coat of sanding sealer to help the finish build faster. The parts are placed one at a time on a piece of plywood that sits on a 3-in.-dia. lazy-Susan bearing, and I rotate the board with my gloved left hand while I spray the sealer. After this coat is dry, I scrub on a coat of Waterlox (see sources of supply at right) with 0000 steel wool and place the parts on the trays for a few minutes before wiping off the excess with a cloth. If the finish is generally smooth, I apply the second and subsequent coats with soft cotton cloth instead of steel wool, to allow the finish to build faster. I apply three to five coats of Waterlox, depending on the gloss desired: Three coats will give a satin finish; Five coats will give a fairly glossy finish. Allow at least six hours between coats, longer if the temperature is below 70° or if the humidity is high. Waterlox is similar to Danish oil, but it builds much faster and is much more water-resistant. It sets up so fast that you should put finish on only four pieces before coming back to wipe them off.

After the finishing is complete, I glue the dowel stems in place by spreading glue in the hole in each top and firmly pressing the stem into place. Keep squeeze-out to a minimum by experimenting with the amount of glue on the first few you do.

Now it's back to the drill press to complete the tops. First drill all the saltshaker tops. Place them upside down in the drilling jig, and with a ⅝-in. Forstner bit, with the point shortened, drill to within ³⁄₃₂ in. of the top. Make sure your depth stop is accurately and firmly set. I use a layer of paper towels to cover the jig bottom and protect the finish from dents and scratches.

To drill the pepper-mill tops for the shaft of the grinder mechanism, you'll use the jig with the 1-in.-dia. hole in its center. With a ¼-in. brad-point bit in the chuck, align the center of the hole with the point of the bit before clamping the board in place. Then, place each pepper-mill top with its stem in the 1-in.-dia. hole, and drill all the way through.

To complete the pepper mills, I vacuum the sawdust from the holes in both the tops and bottoms and then install the grinder mechanisms. To complete the saltshakers, I put all the tops onto the bodies, and using my aluminum guide, drill the five ¹⁄₁₆-in. holes, which are just right for lightly salting food. The drill press is run at top speed, and a sharp bit is used for this job only. The tiny bit of roughness I get, even with a slow and steady entry, is buffed off with a piece of old blue-jean fabric wetted with the tiniest bit of oil. After the holes are drilled, I pull the tops off and vacuum them out. Then, I apply glue to the sides of the hole in the top of the body with a pipe cleaner and press the top into place, turning until the top's sides line up with the body. I set the corks in place, making sure they go in far enough to clear the bottom.

All you need now is a label with a tale about the love and care you put into their construction, how to care for them and how to load the peppercorns. I use a lightweight freezer bag around one of the pair to keep it from rubbing the other, then I seal the pair in a well-fitted ZipLock polybag from my local packaging store to complete the thoroughly professional presentation.

More than any other type of work, producing multiples requires careful planning and execution. A simple, beautiful item that works well *can* be profitable. If all the elements in the "score" are well written and well performed, you've got a symphony. □

Sven Hanson builds custom furniture and teaches woodworking in Albuquerque, N.M.

Sources of supply

Pepper-mill grinding mechanism:
Craft Supplies USA, 1287 E. 1120 S., Provo, UT 84601; (801) 373-0917. (Type-A pepper mills in 4-in. through 18-in. lengths)
Waterlox:
Waterlox Chemical and Coating Corp., 9808 Meech Ave., Cleveland, OH 44105; (216) 641-4877.
Aerosol sanding sealer:
Standard Brands Paint Co., 4300 T.W. 190th St., Torrance, CA 90509-2956; (213) 542-5901.

Turning Balls

by Ernie Conover

First make the cup chuck shown in step **1**. You can chase threads into the endgrain so it will mount directly on the spindle, or you can screw it to a faceplate. Scrape the inside walls to an included taper of 4°, with an opening equal to the diameter of the ball. Take note that if the chuck sits around for more than a day or so it will distort and have to be retrued.

Prepare the stock by turning a cylinder the diameter of the ball. If turning a few balls, make the cylinder long enough to include them all. Then part each ball blank off, completing the cut with a backsaw to avoid tearout.

Force the stock into the chuck and tap it with a hammer until it runs true, turning the lathe by hand. Square off the endgrain with a roundnose scraper, step **2**, then mark the pole point with a pencil dot. Use vernier calipers to measure the radius of the work, and transfer this dimension to mark the equator and the far end of the ball. Also, make two gauge lines parallel to the equator and shade them in—this will help in the final stages of turning.

With a gouge, turn the end of the ball slightly outside true diameter, then reverse the work to round the other end (steps **3** and **4**). Next rotate the work as shown in step **5**, and draw a new equator through the old poles. When the lathe turns, you will see a ghost of a perfect sphere. Scrape down to the image using a square-end chisel—the trick is to cut away the gauge lines without removing the equator. The ball can be further trued by remounting it at random positions. In the final stages, you can knock the work out of the chuck by inserting a dowel through the spindle, or, if you have a solid spindle, by drilling an angled hole from the middle of the cup out through the side of the chuck. Mark a new equator line with each position change and turn just up to it and no further. Have patience, stop the lathe frequently for inspection and don't get excited if you blow a few. □

Ernie Conover works wood and makes lathes in Parkman, Ohio, and thanks Richard Bailey for his help with this method.

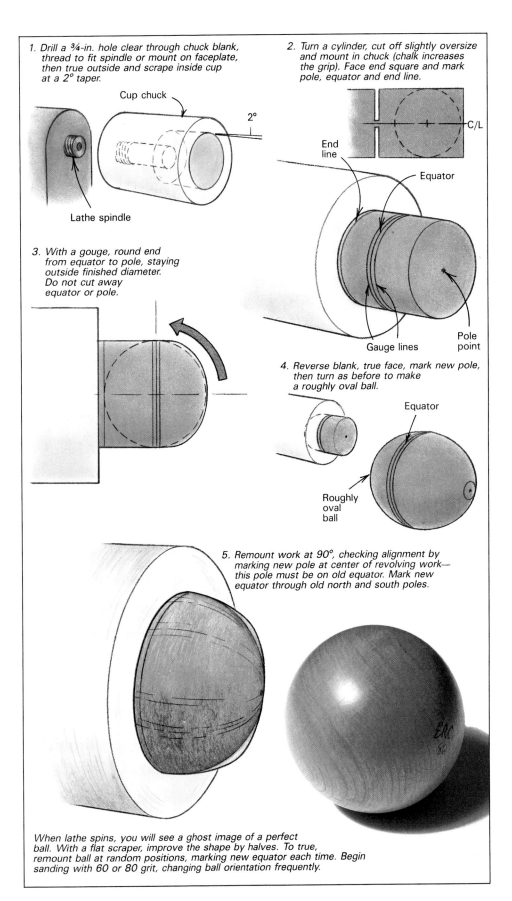

1. Drill a ¾-in. hole clear through chuck blank, thread to fit spindle or mount on faceplate, then true outside and scrape inside cup at a 2° taper.

Cup chuck

2°

Lathe spindle

2. Turn a cylinder, cut off slightly oversize and mount in chuck (chalk increases the grip). Face end square and mark pole, equator and end line.

C/L

End line

Equator

Pole point

Gauge lines

3. With a gouge, round end from equator to pole, staying outside finished diameter. Do not cut away equator or pole.

4. Reverse blank, true face, mark new pole, then turn as before to make a roughly oval ball.

Equator

Roughly oval ball

5. Remount work at 90°, checking alignment by marking new pole at center of revolving work—this pole must be on old equator. Mark new equator through old north and south poles.

When lathe spins, you will see a ghost image of a perfect ball. With a flat scraper, improve the shape by halves. To true, remount ball at random positions, marking new equator each time. Begin sanding with 60 or 80 grit, changing ball orientation frequently.

From *Fine Woodworking* magazine (September 1986) 60:76

Turning a Pool Cue

A hustler shares his secrets

by Colorado Slim

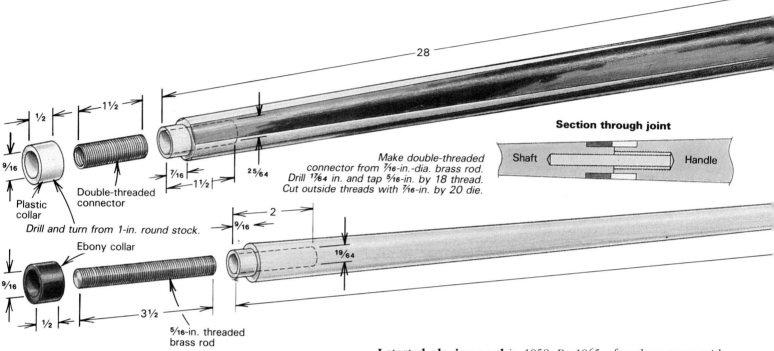

28

Section through joint

Shaft | Handle

Make double-threaded connector from ⁷⁄₁₆-in.-dia. brass rod. Drill ¹⁷⁄₆₄ in. and tap ⁵⁄₁₆-in. by 18 thread. Cut outside threads with ⁷⁄₁₆-in. by 20 die.

1½

½

⁹⁄₁₆

Plastic collar

Double-threaded connector

⁷⁄₁₆

1½

25⁄64

Drill and turn from 1-in. round stock.

Ebony collar

⁹⁄₁₆

½

3½

2

⁹⁄₁₆

19⁄64

⁵⁄₁₆-in. threaded brass rod

I t was a hot, dry August day, and we were shooting nine-ball for dollars at The Wheel, a little cowboy bar in Estes Park, Colorado. The three of us were definitely in our stride by mid-afternoon when a new guy walked in, saddled up to the bar and ordered a beer and a shot. After a while, he just seemed to fade into the crowd.

Jimmy caught the guy's side glance at the pool table. "Hey, Slim," he said under his breath, "I think maybe we got ourselves some action here. How do you want to play it?" If I turned around I'd play my hand, so I waited for my turn on the table to get a better look. Cody was on a roll, and I began to wonder if he was going to scare this fellow off before we'd had a chance to see his dance. Cody wowed the crowd with a three-rail slice into the corner and calmly asked if we'd like to up the stakes. "Nice shot, cowboy," I said as I got up to rack the balls.

The new guy was a real sleeper. He looked good from a distance; almost indifferent, but confident. He was laying back just checking things out. One thing for sure, he was learning more about us than we were about him and that didn't sit good with me at all. Got to get him off that stool before the stakes get too high and he runs. Got to see him bridge that cue—just once— then I'd know for sure. It was time to put on the squeeze.

I slipped Jimmy a twenty that I'd folded around a dime and whispered, "You're out." (The twenty was for beer...the dime let him know he'd get ten percent of the take.) "OK, Cody, $5 and $5, with re-spots only on the nine." I said. If I lost, it was on my shoulders. Cody was ready to flip for the break when the new guy finally opened up..."You fellows want a third?"

I started playing pool in 1958. By 1965, after three years with Uncle Sam, I was hot stuff. I made my first cue stick in 1970. It was a beauty—rosewood, maple, ebony, purpleheart, mother-of-pearl inlays in the handle—everything I'd seen in other cues, and more. The shaft was the best part; bright red padauk. When I walked into a hall with that stick it was "eyes RIGHT!" It didn't matter if I was good or not; this was a lesson in intimidation. Unfortunately, the first time I opened up a full rack there was a sickening sound of splintering timbers, and there I stood with toothpicks all over the table and a large red spike lodged in my left forearm. Red wood, red blood and a red face. Like most other lessons in the game of pool, this was a hard one to learn.

My second cue had two straight-grained sugar maple shafts— one with a tip diameter of 15mm for 3-cushion billiards, and a thinner shaft with a 13mm tip for snooker and the standard money games of 9-ball and one-pocket. By this time I'd worked out this slick design for a self-aligning and self-tightening connecting joint. What I hadn't worked out was how to make that "star joint" in the handle of commercial sticks. I had soaked open an old cue in my parents' bathtub to check out how that joint was made and concluded that some frustrated engineer had mis-spent his youth hunched over a drawing board. The star joint was out.

Unlike my first cue, this one was a real "lady," perfectly balanced and, best of all, it practically shot by itself. The acid test came with a rack of 15 little red snooker balls and a billiard ball used as a shooter. I spent an hour one afternoon splattering those little devils all over the poolroom and never once did that stick buckle or split.

Over the years, I've made a number of sticks for different shooters. The easiest part is the turning, which can be done by any decent spindle turner. The hard part is trying to figure out

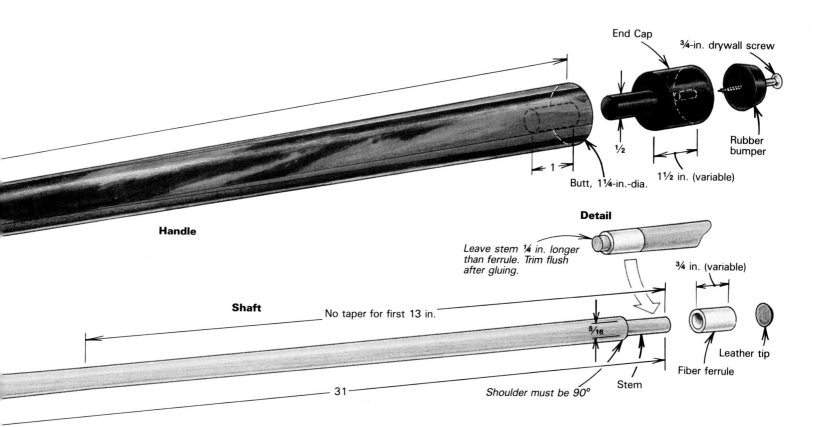

End Cap

¾-in. drywall screw

Rubber bumper

Handle

Butt, 1¼-in.-dia.

½

1

1½ in. (variable)

Detail

Leave stem ¼ in. longer than ferrule. Trim flush after gluing.

¾ in. (variable)

Shaft

No taper for first 13 in.

5/16

Leather tip

Fiber ferrule

Stem

Shoulder must be 90°

31

what the client wants, or thinks he wants, in a stick.

The sticks I make have a "European taper," meaning that the diameter of the shaft remains equal for a distance of 13 inches back from the point of the tip. Then the diameter expands in a straight line directly to the butt of the handle. This way the shooter experiences no increase in shaft diameter as he is stroking through his shot. With an "American taper" the cue tapers in a straight line from the tip to the butt. The shaft gets larger in diameter as it passes through the bridge hand, and this draws the shooter's attention to the stick instead of his game.

Threaded brass connectors—a double-threaded connector in the handle and a threaded rod in the shaft—fasten the shaft and handle together. I make these from brass rod using standard taps and dies. With the aid of the "dummy bar" and "dummy rod" driving jigs shown on the following page, I can chuck up the connectors without damaging the threads. I don't glue the connectors into the cue so, as the joint "settles" with use, it tightens by virtue of the direction of the threads in each element.

A good cue joint should act like a shock absorber to dampen the impact of the cue and the ball. I use a collar of ebony at the end of the shaft which butts up against a plastic collar at the receiving end of the handle, as shown on p. 99. The plastic simply rebounds with the impact of each shot. Using a skew, I turn the plastic collar from a length of 1-in.-dia. Delrin Acetal rod (available from AIN Plastics, 249 E. Sandford Blvd., P.O. Box 151, Mt. Vernon, NY 10550).

The key to a well-balanced cue is equal distribution of weight (mass) throughout the stick. The total weight of the cue (between 15 oz. and 21 oz.) is a matter of preference, but a lighter stick is usually used for snooker, a heavier one for 3-cushion billiards. I've seen big guys use light sticks and little fellows use heavy ones. If the balance is correct, it really doesn't matter. I use a ¾-in.-square maple core for the handle of sticks in the 15 oz. to 18 oz. range, but will switch to a rosewood core for those in the 18 oz. to 21 oz. range. If weights must be added, they should

be placed in both ends of the handle, not just in the butt end. Weight holes can be drilled into the handle just below the double-threaded brass connector, and into the butt end just ahead of the end cap. Each hole receives half the amount of lead to be used, resulting in equal distribution of the added mass throughout the handle. The weights must be glued in place, but don't get any glue on the threads of the brass connector.

The handle design shown here reflects the influence of the star joint. Starting at the butt, the padauk laminates taper to a point near the middle of the handle, where they finally disappear. At this same point, the edge of the square maple core piece begins to emerge from beneath the ebony, creating a mirror image of the padauk as the maple extends toward the joint. Laminated handles can easily become more elaborate. I don't mind a few inlays for glitz, but I've seen some cues that look like rejects from a tattoo parlor and I was not impressed.

The drawing on the next page shows how to glue up the handle blank. After jointing the pieces, I smooth up the mating surfaces with a cabinet scraper before gluing. I use Hot Stuff cyanoacrylate glue (available from Craft Supplies USA, 1644 S. State St., Provo, Utah 84601) as it bonds well with exotic woods, but epoxy may be just as good. Make sure that clamping pressure is distributed evenly along the length of the blank.

By means of a jackshaft setup, I can reduce the speed of my lathe down to 36 RPM or 50 RPM so that I can drill and thread the brass parts on the lathe with the aid of a 3-jaw engineers' chuck and a drill-press chuck in the tailstock. I cut outside threads with the die chucked in the 3-jaw and the brass rod in the tailstock chuck. The inside threads on the handle insert are cut with the tap in the tailstock chuck. If you don't want to gear down your lathe, drill the brass at your lathe's slowest speed then rotate the 3-jaw chuck by hand to cut the threads.

To keep the turning from whipping around as it gets thinner, I've rigged up a steady rest made from a pillow-block bearing, shown in the photo on p. 99. I turned maple sleeves to fit the inside of the bearing. Each sleeve has a different sized hole in the center to fit over different diameters along the tapered shaft and handle.

As with any spindle turning, I work from specific lengths and

Handle blank

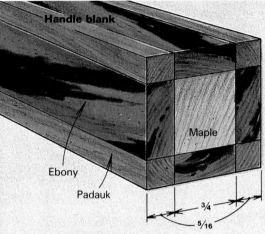

Ebony

Padauk

Maple

¾

⁵⁄₁₆

Dummy-bar driving jig

Make dummy bar from ⁷⁄₁₆-in.-dia. brass rod. Drill with ¹⁷⁄₆₄-in. twist drill. Thread with ⁵⁄₁₆-in. by 18 tap.

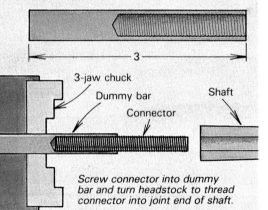

3

3-jaw chuck

Dummy bar

Connector

Shaft

Screw connector into dummy bar and turn headstock to thread connector into joint end of shaft.

Dummy rod

Make dummy rod from ⁵⁄₁₆-in.-dia. brass rod. Thread with ⁵⁄₁₆-in. by 18 die.

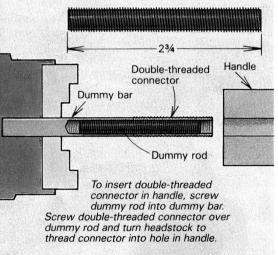

2¾

Double-threaded connector

Handle

Dummy bar

Dummy rod

To insert double-threaded connector in handle, screw dummy rod into dummy bar. Screw double-threaded connector over dummy rod and turn headstock to thread connector into hole in handle.

Turning the handle

Glue up the blank as shown in the drawing at left. Glue and clamp the ebony strips to the maple core two at a time, then glue the padauk strips in the corners. Next, drill the connector hole in the joint end. Chuck a ²⁵⁄₆₄-in. drill in the 3-jaw chuck, hold the joint end of the blank with one hand and bring the tailstock center up against the butt end. Turn the tailstock handwheel to advance the handle blank into the drill. Chuck up the dummy bar, dummy rod and the double-threaded connector as shown in the drawing (bottom, left), and thread the connector into the handle at a very slow speed (top, right). Chuck the handle by the connector and turn the handle to size. For final cuts, draw the skew toward you for a more accurate taper (below). Turn down the joint end (right) and glue on the plastic collar. Replace the tailstock center with a Jacobs chuck and drill the butt for the end-cap tenon. Glue on the end cap and trim with a skew. Sand with the grain using 320-grit paper and apply finish.

The shaft and handle join with a self-aligning, self-tightening joint which consists of a threaded brass connector in the shaft that screws into a female brass connector in the handle. The ¹⁄₁₆-in. maple shoulder on the end of the shaft (right) fits into a corresponding recess on the end of the handle.

Turning the shaft

Support the rough-turned shaft blank with the steady rest (shown at left) and bore a ¹⁹⁄₆₄-in.-dia. hole for the connector. Next, chuck up the dummy bar and connector, as shown in the drawing on the preceding page (left, center), and thread the connector into shaft. Turn the shaft, then fit the ebony collar. Sand with the grain and apply the finish, then turn the tip for the ferrule (right).

diameters in the critical areas of the cue's parts. I then use a straightedge as a guide in the roughing stages, but the final turning is done by eye. I rough out the shaft and handle with a 1½-in. spindle gouge at about 600 RPM, then finish turn with a ½-in. skew at 2,000 RPM. In the final stages, I draw the skew toward me instead of pushing it away. With the palm of my left hand I can feel all the imperfections on the surface before they reach the edge of the skew. Also, I'm less likely to make mistakes with my hands moving toward my body than if they were extending away to the outer limits of my reach.

I turn the shaft in progressive stages between centers, allowing the wood to dry and settle out between each stage. Several weeks may go by before the wood is ready to be re-turned, depending on how soon it reaches moisture equilibrium. To compensate for warp between stages, I sometimes have to relocate the center points slightly when I remount the spindle. When the shaft is straight, about ⅞ in. dia., and doesn't deflect or buckle when struck solidly on the tip end with a rubber mallet, I drill the hole for, and install, the brass connector. With the connector (protected by the dummy bar) in the chuck, I finish turning the shaft.

Care must be taken that the holes in the shaft and handle for the threaded brass connectors are exactly centered. This can be done by using the steady rest to begin the initial boring operations. The ebony and plastic collars, as well as the end cap, can also be turned and drilled from longer stock in the same manner. All these parts must fit so exactly that they "slip" into position. If they must be press-fit they are too tight and the collars will eventually split. Glue should be used, but not to fill gaps from a sloppy fit.

The end cap of the handle may be made from a variety of exotic woods, depending on personal taste and whether you wish to add or subtract a little weight in balancing the cue. The actual amount of weight involved will probably be no more than ½ oz. The end cap is turned with a post about 1 in. long, which is later glued into a hole drilled in the butt end of the handle. Again, proper centering is essential.

Turning the end of the shaft to receive the ferrule is something

I always save for last, and it must be done with absolute perfection. I use a fiber ferrule that comes pre-drilled to ⁵⁄₁₆ in. (Ferrules, tips and rubber bumpers are available from Penn-Ray Sutra Corp., P.O. Box 1088, Bensalem, Pa. 19020.) Turn the maple stem with the skew to the exact diameter of the hole in the ferrule and ¼ in. longer than the ferrule itself. Slip on the ferrule and turn the exposed end off flat with the point of the skew. Then reverse the ferrule and check that it fits perfectly square to the shaft. If it doesn't, the ferrule will split with use. Glue it in place and turn down with the skew to match the shaft diameter. True up the end to receive the leather tip and trim off the ¼-in. of maple protruding from the center. The tip can now be glued on with contact cement. Score the surfaces of tip and ferrule with a sharp knife for additional traction, coat each surface, let dry, then attach. Beat the tip down with several strikes of a hammer to ensure a perfect bond. I always use an oversized tip and then turn off the excess with the skew by remounting the shaft on the lathe using the brass dummy-bar in the 3-jaw chuck and a cup center against the tip in the ball-bearing center. This avoids sanding the leather tip and can be repeated whenever a new tip is needed.

The finish on any pool cue probably relates more to the desires of the shooter than to any prescribed formula. Most people want the pores of the wood to be sealed so that the wood won't discolor from use. Any hard urethane sealer will work, but be sure to remove the high gloss with 0000 steel wool so that a sweaty hand won't stick to the shaft. Waterlox is another good product which I cut with 50% naptha, applying many coats. My original stick (the 2nd one) has no finish at all on the shaft—just sweat, grime and a slight greenish hue from years of chalking the tip. It has a beautiful patina and still feels like satin. I don't know if that makes it a better finish than others, but for all the nerves I've rattled with it over the years, who cares? □

———————

Colorado Slim is the pool-hall alias of a retired hustler who now turns wood for a living.

Designing Wooden Clockworks

Movements and how they work

by Wayne Westphale

From *Fine Woodworking* magazine (January 1986) 56:30-35

I suppose I am only one of many readers of *Fine Woodworking* intrigued by wooden-works clocks. My first efforts were only nominally successful (in large measure because I can be impatient—I wanted to build the whole clockworks and sit back and watch it run). Well, it ran, but it had so much internal friction that it required 12 lb. of drive weight. Beyond that, its ticktock was not as consistent as even a novice clockmaker would like. Although it won a best-in-show in one woodworking exhibition, it did not satisfy me. In fact, a couple tried to buy it at a show in Philadelphia, but luckily—for them as well as for my reputation—I was able to persuade them to wait a few weeks for the improved model.

Clock construction is a study in perseverance, patience and forethought. Dad charges, "Boy, you're in too much of a hurry. You've never got enough time to do a job right the first time, but you've always got time to do it over." Like most fathers, mine proves to be right with uncanny, and sometimes irritating, frequency. Nevertheless, I have to wonder if "doing it right the first time" is even possible with clocks—mine seem to work better with each one I build. The grandfather clock described in this article runs two days on a winding and carries two 3-lb. drive weights. It is accurate to about a half-minute per day.

One of my latest clocks, which I call the Oval, ran in the workshop on an astonishing 1¾ lb. of weight. I am hoping to get my next generation of grandfather clocks to run five or six days on 6 lb. of weight. This kind of performance requires great precision. Are setups and measurements with a machinists' dial caliper going too far? Perhaps, I can't say for sure—I only know I feel better for doing the best I know how. Doing less would reduce the pleasure of the craft and result in something other than the heirloom timepieces I intend my work to become.

What is a clock?—In the strict definition, a clock is a timepiece that signals the hours by striking a bell. But in broader terms a clock is a mechanical device designed to release stored energy in small, equal increments over a period of time.

The energy in purely mechanical clocks is typically stored in one of two ways, either in a coiled spring or in a falling weight or weights. In a spring-driven clock, a fully-wound mainspring delivers maximum drive energy, but this force decreases constantly as the clock runs down. Spring-driven clocks, therefore, require special compensating mechanisms that are beyond the scope of this article.

The most practical power source for mechanical clocks is the energy provided by a falling weight, which remains constant for the duration of the weight fall. It is a simple matter to compensate for the internal friction of the clock movement by increasing the drive weight. Of course, too much weight will accelerate wear, deform bearings and possibly even bend the weight arbor.

As shown in the drawing on p. 103, the weights in my clock are wound around a drum 1 in. in diameter, which acts as a lever—the larger it is, the more force it will transmit, but the faster the weights will fall and the sooner the clock will have to be rewound. The less internal friction in a clock (and the more efficient it is in general), the smaller the drum can be, and the longer the clock will run with any given weight.

Converting weight into time—At first glance, a clock seems a confusingly complex mechanism, but a few minutes' study will prove that a basic timepiece such as this one is surprisingly straightforward. The clock turns energy into time by means of two gear trains, a *drive train* (or going train) and a *dial train*,

which moves the hands. An *escapement* mechanism controls the rate at which the energy stored in the weights is released. The escapement mechanism consists of an escape wheel, an escape lever, a pendulum and a crutch.

The weights connect to a weight arbor at the beginning of the drive train, and from there a series of gears increases the speed at which each successive arbor turns (the arbor is the shaft the gears are mounted on). This sort of gear-up drive, where large wheels are driving smaller pinions, is unique to horological applications. In most other gear trains, pinions (the small gears) turn wheels (the large gears) in order to convert the fast, low-power revolutions of a motor shaft to an output shaft that turns slower but has more torque. Because the drive train of a clock is a gear-up train, the tooth profiles on its wheels and pinions are not the same as those in most other gear trains, a consideration discussed in the box on p. 104.

The speed of the drive train triples from the 48-tooth wheel on the weight arbor to the first pinion, then increases by eight, then by eight again. The result is that the escape wheel wants to turn 192 times faster than the weight-arbor wheel. Ignoring all internal friction for the moment, this means that the clock's 6 lb. of weight (or 96 ounces) can be stopped by a ½-ounce force applied to the pinion on the escape-wheel arbor.

If we apply the force to the escape wheel itself, which is much larger than the pinion, the stopping force decreases to about 1/16 ounce. And when we introduce the power losses due to the clock's internal friction, which occurs not only at the bearings but also between the pairs of teeth as they engage and disengage, we see that it takes very little force to prevent the escape wheel from turning.

Thus the escape wheel is a good place in the drive train to

James Canfield

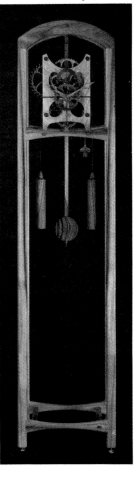

Westphale's first clock, above, ran but required 12 lb. of drive weight. He has since refined the designs—the contemporary grandfather clock, at right and on the facing page, will run on 4 lb. (the less weight, the less stress on the bearings) and is accurate to a half-minute per day. It sells for $6,000.

regulate the rate of release of the energy stored in the clock's weights—because little force is involved, the acting parts can be light in weight and, further, they will be subjected to little wear.

The escapement mechanism—The drawing on the facing page traces the path of the drive force of a clock by starting at the weights. But in designing a clock, the escapement is where you would start, because all clocks depend on the following inter-relationship: the internal gearing determines the length of the pendulum; the length of the pendulum suggests the internal gearing. For those interested, I've included a mathematical discussion of gear ratios and pendulum lengths (at right).

The pendulum regulator developed around 1675. It superseded the verge escapement, the earliest escapement known, which dates from the 13th century. Verge escapements required a large oscillation of about 100° of arc and were, therefore, not very accurate. With the development of the recoil escapement, the pendulum oscillation was reduced to between 5° and 10° of arc. Within this range, the period of a pendulum (the length of time it takes to swing from right to left or from left to right) is constant, or nearly so. It is this principle upon which all pendulum regulators are built.

The exact period of a pendulum can be calculated mathematically, at least in theory. In the real world, theory and actuality do not quite correspond, but it remains true that to lengthen a pendulum's period, you lengthen the pendulum; to shorten the period, you shorten the pendulum. In my grandfather clock, the bob—the weight on the end of the pendulum shaft—is adjustable up and down. By moving the bob, the pendulum can be adjusted to swing faster or slower, thus speeding or slowing the clock.

With each oscillation of the pendulum, one tooth of the escape wheel is released and the entire gear train of the clock is allowed to advance proportionally. More specifically, the escape wheel and escape lever constitute the release/relock mechanism. As shown in the drawings below, the pendulum, working through the crutch, rocks the escape-lever arbor back and forth, so that the escape lever will stop and release each tooth on the escape wheel according to how fast the pendulum is adjusted to swing. It is important to keep in mind that though the pendulum controls the movement of the crutch and, therefore, of the escape lever, it would stop without the impulse it receives from the escape wheel and the escape lever through the crutch. This push is essential, because it is the force that keeps the pendulum swinging. There are at least a dozen major clock escapements, all designed to solve one problem or another, but only two—the

Clock math

The internal gearing of a clock must relate to the length of its pendulum. The period of a pendulum of small oscillation is mathematically defined as:

$$t = \pi\sqrt{p/g} \quad \text{or} \quad p = t^2 g/\pi^2, \text{ where:}$$

t = one oscillation in seconds

π = 3.14

p = length of pendulum in feet

g = acceleration of gravity (32.17 ft./sec.²)

If t = 1 second, then, p equals $(1^2 \times 32.17) \div$ by 3.14^2, which equals: $32.17 \div 9.86$, which equals: 3.26 ft. (or 39.12 in.). Therefore, a "seconds" pendulum is one meter long, at least in theory.

The mathematics of the internal gearing (the drive train gearing) is equally straightforward. Horologists call the large gears wheels, and the small ones pinions. The number of beats per hour is equal to the product of all the wheel teeth divided by the product of all the pinion leaves. The number of teeth on the escape wheel must be counted twice because each acts twice on the escape lever—once on the entrance pallet, once on the exit pallet.

For a seconds pendulum, any combination of wheels and pinions may be used that yields 3,600 beats per hour. A typical grandfather clock with a seconds pendulum might employ a 30-tooth escape wheel, 60-tooth second and 64-tooth center wheels, with two 8-leaf pinions:

$$2 \times 30 \times 60 \times 64 \div 8 \times 8 = 3,600$$

A design parameter of my grandfather clock was a 3-ft. pendulum. A slight modification in the drive train gearing was all that was necessary to accomplish this.

I've also designed a mantel clock with a pendulum just over 12 in. long. It beats 6,400 times per hour. This clock required an extra wheel and pinion to absorb the additional beats of this much shorter pendulum. Consequently, its escape wheel rotates counterclockwise.

My general rule in designing a gear train is to use pinions of 8, 10 and 12 leaves whenever possible. Pinions having fewer than 8 leaves are troublesome. Pinions having more than 12 leaves yield smooth engagement patterns but become inefficient because the mating wheels must be so much larger to maintain the 8:1 wheel-to-pinion ratio common to clocks. Much higher ratios are not desirable; lower ratios require more wheels and pinions in the train, introducing more friction. Whatever their size, good pinions are critical. —*W.W.*

How the escapement works

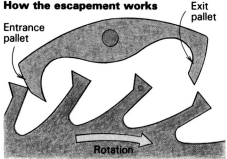
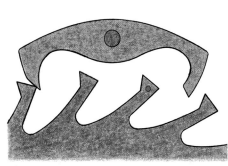
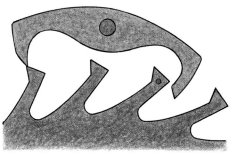

1. "TICK." The escape wheel advances freely until stopped (producing the sound) by the entrance pallet on the escape lever. The pendulum's arc is at its maximum point to the right; as it swings back to the left, it rocks the escape lever toward the position shown in 2.

2. As the pendulum continues to swing left, the impulse plane of the escape wheel, powered by the clock's weights, advances across the escape lever. This motion gives a small impulse to the pendulum, just enough force to keep it swinging.

3. The escape wheel eventually advances far enough so that a tooth can drop freely onto the exit pallet. The opposing planes between the wheel and the lever must be designed so that they never become parallel; otherwise there would be too much friction.

How a clock tells time

Energy in the drive train moves from the weight-arbor wheel (1) through the blue gears and arbors up to the escape wheel (4). One revolution of the weight-arbor wheel produces 192 revolutions of the escape wheel, as shown. The escapement (escape lever, crutch and pendulum) regulates the speed the escape wheel can turn, as shown in the sequence at the bottom of this page. The clock is geared so that the center arbor turns once per hour, carrying the minute hand. The dial train, which regulates the hour hand, is located outside the front plate (see photo, p. 100). The 16-tooth pinion (5) turns once per hour and works a gear-down train (red gears) so that the 48-tooth wheel (7) attached to the cannon tube (see detail) revolves ¹⁄₁₂ turn per hour.

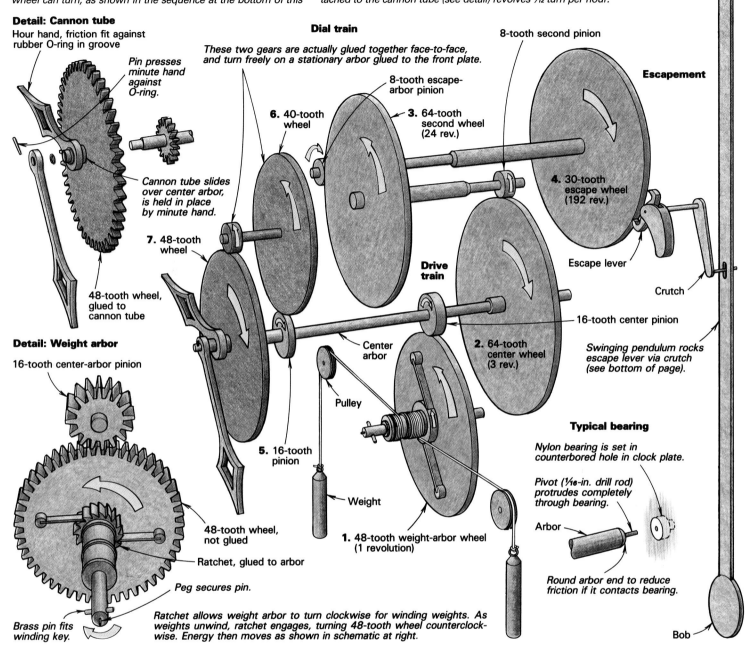

Pendulum shaft, hinged to clock case

Detail: Cannon tube

Hour hand, friction fit against rubber O-ring in groove

Pin presses minute hand against O-ring.

Cannon tube slides over center arbor, is held in place by minute hand.

7. 48-tooth wheel

48-tooth wheel, glued to cannon tube

Dial train

These two gears are actually glued together face-to-face, and turn freely on a stationary arbor glued to the front plate.

8-tooth escape-arbor pinion

6. 40-tooth wheel

3. 64-tooth second wheel (24 rev.)

8-tooth second pinion

Escapement

4. 30-tooth escape wheel (192 rev.)

Escape lever

Crutch

Swinging pendulum rocks escape lever via crutch (see bottom of page).

Drive train

Center arbor

5. 16-tooth pinion

2. 64-tooth center wheel (3 rev.)

16-tooth center pinion

Detail: Weight arbor

16-tooth center-arbor pinion

48-tooth wheel, not glued

Ratchet, glued to arbor

Peg secures pin.

Brass pin fits winding key.

Pulley

Weight

1. 48-tooth weight-arbor wheel (1 revolution)

Typical bearing

Nylon bearing is set in counterbored hole in clock plate.

Pivot (¹⁄₁₆-in. drill rod) protrudes completely through bearing.

Arbor

Round arbor end to reduce friction if it contacts bearing.

Bob

Ratchet allows weight arbor to turn clockwise for winding weights. As weights unwind, ratchet engages, turning 48-tooth wheel counterclockwise. Energy then moves as shown in schematic at right.

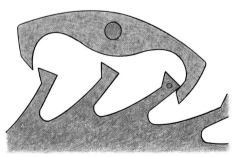

4. "TOCK" sounds when the escape wheel's free advance is stopped by the exit pallet. The pendulum is at the far left of its arc and begins to drop back to the right, rocking the escape lever so the wheel can move to the position shown in the next drawing.

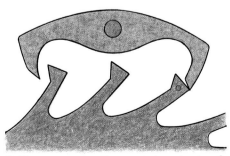

5. The process continues much as in step 2. The right-moving pendulum rocks the lever, allowing the escape wheel to advance. Again the escape wheel contributes a small impulse to the pendulum as the opposing, non-parallel planes traverse each other.

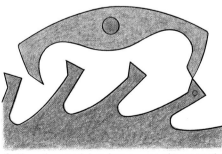

6. Here the pendulum has swung almost to the farthest right, and the escape wheel is poised to advance freely onto the entrance pallet. This will sound the next tick and start the cycle over again. The time each cycle takes is determined by the length of the pendulum.

Wooden gears

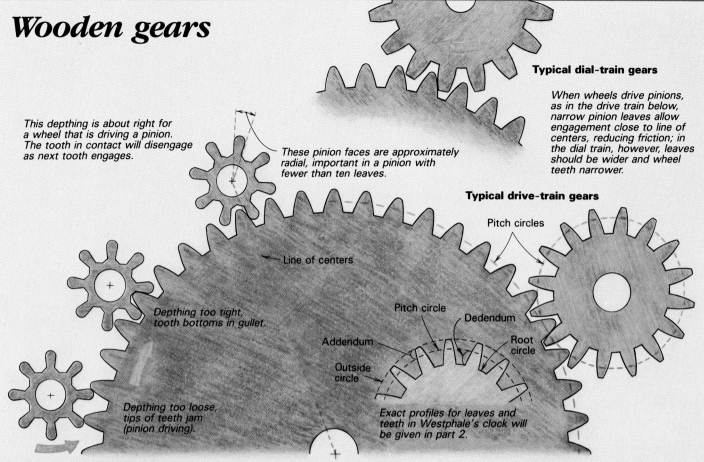

This depthing is about right for a wheel that is driving a pinion. The tooth in contact will disengage as next tooth engages.

These pinion faces are approximately radial, important in a pinion with fewer than ten leaves.

Typical dial-train gears

When wheels drive pinions, as in the drive train below, narrow pinion leaves allow engagement close to line of centers, reducing friction; in the dial train, however, leaves should be wider and wheel teeth narrower.

Typical drive-train gears

Line of centers

Pitch circles

Depthing too tight, tooth bottoms in gullet.

Pitch circle

Dedendum

Addendum

Root circle

Outside circle

Depthing too loose, tips of teeth jam (pinion driving).

Exact profiles for leaves and teeth in Westphale's clock will be given in part 2.

Much of what will be covered here pertains specifically to clocks, but the principles can be applied to any set of wooden gears, including kinetic sculptures, models for teaching and demonstration, and an infinite variety of whimsical mechanisms.

I use eight different tooth shapes in my grandfather clock. This discussion will explain why. In part 2, I'll describe exactly how I make the gears and adjust their fit.

There are several rules that pertain to gear cutting in horological application: For wheels and pinions to mesh smoothly, they must have the same diametral pitch, that is, the same number of teeth per inch of diameter of the pitch circle (approximately the circle of initial tooth contact, as shown in the drawing). D.P. = Number of teeth divided by the pitch diameter in inches. The smaller the D.P., the larger each tooth will be. It is convenient, though not necessary, to use the same pitch throughout. Mine are 10 D.P.

Also, the wheels must be adequately spaced (or depthed) so that the tooth of one does not bottom in the gullet of the mating gear, but they must not be too widely spaced or the tips will contact point to point rather than engage, as shown above. There must also be a small amount of backlash—play between the teeth.

Beyond this, the object is to achieve constant rotational velocity and, as much as possible, avoid engagement before the line of centers (an imaginary line through the pivots of mating gears). The friction of engagement, approach friction, is greater

than the friction of disengagement, recess friction. The principal means of reducing friction within a clock is to minimize approach friction by designing appropriate tooth profiles. Historically, this has been accomplished in a variety of ways.

The most common tooth profiles are derivations of involute and cycloidal curves. These are mathematically defined curves capable of providing constant rotational velocity. Each profile has its advantages and disadvantages.

Involute profiles are what you will typically find in mechanical equipment. Their primary advantages are (1) milling cutters are available in a variety of tooth sizes; (2) constant rotational velocity is relatively insensitive to depthing.

The primary disadvantage of involute gearing when used in a gear-up drive train is that there is considerable engagement friction. Involute gearing was designed for bi-directional running with minimal backlash to reduce noise at high RPMs. Engagement friction is not a concern under these high-power conditions.

The primary disadvantages of cycloidal profiles are (1) cutters are not generally available in the sizes we need for a wooden clock and (2) constant rotational velocity of mating gears is depth sensitive.

The considerable advantage of cycloidal profiles in drive trains is that approach friction can be eliminated or substantially minimized. Further, it is not unreasonably difficult to create cutters to produce approximate cycloidal profiles, as I'll ex-

plain in part 2. For these reasons I recommend cycloidal tooth profiles in the drive train. Involute profiles are acceptable in the dial train, but cycloidal profiles work well there too.

A very usable tooth profile is shown in the drawing: these teeth do not correspond exactly to what the theory calls for, but they have the advantage of being fairly forgiving. They are less depth-sensitive than "ideal" teeth, and their width can be varied a little both ways to accommodate the different requirements of both the drive train and the dial train.

For best results, pinions in the drive train should have leaves about one-third the circular pitch—where the pinion is driven, the leaf must be narrower to minimize engagement friction. In the dial train, where wheels and pinions both drive, ideally the wheel teeth should be a bit thinner and the pinion leaves a bit thicker, because both wheels and pinions contribute to circumferential clearance (i.e. backlash).

In spite of what has been said so far, involute profiles can be used in the drive train if mated with lantern pinions instead of involute pinions (which are uncommon below 12 leaves). I used lantern pinions in my first clock, and they are visible in the photo on p. 101. Lantern pinions have no appreciable dedendum and so engagement friction is substantially reduced. But don't use them in the dial train. Even though I got away with it in my first clock, it really isn't good practice.   —W.W.

recoil and the dead beat—seemed practical for me to construct in wood. The recoil is so named because there is a small counter-rotational movement of the escape wheel for each swing of the pendulum.

The dead beat escapement, a significant refinement, was invented by George Graham about 1730. In a weight-driven clock with a long pendulum, it is probably the best escapement to use. It gives a steady, constant beat—and with no recoil, the drive train moves in only one direction. My version of the dead beat uses a "club foot" escape wheel—it is a bit more difficult to construct than the standard recoil, but it offers larger wear surfaces that should allow a wooden mechanism a long life.

The dial train—With this much accomplished, we have a mechanism that will keep time, in the sense that the pendulum will swing at a steady rate until the weights have fully unwound. It remains for us to translate the mechanism's rate of time to our own, by gearing the clock to indicate hours and minutes.

The typical arrangement, which I use in the grandfather clock, is to design the escapement and gearing so that the center wheel of the drive train rotates once each hour. Then the minute hand can simply be mounted on the end of the center wheel arbor.

To turn the hour hand, we need a train of gears called the dial train, shown on p. 103. This is simply a four-gear 12-to-1 reduction system that takes its power from the center arbor and causes the hour hand to rotate once for each 12 rotations of the minute hand. In other words, as the minute hand cycles through 12 hours, the hour hand moves from midnight to 12 noon.

In order that the hour hand and the minute hand can both be centered on the clock face, the dial-train gearing is "folded back" upon itself, and the hour hand is mounted on a short hollow arbor, called the cannon tube, concentric with the minute-hand arbor. The hands are friction-fit against rubber O-rings on the center arbor and the cannon tube, so that the hands can be set without turning the clock's gears.

Holding it all together—The clock's moving parts must be held in precise alignment with each other. Wheels and pinions are mounted on wooden shafts called arbors. In general terms, arbors turn in bearings set into the front plate and the rear plate. Wooden clocks in the past have successfully used bearing materials such as brass, ivory and bone. Ivory and bone make particularly handsome bearings, but I am shifting away from them to nylon, which I find superior. Materials such as Teflon are too soft.

My arrangement is to bore the clock plate to accept a ⅜-in.-dia. plug of nylon, which has ¹⁄₁₆-in.-dia. hole through its center. A pivot, a steel pin on the end of the arbor, fits the bearing hole and runs with little friction. The pivot must be perfectly centered in the end of the arbor or the wheels will turn eccentrically.

The clock's plates are held rigidly in relation to each other by concealed threaded rod, making a unit of most of the moving parts. The plate assembly is supported by a case or a frame tall enough to contain the pendulum and allow room for the weights to drop. In my grandfather clock the pendulum is attached directly to the frame, not to the clock's rear plate.

Wood for clocks—Anything made of solid wood will change size or shape across the grain as the humidity of its environment changes. For this reason I use laminated wood wherever possible. Since solid-core plywood of the quality I need is not commercially available, I make my own of ⅛-in.-thick layers, alternating each ply at 90°. For parts that will be subject to wear, I choose dense, tight-grained rosewoods that contain a high degree of natural oil. For parts not subject to wear, such as clock plates, I laminate various domestic and imported hardwoods, choosing these as much for beauty as anything else.

Be sure the wood is dried to a moisture content compatible with the intended environment. Select good, flat, preferable straight-grained wood, joint one face and edge, then thickness so that the stock is absolutely uniform. Proceed to make your own sawn veneer.

I have found epoxy to be the best adhesive. Since it cures chemically, it has no effect on the moisture content of the wood. It adheres well to all the woods I've used, and it's an excellent gap filler, if needed as such. I use T-88 two-part epoxy (from Chem Tech, Inc., Chagrin Falls, Ohio). I apply it evenly, using a serrated applicator that I made from a hacksaw blade. I make sure all surfaces are covered evenly—no lumps and no voids. I've found that coating one side of each ply is adequate. I press the parts together by hand with a slight circular motion to assist glue transfer, then clamp between cauls overnight.

The woods I use are heavy, so I lighten the wheels by cutting away as much unnecessary wood as possible. This provides me with an opportunity to add to the clockwork's visual appeal. I try to design spoke patterns that are interesting in themselves and that also allow a viewer to look through into the clock's interior to watch everything in motion. I'll describe my methods of cutting spokes in part 2.

More to come—This first article has provided an overview of how a clock works and some of the theoretical considerations. In the next part I'll give exact sizes and relationships and I'll cover the methods I use to achieve the necessary precision. I'll also talk about problem-solving and fine-tuning. I hope I've tempted you so far to try to build a clock of your own. But hold off for just a while longer—I may be able to help you steer clear of dead ends, backtracking and trouble spots. I've been there once already, and believe me, trial-and-error is the long way to get through the maze. □

Wayne Westphale designs and builds a variety of limited-edition and custom clocks at his shop, Contemporary Time, in Steamboat Springs, Colo.

References

National Association of Watch and Clock Collectors, 514 Poplar St., Columbia, Pa. 17512. Members receive a regular bulletin and may borrow books by mail from the association's extensive lending library.

Adams Brown Co. Catalog of Horological Literature, 26 N. Main St., Box 357, Cranbury, N.J. 08512.

Clock and Watch Escapements, W. J. Gazeley, 1956, Butterworth Publishers, Inc., 19 Cummings Park, Woburn, Mass. 01801.

Watch and Clock Making and Repairing, W.J. Gazeley, 1958, Van Nostrand Reinhold Co., 135 W. 50th St., New York, N.Y. 10020.

Clock Wheel and Pinion Cutting, J. Malcolm Wild, 1983, Argus Books Ltd., Wolsey House, Wolsey Rd., Hemel Hempstead, Herts. HPZ 45S, England.

The Modern Clock, Ward L. Goodrich, 1905. (Sold by Arlington Book Company, Box 327, Arlington, Va. 22210.) This company has an extensive catalog of horological material and regular mailings of additions, revisions and special sales.

Making a Wooden Clockworks
Part two: Getting things ticking

by Wayne Westphale

In part 1 we discussed the theory of how a clock works. Now is the time to make one. There are a variety of ways to cut gear teeth, methods that cover a broad range of accuracy, speed and expense. The method you choose will depend on your goal, your shop equipment, and your budget.

As an example of how low-tech clockmaking can be, for my first clock I turned the arbors on a lathe setup that consisted of an electric drill (as a headstock) clamped to a 2x4 (the lathe bed). A piece of angle iron, drilled and tapped to carry a pointed bolt, became a tailstock. A chisel served as a lathe tool and a piece of scrap as a tool rest. My first tooth cutters were reground spade bits, as shown in the bottom right photo on the facing page. Needless to say, this was doing it the hard way.

I've always tried to surpass each clock I've built with a better one, and along the way I've invested in some pretty sophisticated equipment—machines more often found in a metalworking shop. These are not essential to building a good clock, but they allow me, as a matter of routine, to achieve repeatable accuracy with little fuss. Expect this clock to tax your ingenuity in getting the necessary precision from your own machines and tools. There are ways around every problem as long as you understand the features in a clock that are critical to its operation.

Horologists don't speak of gears, but of wheels and pinions. Wheels, the large gears, have teeth; pinions, the small gears, have leaves. I cut teeth and leaves on two different machines, but the process is basically the same—I use a set of reground router bits to cut the gullets between the teeth.

The preparatory step, laminating plywood gear blanks, was described in part 1. The photos on the facing page show some of the actual cutting, including my jig for bandsawing circles. To cut the wheel teeth, I mount a stack of gear blanks on a mandrel and mount the mandrel on an old metal lathe, which I also use to turn clock arbors. The tool-bit holder on the lathe's cross-slide and compound has been adapted to carry a router, with the router bit perpendicular to the lathe centerline. By cranking one of the lathe's control wheels, the router bit can be positioned closer to or farther from the work, then locked in position to give a cut at a set depth. By means of another control wheel the router can be moved precisely along the length of the work.

The first step in cutting the teeth is to turn the lathe on at slow speed, then use an end mill or hinge-mortising bit in the router to trim the blanks to true round, sizing them to the correct diameter at the same time. This ensures that the arbor hole will be exactly centered.

The lathe is then turned off, and the blanks are indexed by a pin and a shopmade plate. The router roughs out the gullets one by one by traversing horizontally along the stack. I crank the router from the tailstock end up to the headstock end to cut a tooth gullet. Then I crank the router back to the tailstock end, turn the stack of wheel blanks to the next index location and repeat the process. (The escape wheel is a special case. It has three very critical surfaces on each tooth, and I make these as shown in figure 3 on p. 110.)

To minimize chipping—and maximize cutter life—I make several passes, each with a different cutter. The first cutter, as shown in figure 1, has straight faces, is easy to sharpen, and has an included angle of about 32°. It is a wasting cutter. I set it to about 80% of full depth. The next cutter profiles the tooth face and cuts to final depth. The last cutter eases over the tooth tip. The relief angle of this cutter is only 2° to 3°—the desired effect is to round over and burnish the tooth tip in one pass. Next, I lightly sand with 400-grit paper over a soft block to remove the burr left at the tips of the teeth.

This produces a stack of identical chip-free wheels. The method suits itself both to small-scale production or, if you are making just one clock, to making any identical wheels that may be in it (there are two identical pairs in my grandfather clock). Pinions are cut in a similar way on a milling machine, as shown in center photo. The same operation could be accomplished with a drill press fitted with a compound table (available from Sears for under $80 and from time to time in various bulk-mail catalogs for even less) and a properly contoured cutter.

I profiled my cutters in a series of steps, as shown in figure 1. I began with a full-size drawing of each of the gear-tooth profiles. Figure 2, on p. 109, shows the exact profiles of the teeth and leaves in my grandfather clock. To achieve the necessary variety with the fewest number of cutters, I taper my cutters slightly at the tip, so that the tooth size, the width at the pitch circle, can be controlled by depthing the cutter as required. Pitch circle and other technical terms are explained in part 1.

Arbors and bearings—I turn arbors in the metal lathe—it is fast and sure and will maintain 0.001-in. tolerances (exact sizes are shown in figure 2). I strive for a snug fit of wheel to arbor. A metal lathe is not absolutely necessary, though I would not recommend using dowels straight from the hardware store either. You'll find that commercial dowels are only approximately sized and only approximately round.

I recommend a piece of tool steel or 1/16-in. drill rod be pressed into the arbor to serve as a pivot. Wood-on-wood is too inefficient at this point from the standpoint of friction as well as durability. The pivot must be accurately centered. If your lathe has a

From *Fine Woodworking* magazine (March 1986) 57:58-65

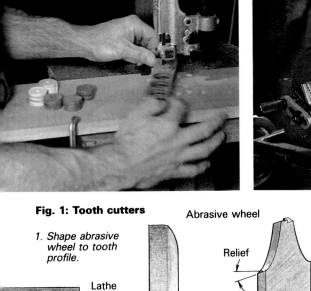

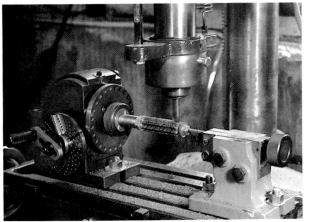

At left, large gears are cut by a router mounted on the cross-slide and compound of a South Bend metal lathe, which the author bought used for $4,000. The blanks are indexed by the pin opposite the router bit. Above, Westphale cranks the router along a stack of six wheel blanks, backed up at each end by a hardboard blank to prevent tearout.

Left, a milling machine is the metalworker's precision version of a drill press, equipped with a table that can be moved horizontally on X and Y axes by hand cranks. The stack of pinion blanks is indexed by a dividing head, which calculates angles by means of perforated plates and a gearbox. It takes forty turns of the crank handle to rotate the output shaft one full turn. Far left, an efficient circle-cutting jig: The board has a runner on the bottom that rides in the bandsaw's miter-gauge slot, and a number of axle holes to suit the various gear sizes.

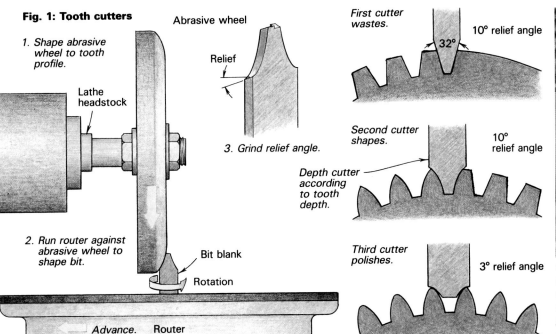

Fig. 1: Tooth cutters

1. Shape abrasive wheel to tooth profile.

Abrasive wheel

Lathe headstock

Relief

3. Grind relief angle.

2. Run router against abrasive wheel to shape bit.

Bit blank

Rotation

Advance. Router

First cutter wastes.

32° 10° relief angle

Second cutter shapes.

10° relief angle

Depth cutter according to tooth depth.

Third cutter polishes.

3° relief angle

Cutters are reshaped as shown in the drawing at left. Tooling need not be high-tech. Westphale shows two of his early gear cutters, reground spade bits, alongside the highly evolved ones he uses today.

Drawings: Lee Hov

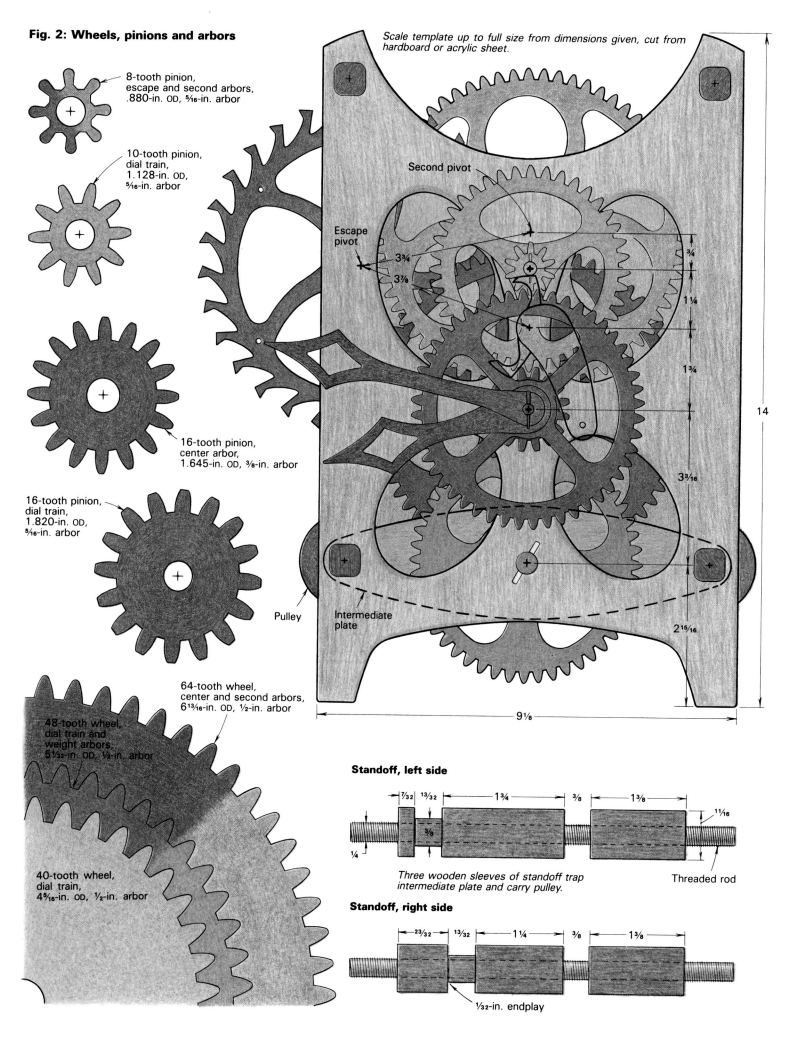

Fig. 2: Wheels, pinions and arbors

8-tooth pinion, escape and second arbors, .880-in. OD, 5/16-in. arbor

10-tooth pinion, dial train, 1.128-in. OD, 5/16-in. arbor

16-tooth pinion, center arbor, 1.645-in. OD, 3/8-in. arbor

16-tooth pinion, dial train, 1.820-in. OD, 5/16-in. arbor

64-tooth wheel, center and second arbors, 6 13/16-in. OD, 1/2-in. arbor

48-tooth wheel, dial train and weight arbors, 5 1/32-in. OD, 1/2-in. arbor

40-tooth wheel, dial train, 4 5/16-in. OD, 1/2-in. arbor

Scale template up to full size from dimensions given, cut from hardboard or acrylic sheet.

Second pivot

Escape pivot

3 3/4

3 7/8

3/4

1 1/4

1 3/4

3 9/16

2 15/16

14

9 1/8

Pulley

Intermediate plate

Standoff, left side

7/32 13/32 1 3/4 3/8 1 3/8

3/8

1/4

11/16

Three wooden sleeves of standoff trap intermediate plate and carry pulley.

Threaded rod

Standoff, right side

2 3/32 13/32 1 1/4 3/8 1 3/8

1/32-in. endplay

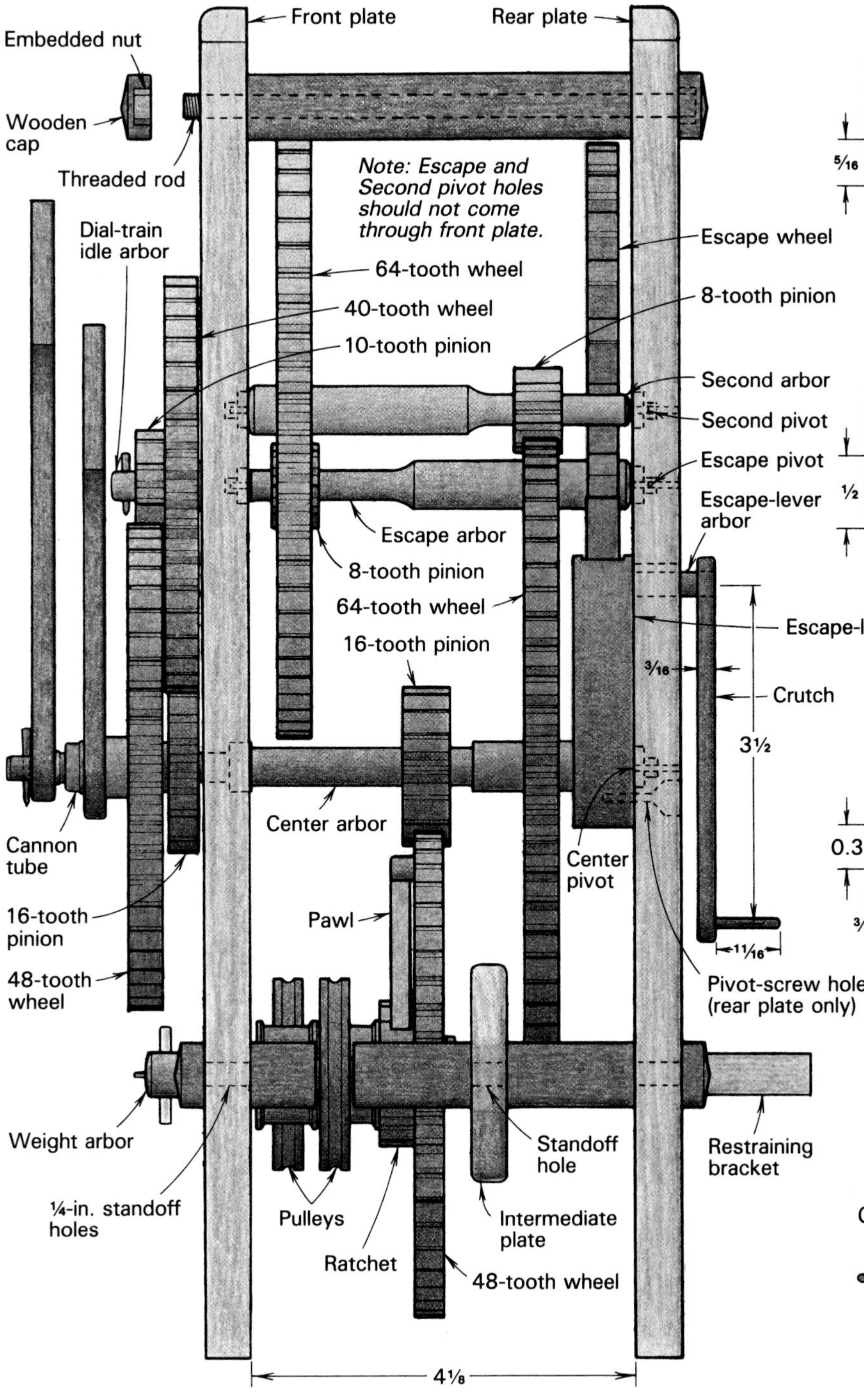

Front plate
Rear plate
Embedded nut
Wooden cap
Threaded rod
Note: Escape and Second pivot holes should not come through front plate.
Dial-train idle arbor
Escape wheel
64-tooth wheel
40-tooth wheel
8-tooth pinion
10-tooth pinion
Second arbor
Second pivot
Escape pivot
Escape-lever arbor
Escape arbor
8-tooth pinion
64-tooth wheel
Escape-lever bracket
16-tooth pinion
3/16
Crutch
3½
Center arbor
Cannon tube
Center pivot
16-tooth pinion
Pawl
48-tooth wheel
1 1/16
Pivot-screw hole (rear plate only)
Weight arbor
Standoff hole
Restraining bracket
¼-in. standoff holes
Pulleys
Intermediate plate
Ratchet
48-tooth wheel
4⅛

Escape arbor

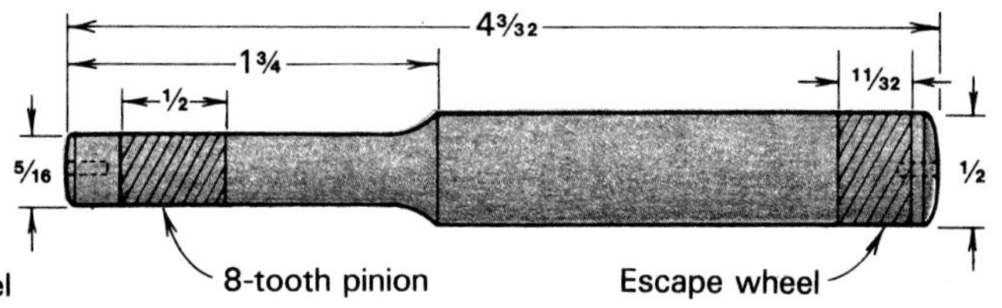

4 3/32
1¾
½
11/32
5/16
½
8-tooth pinion
Escape wheel

Second arbor

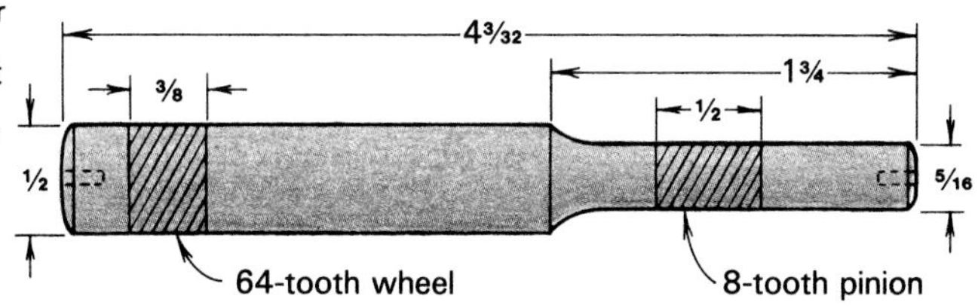

4 3/32
1¾
⅜
½
½
5/16
64-tooth wheel
8-tooth pinion

Dial-train arbor

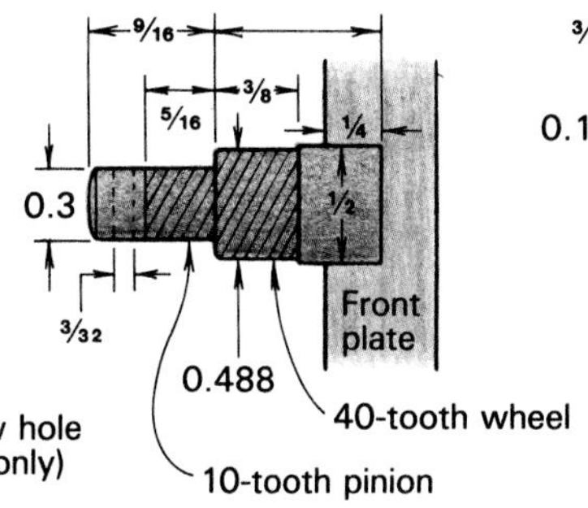

9/16
⅜
5/16
¼
0.3
½
Front plate
3/32
0.488
40-tooth wheel
10-tooth pinion

Escape-lever arbor

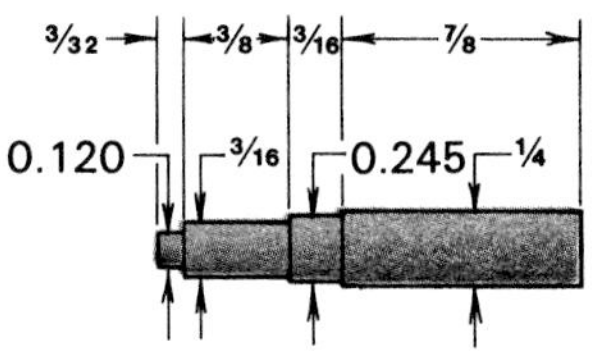

3/32
⅜
3/16
⅞
0.120
3/16
0.245
¼

Weight arbor

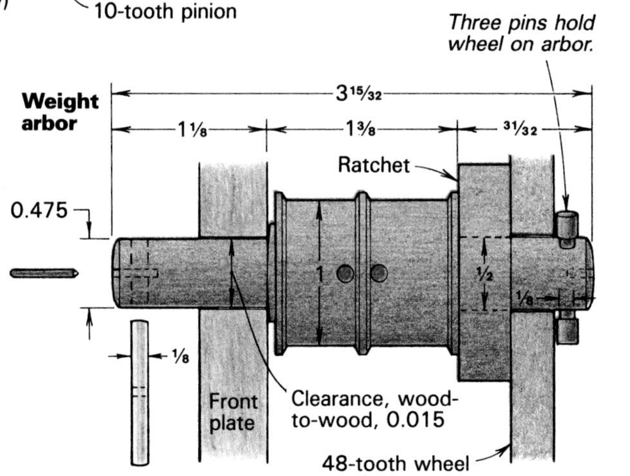

Three pins hold wheel on arbor.
3 15/32
1⅛
1⅜
31/32
Ratchet
0.475
1
½
⅛
⅛
Front plate
Clearance, wood-to-wood, 0.015
48-tooth wheel

Cannon tube

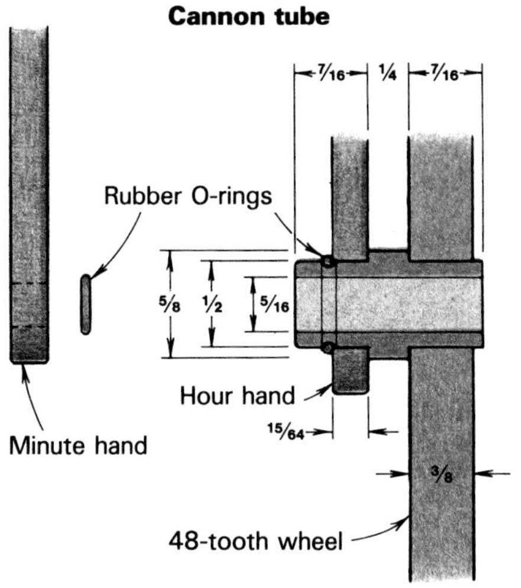

7/16
¼
7/16
Rubber O-rings
⅝
½
5/16
Hour hand
15/64
⅜
Minute hand
48-tooth wheel

Center arbor

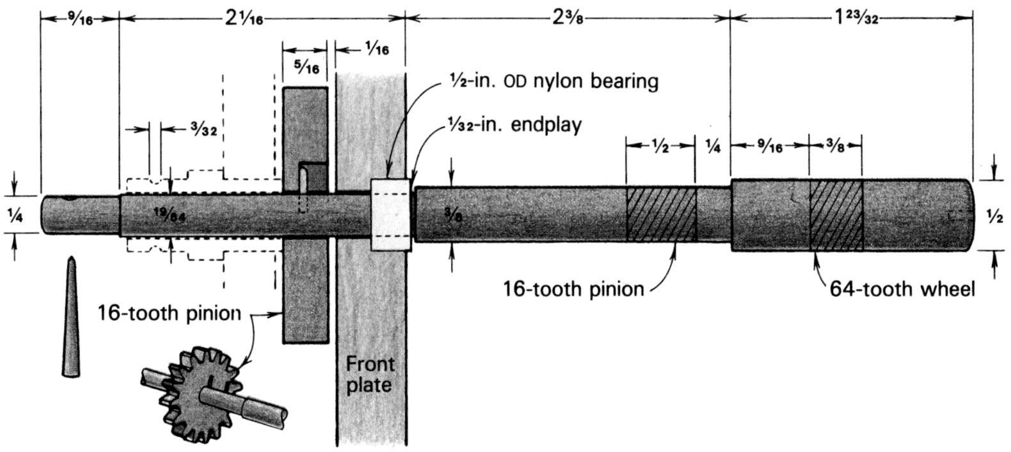

9/16
2 1/16
2⅜
1 23/32
5/16
1/16
½-in. OD nylon bearing
3/32
1/32-in. endplay
½
¼
9/16
⅜
¼
19/64
⅜
½
16-tooth pinion
64-tooth wheel
16-tooth pinion
Front plate

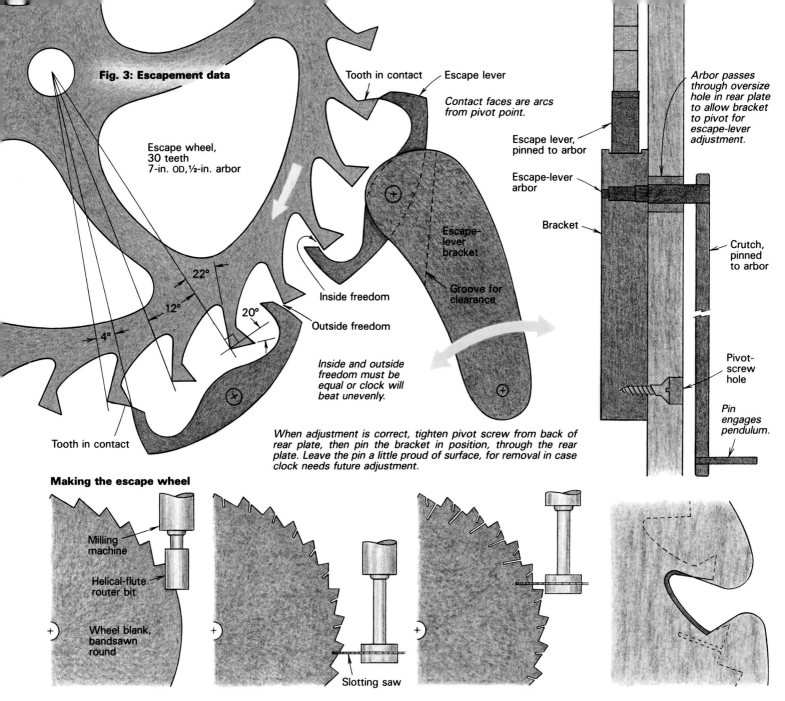

Fig. 3: Escapement data

Escape wheel,
30 teeth
7-in. OD, ½-in. arbor

22°
12°
4°
20°

Tooth in contact

Inside freedom

Outside freedom

Tooth in contact

Contact faces are arcs from pivot point.

Tooth in contact — Escape lever

Inside and outside freedom must be equal or clock will beat unevenly.

Escape-lever bracket

Groove for clearance

When adjustment is correct, tighten pivot screw from back of rear plate, then pin the bracket in position, through the rear plate. Leave the pin a little proud of surface, for removal in case clock needs future adjustment.

Arbor passes through oversize hole in rear plate to allow bracket to pivot for escape-lever adjustment.

Escape lever, pinned to arbor

Escape-lever arbor

Bracket

Crutch, pinned to arbor

Pivot-screw hole

Pin engages pendulum.

Making the escape wheel

Milling machine

Helical-flute router bit

Wheel blank, bandsawn round

Slotting saw

Westphale makes the teeth on his escape wheels with a series of straight cuts, as shown above, then routs out the curved shape of the gullets using a template and guide bushing (far right). The escape-wheel blank (or a stack of blanks) is mounted on a mandrel through the arbor hole, and the mandrel is fixed to a divid-

ing head. The dividing head rotates and locks the wheel blank a fixed amount for each cut, ensuring even tooth spacing. Cutters are held in the chuck of a milling machine, the metal-working equivalent of a drill press. The milling machine adjusts precisely in three planes to locate the cutter relative to the work. The divid-

ing head is attached to a sliding table, worked by hand cranks, that moves the work horizontally past the cutter and back again for the next cut. When routing the gullets, the work is indexed under the template by the dividing head. Spokes are routed the same way (photo, facing page) then rounded over on a router table.

hollow headstock you can drill the pivot holes as I do, with a bit in the tailstock. If not, I'd suggest clamping a piece of scrap to your drill-press table and drilling a hole the diameter of your arbor through the scrap just off the edge of the table. Maintain the setup but change the drill to a size a few thousandths smaller than your pivot material; I find that a #53 drill bit works well. Insert the arbor from the bottom and drill carefully into the end. As the arbors are different diameters on each end, at least two different setups will be required.

Bearings, which I make from nylon rod, can be drilled with a similar setup. In this case, just drill part way through the scrap. For instance, if you use ⅜-in.-dia. bearing stock, drill a ⅜-in. hole ⅛ in. deep with a Forstner bit into the clamped scrap. Then drill a ¼-in. hole all the way through. Cut your bearing stock into ⅛-in.-thick wafers. Insert the wafer, drill the appropriate size pivot hole, then push out the completed bearing from below.

Engagement testing—Test wheel-and-pinion engagement patterns at various center distances. In a scrap of plywood, drill a hole for a pin that will represent the wheel arbor. Around it, draw a series of pinion-arbor holes, one at the nominal distance from center, the others at ⅟₃₂-in. increments from the ideal. Mount the pinion on a pin in various holes, revolve the gears, and note how the teeth mesh. Part 1 explains what to look for. Choose the distance that gives the smoothest action. There is some latitude, but many times, while working out the tooth profiles of the grandfather clock, I had to refine the contour of one cutter or the other, and sometimes both. You don't have to go with the exact tooth profiles and distances I've worked out, but they work well and I recommend that you try to match them.

Once the teeth have been cut, the wheels can be lightened with any number of spoke configurations. Spoke shapes are limited only by what is practical and aesthetically pleasing. My

The escape wheel nearing completion. The acrylic template remains stationary, with its far end clamped to a block on the workshop wall. To rout successive spoke holes, the work is turned by the dividing head, which has been set in position to hold the wheel horizontal. Spoke-hole patterns for some of the other wheels in the clock are also visible in the photo.

spoke template is shown in the photo above. I use a router and guide bushing with a ⅛-in. veining bit. Some of my spoke patterns are a series of round holes of various sizes, which can be cut with a drill or a circle cutter as size dictates.

Next the spokes can be rounded over on a router table, using a regular piloted roundover bit. After that, I seal the wood with a mixture of tung oil, polyurethane and mineral spirits, equal parts of each. I soak the wheel for a few minutes, then wipe off all the surplus. At the teeth surfaces, I use high-pressure air to blow away all external traces of the sealer—all I want left is what has soaked into the wood. After drying, I repeat the sealing step a couple of times until there is enough finish on the wheel to be buffed and polished. The final step is to wax the surface and buff it, but take care not to wax the tooth surfaces—they must run dry.

After finishing, the escape wheel gets a little extra treatment with 400-grit paper to polish the contact surfaces of the teeth.

The wheels can now be balanced. Do this after the wheel and pinion are secured to the arbor (I use both glue and brass pins, driven at an angle). Wood density varies and sometimes wheels that you would reasonably expect to be balanced are not. To test them, I rest the pivots on the open jaws of a machinists' vise. The heavy side of the wheel will stop at the bottom. Rotate the wheel one-quarter turn and release. If the wheel stops in the same position, it needs balancing; if it doesn't turn, or the stopping position is random, it doesn't require balancing. Usually it will.

Mark the light side of the back of the wheel near the perimeter and drill a hole about halfway through the wheel. Insert a small lead plug or piece of lead shot and test again. Add more weight if required until the stopping pattern becomes random, then use a small nailset or punch to expand the lead in the hole. You can plug if you wish—I usually leave the hole open as evidence the wheel was balanced.

Setting up—The clockworks are supported by two outside plates. An intermediate plate carries the back end of the weight arbor. My template for the plates is shown in figure 2. Distances between pivots are critical, and should be adjusted in your clock according to how each wheel/pinion pair functions in the engagement testing described earlier.

My clock case is an open frame that is 76 in. high, 18 in. wide, and 11 in. deep. The clock plates are attached to the frame's crosspieces with screws from beneath. A photo of my finished clock was shown in part 1, and you are welcome to copy my case design as closely as you care to, but feel equally free to design

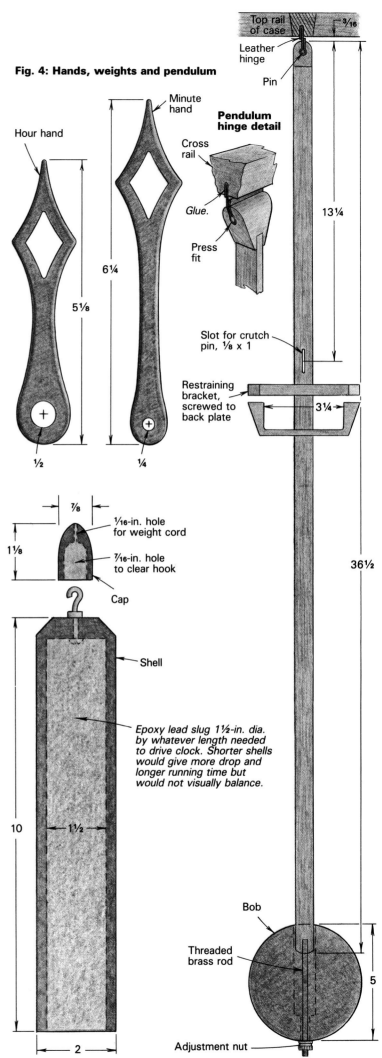

Fig. 4: Hands, weights and pendulum

Hour hand

Minute hand

6¼

5⅛

½   ¼

Pendulum hinge detail

Cross rail

Glue.

Press fit

Top rail of case

Leather hinge

Pin

3/16

13¼

Slot for crutch pin, ⅛ x 1

Restraining bracket, screwed to back plate

3¼

36½

⅞

1⅛

1/16-in. hole for weight cord

7/16-in. hole to clear hook

Cap

Shell

Epoxy lead slug 1½-in. dia. by whatever length needed to drive clock. Shorter shells would give more drop and longer running time but would not visually balance.

10

1½

2

Bob

Threaded brass rod

Adjustment nut

5

Rout-a-clock

by Jim Cummins

While editing Wayne Westphale's article, I had occasion to visit him in Colorado and watch him at work. He relies on precision metalworking equipment, which most woodworkers don't have, so I began trying to think of other ways to make a clockworks, using tools that might be found in any shop.

The various options seemed: to rig up a carriage on the drill press in imitation of Westphale's dividing head and milling machine, to rig up my lathe with a traveling router, or to focus on the indexing setup. I chose the last course and devised the router-template jig shown in the photos. Here are the basics:

The index wheel turns on a ½-in.-dia. pin that sticks up through a particleboard base. My index wheel is acrylic plastic (though it could be hardboard, etc.) with four concentric circles drilled for 64, 48, 40, and 30 holes (various increments of these give all the necessary divisions in Westphale's design).

Mark what will be the centerpoint on the wheel, then use a compass to lay out the four index circles. I worked out the spacing for the holes by using a circle division table (which provides a quick way to figure out how to divide a circle into equal parts). For those who don't have access to such a table, here's how it works: Measure the exact diameter of the circle in inches, then multiply by one of the following factors: for 64 holes, 0.0491; for 48, 0.0654; for 40, 0.0785; and for 30, 0.1045. Work things out to as many decimal places as your calculator will allow. Set sharp dividers to the figure (you can measure with a machinists' rule in hundredths, or convert things to sixty-fourths as I did) and step off around

At left, routing an escape wheel on the indexing jig. The rough shape of the teeth can be cut using the template as shown. A second template is then needed to square off the tops of the teeth. Minor tearout can be patched with epoxy and sawdust. Pinion blanks (above) are too small to be screwed to the index wheel, but they can be glued to an oversize spacer for routing. The newspaper allows the finished pinion to be split free.

one of your own. Just be sure your design will accommodate the pendulum pivot as shown in figure 4.

Mount the plate assembly on the clock frame and hook up the pendulum and weights, shown in figure 4. My standard weights are three pounds each, but you may find that your clock will run on less (mine do, but I allow a 50% safety margin for customers).

The clock should be set level, and the escape lever must be adjusted so that it performs as shown in the tick-tock sequence in part 1. Let the clock run for a while, as a test to see whether it is fast or slow, then adjust the pendulum bob a little to correct it. If the clock is running slow, shorten the pendulum, and vice versa. Keep a record of how often you make adjustments and of how many turns of the adjustment nut you make each time.

You will probably have to make many adjustments to get the clock just right. Clocks don't really run at a steady rate, but speed up and slow down minutely according to the weather and which particular teeth are engaged at any one time. But these slight irregularities average out. My grandfather clock is accurate to a few seconds per day. For the final bob adjustments you may have to let it run a week or more before you can tell whether it is gaining or losing time.

If your clock has problems, a careful rereading of part 1 should allow you to understand what they are. Clocks are fascinating and magical, but they follow physical rules. The important checkpoints are summed up here: The perimeter of wheels and pinions must be concentric with the arbor and the pivots must be

the circumference to show the location of the holes. If it doesn't come out exactly right, adjust the dividers minutely and try again until it does.

When the hole locations are scribed, drill the center hole. Next mount the wheel on its pin through the base, clamp the base to the drill-press table, and pivot the wheel around to drill the series of holes in each circle. I used a ⁹⁄₁₆-in. twist drill (the plastic will ruin a brad-point).

Next, fit your router with a ⁵⁄₁₆-in. guide bushing and a ⅛-in. straight bit with at least a ⅜-in.-long cutting flute. Shopping locally, I found that Black and Decker bits were longer than Master Mechanic bits, so I bought a half-dozen at $2.49 (I'm going to need at least that many more before I'm done). A router bit will give you a round bottom to the gullet, not as nice looking as Westphale's square corners, but perfectly functional.

Screw the wheel blank to the index wheel from beneath, with the screw holes where the spokes will eventually be. Use a spacer between (I used lauan plywood scraps) so the router bit doesn't chew up the index wheel. For the small gears, the pinions, I had to make two stepped-down center pins for the jig, one for a ⅜-in. arbor hole and another for a ⁵⁄₁₆-in. arbor hole. The smallest pinions don't have enough wood in them for anchor screws, so I glued them to an oversize spacer with paper in the joint, as shown in the photo on the facing page.

Make templates that will rout the shapes of the gullets shown on p. 109. To use the jig, rout a gullet, turn the wheel a notch and rout the next, continuing until done. One critical point is to keep a sharp bit and to rout against the rotation, a technique called climb cutting. This helps prevent tear out.

My lauan plywood templates took me several tries each before I was satisfied, but each practice run of a few teeth will show you exactly what modifications are

The teeth and spokes of this 48-tooth dial-train wheel were routed using the plywood template shown. To make the spoke template, the author bandsawed the spoke hole pattern, closed the entrance kerf by gluing a strip of veneer in it, then trued the shape with a rasp. Next step will be to round over the spokes with a piloted router bit.

needed to come down to the correct shape. The template should be indexed by riding on the center pin—this ensures that the final wheels will be the same diameters as the practice pieces—and can be clamped as shown in the photo.

Spokes are routed similarly. Make a template for one spoke hole, then use the index wheel to rotate the wheel the correct amount to space them equally. The spoke edges can be rounded over using a piloted bit in a router table, if you have one (I just clamped my router upside down in a vise).

All this has taken me about five weekends so far, with a good part of the time

just spent musing about the myriad little decisions to be made at each step. I remember that it took me the best part of an evening to realize that I couldn't rout a tooth, but had to rout a gullet. Things like that.

In all, it's been as much of a challenge as Westphale promised and I've enjoyed the project thoroughly. My clock won't be ticking for at least a few more weekends, but the results so far are very promising, and I think I'm on the way. □

Jim Cummins, who putters weekends away at his frame shop in Woodstock, N.Y., is an associate editor at FWW.

at dead center of the arbor. Pivots must be straight, not bent (set the complete arbor, with wheel and pinion mounted, on the open jaws of a vise, then rotate the shaft briskly to check for wobble, warping, etc.). Allow ¹⁄₃₂-in. endplay between the arbors and the clock plates (even so, if the plates warp the arbors may bind). Check for teeth jamming (bottoming or tips butting). Remove the escape lever assembly to check whether the rest of the gear train spins freely. Test pinion leaves for uniform spacing with a micrometer. Never use oil.

I've found that the most likely problem is eccentric wheels, pinions or arbors. One diagnostic trick, which I hope you will never need to use, may pinpoint an intermittent fault. If your clock regularly stops for no apparent reason, mark each pair of

engaged teeth with small dots of masking tape. Then start the clock again. The next time it stops, look with suspicion at any taped pairs of teeth that are engaged as they were before. If it's not the teeth, the same test may pinpoint two gears that are slightly out-of-round, and that bind only when their long axes are aligned. A little work with a file may be all that's needed to put everything right. □

Wayne Westphale designs and builds clocks at his shop, Contemporary Time, in Steamboat Springs, Colo. His grandfather clock took two years to develop, and is copyrighted. Westphale extends to individuals the right to make a copy of his clock for their own use, but not for commercial purposes.

Jigsaw Puzzles

Brain twisters can be works of art

by Steve Malavolta

I first got involved in making puzzles when I needed a gift for my nephew eight years ago. A woodworker friend and I decided that it should be a stand-up dinosaur, in pieces. This led us to make some puzzles out of nicely grained wood cut into somewhat undefined pieces. They were a success on the arts and crafts circuit, so my friend and I formed a partnership and made puzzles full blast for a few years. When the partnership split up, I continued on my own.

A good puzzle should have at least two qualities. The design should be nice to look at and the puzzle should be challenging to put together. I live in the Southwest and derive many of my designs from landscapes. These are fun to make into puzzles, and my patrons seem to prefer them. I also do some abstract designs, and any custom designs a client might ask for.

Over the years, I have tried to expand my notions of what a puzzle can be. The standard jigsaw puzzle is flat. You can make a puzzle a lot more interesting by layering it, making one puzzle fit over another. I've worked up to 10 layers deep and cut up to 1,500 pieces in a single puzzle. I'm constantly working on new ideas, but cutting and finishing each puzzle takes time, and many designs never make it out of the sketchbook.

The jigsaw—Just a note or two about the jigsaw. Any reciprocating jigsaw will do the job, but I'm presently using Delta's new scroll saw and find its electronic speed control very helpful. I work anywhere from 800 to 1,400 strokes per minute, depending on the thickness I need to cut and the number of teeth per inch (tpi) on the blade. I mainly use two blades, both a #0 size, with the same thickness of about 0.011 in. and width of 0.023 in., but one has 22 tpi and the other 32 tpi (available from Woodworker's Supply, 5604 Alameda N.E., Albuquerque, N.M. 87113). I use slower speeds, along with the 32-tpi blade, on thinner or softer material for a slower cut and more control.

Tension is important. I tighten my blade so it vibrates at about a D# when plucked—you can check the note with a pitch pipe, a harmonica or a guitar tuner—but the best tension (and musical pitch) for you will vary according to your jigsaw and blade size. You should experiment. A blade that's too tight will break with slight stress and a blade too loose will bevel the cut, not allowing the pieces to slide in and out of each other smoothly.

Whatever your jigsaw, some fine tuning is needed if you want to work to close tolerances. Viewed from the front, the blade must stroke perpendicular to the table, with no movement from side to side. You can adjust this, on most of the older jigsaws, with a large bolt on the upper back portion of the frame—you simply loosen, adjust and retighten. If in doubt, consult your owners' manual. My new Delta required some shimming at the blade clamps to get the blade absolutely perpendicular.

I remove all guides and hold-down mechanisms from the machine. Guides cause friction on the blade, shortening its life. Hold-downs get in the way when I want to maneuver wood quickly and they block the line of sight.

Cutting without guides and hold-downs takes a bit of practice. The work must be held down firmly by hand or it will lift with each upstroke and slam back down with each cutting stroke. This is not only hard on the blade, it's hard on fragile puzzle pieces.

From *Fine Woodworking* magazine (September 1986) 60:66-69

Below and at left, a puzzle with 88 pieces of kingwood, padauk, bird's-eye maple, wenge and camphorwood, 4⅜ in. by 9¾ in. The pieces removed at the far corner (facing page) show the three layers. To make a jigsaw puzzle, the main elements are cut out in a stack (photo right), then jigsawn into pieces. Below right, an eight-layer puzzle of wenge and maple, about 8 in. square, contains 250 pieces.

Photo: Pat Berret

Despite the firm holding pressure, you have to be sensitive enough to turn the work carefully when cutting curves—if the blade does not remain exactly tangent to the curve, it will stress sideways, either angling the cut or breaking.

Even with every precaution, a good new blade lasts only about ten minutes before it dulls and breaks, and some blades seem to have too little set and break even faster. With that in mind, a machine with quick-change blade holders is an asset. Older saws can be modified by removing the Allen holding screws and replacing them with thumbscrews.

Planning a puzzle—Choose nicely figured hardwoods, free of checks and with fine grain structure. For example, cutting oak is difficult because of its inconsistent and porous grain. In the thicknesses I work with, oak and similar woods are liable to break. Walnut and maple work well, as do tropical hardwoods such as bubinga, wenge, zebrawood, ebony and purpleheart.

I bandsaw the wood into slabs approximately 5/16 in. thick using a ¾-in., 3-tpi hook-tooth blade, then thickness sand them to approximately 5/32 in., with a 180-grit finish.

Figure 1, on the following page, is a simplified, overall view of the steps in cutting the wood into two different types of puzzles, flat and layered. Here are some of the fine points.

I select up to four different pieces of wood and stack them, tacking them together with quick-set epoxy at the corners. If the woods are very dense, I stack fewer layers. I always run the grain in the same direction throughout the stack and examine each piece so that I can orient it effectively. For example, in a land-

scape scene I will position each layer so that the wood that looks most like a sky will be in the sky part of the finished puzzle. Also, the bottom wood of the stack should be the most dense to minimize any chipping during the cut. And, the uppermost piece of the stack should be the lightest in color so the pencil lines of the drawn design stand out clearly.

I now draw the main sections of my design—the areas such as mountains, moon, sky. These are the areas that will later be cut into puzzle pieces, and I take care not to draw any section too small or too fragile. I cut along the drawn lines, as shown in the top photo. In theory, the jigsaw would allow me to cut totally enclosed shapes—such as a full moon not touching the horizon line—by drilling a tiny starting hole through the work, threading the blade through it, then clamping the blade in the saw. But, in practice, the starting hole leaves a nasty little indent on the edge of the puzzle piece. So in all cases, I begin the cut at the edge of the puzzle, just as if using a bandsaw.

I draw my designs so that the puzzle pieces will be held in an outer frame that's glued to a backboard. In a puzzle such as the one in the large photo above, the outer frames are cut so that pieces of them can be used to build up depth in the foreground. Another approach is to glue the frame as a boxlike border, such as in the puzzle with circles, which is also shown.

Regardless of which type of puzzle you are making, the inner border of the frame must be cut through the entire stack at once. How much of the outer frame should be cut into pieces at this time depends on the design. Sometimes, figuring out the cutting sequence for a complicated puzzle reminds me of what the

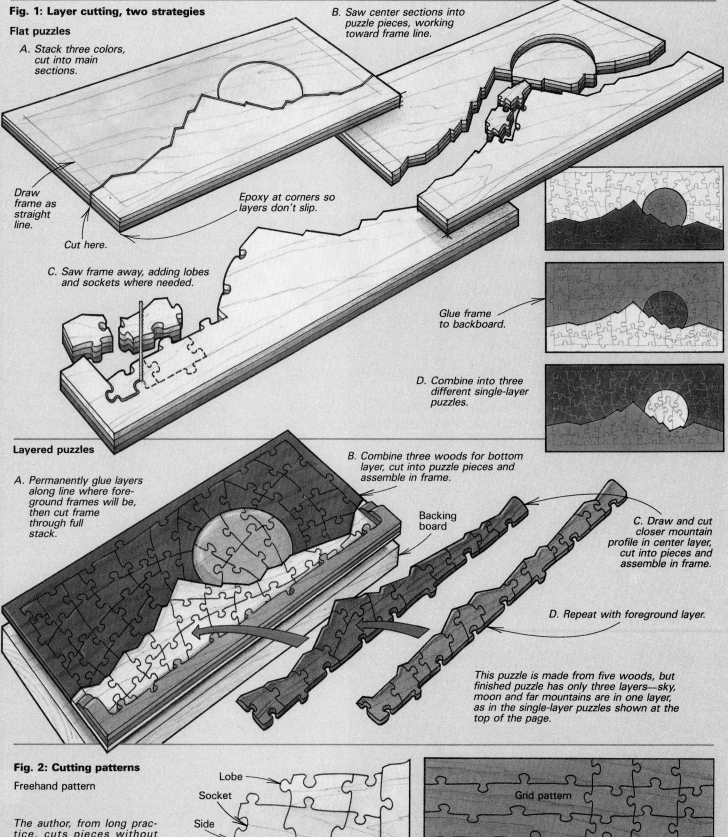

Fig. 1: Layer cutting, two strategies

Flat puzzles

A. Stack three colors, cut into main sections.

B. Saw center sections into puzzle pieces, working toward frame line.

Draw frame as straight line.

Cut here.

Epoxy at corners so layers don't slip.

C. Saw frame away, adding lobes and sockets where needed.

Glue frame to backboard.

D. Combine into three different single-layer puzzles.

Layered puzzles

A. Permanently glue layers along line where foreground frames will be, then cut frame through full stack.

B. Combine three woods for bottom layer, cut into puzzle pieces and assemble in frame.

Backing board

C. Draw and cut closer mountain profile in center layer, cut into pieces and assemble in frame.

D. Repeat with foreground layer.

This puzzle is made from five woods, but finished puzzle has only three layers—sky, moon and far mountains are in one layer, as in the single-layer puzzles shown at the top of the page.

Fig. 2: Cutting patterns

Freehand pattern

The author, from long practice, cuts pieces without drawing guide lines, keeping the following rules in mind: He interlocks at least every other perimeter piece to the frame. Within the puzzle, he interlocks each side of a piece with the piece next to it. About every 5th to 10th piece, he makes two-to-one connections, as shown in the drawing, to help tighten the slack created by the sawkerfs.

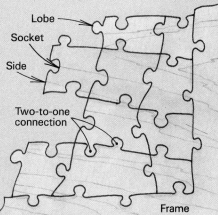

Lobe

Socket

Side

Two-to-one connection

Frame

Grid pattern

The grid pattern is much simpler to plan and cut, but is less suited to puzzles of irregular shape. First draw a series of horizontal grid lines with lobes and sockets alternating along their length. Then cross the horizontal lines with vertical lines to produce an interlocking pattern containing a locking joint at each side of each piece.

Drawing: David Dann

puzzle's buyer will have to go through when putting it together.

If you're making flat puzzles, the sections can be sawn into puzzle pieces while they are still stacked. But layered puzzles are sawn into pieces with the sections split apart, so that you don't end up with one identical puzzle piece over another in the finished puzzle. I split the layers apart using a sturdy utility knife, working with the grain.

Beveling the edges of the sections gives the illusion of more depth than the puzzle actually has. For example, in the landscape puzzle shown in this article, the sky, moon and far mountains are all on the puzzle's bottom layer. I usually bevel pieces on a 60-grit, 6-in. by 48-in. belt sander. I work primarily on the front roller and sand off a shallow angle, half the thickness of the wood, on the desired edges. I finish sand the bevel on a 3-in. pneumatic drum sander with a well used 180-grit sleeve.

Cutting pieces—The sections are now ready to be cut into puzzle pieces. Some puzzle makers draw out a grid system as a basis for their pieces, a process illustrated in figure 2. But because I cut within such irregular shapes (and have years of practice), I freehand all my cuts, as I am doing in the photo at right. I plan out pieces in my mind about three or four ahead of the one I'm cutting and aim to keep each piece about ½ in. to ¾ in. square. I've always forced myself to make them as small as possible within the limits of my equipment.

Mass-produced cardboard puzzles are stamped out by machine, resulting in virtually no space between pieces. A wooden puzzle, in contrast, always has some slack from the sawkerf, and the interlocking pieces should be shaped so that they cannot slide apart. This requires a lobe-and-socket connection on each side. As further security, on about every fifth to tenth piece, depending on the size of the puzzle, I make pieces with two-to-one connections, as shown in the drawing.

As I cut each piece, I assemble the puzzle on newsprint paper so I don't lose track of which piece goes where. When all the pieces are in place, I put the frame around the puzzle so that I can sand the surface to remove any burring from the cutting. Next I polish with 00 steel wool.

To flip the puzzle without jumbling the pieces, I use a manila file folder, placing the edge of the puzzle at the crease, closing the folder, turning it over and reopening it.

I finish the centers of the puzzles first, leaving the frames for later. I brush the assembled pieces with Watco oil on both sides, flipping the puzzle as before and placing it back on newsprint. After a few hours, I wipe off the excess oil. The next day, I wipe both surfaces with tung oil.

I glue the frame pieces to a backing board of 4/4 alder, trim the assembly square with the radial-arm saw, then sand the back and sides to round and soften the edges. Using a Foredom tool with a small Dremel burr, I inscribe the back of the puzzle with the different kinds of woods used, my signature, the date, and the title if applicable. After a bit more hand sanding and steel wooling, the backed frame is ready for oiling. After the oil is dry, I slide the puzzle pieces off the newsprint into the frame and wipe on a final coat of tung oil.

To get away from woodworking for a moment, many of my puzzles contain inlaid metal—sterling silver wire, for example, used as stars in landscape scenes. Inlaying can be done before or after relief beveling, but is best done before cutting the puzzle pieces, because it's much easier to manipulate the work. I drill clear through with various small drills equal in diameter to the gauges of silver wire (available at most jewelry stores with repair

Edge-beveling, which gives an illusion of depth, can be roughed out over the end roller of a belt sander.

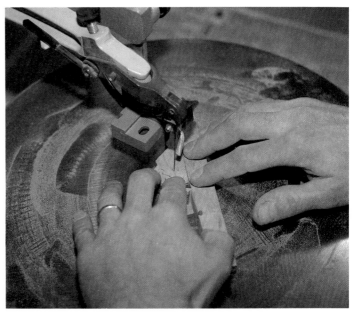

Each segment of a layered puzzle is sawn into interlocking pieces. Typical sawing patterns are shown on the facing page.

departments or from jewelry supply houses). I epoxy the wire into place, then snip it off, leaving a small amount extra on both top and bottom to be sanded flat later.

The puzzle now waits to be dumped and played. Although some of the puzzles have as few as 30 pieces, they still can be quite an entertaining challenge. Since the pieces are finished on both sides, the puzzle builder has to determine whether each piece is right side up or not—the trick is to learn to visualize each piece in reverse. Some of the larger puzzles become very challenging. The use of layering not only adds depth but also difficulty. Each layer goes completely underneath the one above it with different shaped pieces and, in some cases, with the same wood. So one can easily start constructing the edge pieces on the wrong level only to discover this false start later, when trying to assemble the interior pieces. This may seem like a dirty trick, but it's the sort of deception that delights puzzle fans. □

Steve Malavolta also makes letter openers and sculptural lighting fixtures at his studio, Selected Grains, in Albuquerque, N.M. Photos of work in progress by Marc Coan.

Christmas Ornaments

Constructing a blizzard

by Steven J. Gray

People are always looking for inexpensive but well-crafted novelty items. The trick to satisfying these sometimes contradictory requirements is to develop a method for easily reproducing saleable items. I've always admired high-quality mass production, but because most craft items are made one at a time, it's difficult for small-shop woodworkers to find production shortcuts without compromising on quality.

My search for an easily reproduced product turned up some wooden snowflakes that apparently were punched out of thin laminate made up from several different woods with contrasting color and grain. Because the wooden flakes were intricate and fragile, I assumed reproducing them would be complicated and expensive. And, I was not interested in jigsawing copies one at a time, so I put the idea aside. A few years later, while preparing for the Christmas craft shows, I remembered the snowflakes. In my mind, I could see the results I was after; all I needed was a little inspiration in the fabrication area.

What I came up with was a snowflake made up from six identical diamond-shape sections joined together to form a star shape. I decided to shape the cross section of each diamond, then glue up the required number of sections to form a bar of "snowflakes." I would then cut off thin slices to produce each individual snowflake. The drawing on the facing page outlines the process for a six-point snowflake, but the principle is the same for any configuration.

Initially, my snowflakes were a bit crude: They had gaps between their glued-up sections, which were often poorly aligned. Still, friends seemed to like them and even said they would buy them—if I could eliminate the gaps and poor fit. I thought these problems could easily be fixed by using jigs to hold the small, fragile snowflakes during their construction. The jigs would allow me to keep my fingers and hands clear of the cutting edges of the tools so I could concentrate more fully on the shaping operations and quickly achieve accurate and reproducible results.

Construction process—Wood color and grain are important aspects of the snowflake, so I'm fussy about selecting lumber. I like to imagine how the finished snowflake will look against an evergreen tree. Redwoods and light-color woods are visually appealing, making them the most popular. Closed-grain woods, like maple and padauk, also sell well; they also are less apt to chip, and their glue joints hold up a little better.

The shaping process removes a lot of wood (as much as 50%) and increases the piece's surface area significantly. This makes the segments more susceptible to humidity changes and subsequent wood movement, so I try to use clear, kiln-dried lumber whenever possible. For most of my designs, I use ¾-in.- to 1-in.-thick stock. Each board should be as wide as possible to maximize the output of snowflakes. My jointer-planer width limits me to about 10 in., which yields 60 to 80 snowflakes.

I begin by jointing one surface of the board flat and planing the flip side to the desired thickness. Then, I joint one of the long edges to provide a good reference surface for crosscutting the diamond sections on the tablesaw. The sawblade angle at this point is crucial in determining whether the sections will fit together snugly. Invest the time and effort to set the blade accurately. Any cumulative cutting errors will be minimized along with a lot of frustration, wasted time and material loss later on. The appropriate angle depends, of course, on the number of points in the snowflake; it can be determined simply by dividing 360° by the number of snowflake points. For the six-point snowflake described here, the diamond sections are cut to 60°. On my tablesaw, this requires setting the blade 30° from the vertical.

All four sides of the diamond section must be the same length, which means that the width of the cut piece must equal its thickness. I make a sample cut, flip the cut section end for end, rotate it 90° and slide it back up against the board from which it was cut. If there is any difference in height between the pieces, I adjust the fence and try again. Once the angle and width are set properly, I proceed to make all my cuts. I need six pieces for the six-point snowflake, but I make at least seven in case something goes wrong. At this point, I tape six of the pieces together to make a final check on the fit and alignment. If my setup is done properly, everything should fit, but occasionally a minor saw adjustment is necessary. One more thing: I save two waste pieces cut from the end of the board, because these have the correct angles for the jig and the fence needed to shape the segments.

The fun part of the construction process is shaping the sections. I don't plan this. I simply start making full-length cuts along the diamond sections using a thin-kerf blade on my tablesaw and a variety of straight and curved bits in my router (inverted and mounted in a router table). To move the segments safely past the cutters, I screw a combination hold-down/handle and an end stop to one of the waste pieces I saved, as shown in the top photo on the facing page. I clamp the second waste piece to the saw table or router table to serve as a fence.

From *Fine Woodworking* magazine (November 1988) 73:68-70

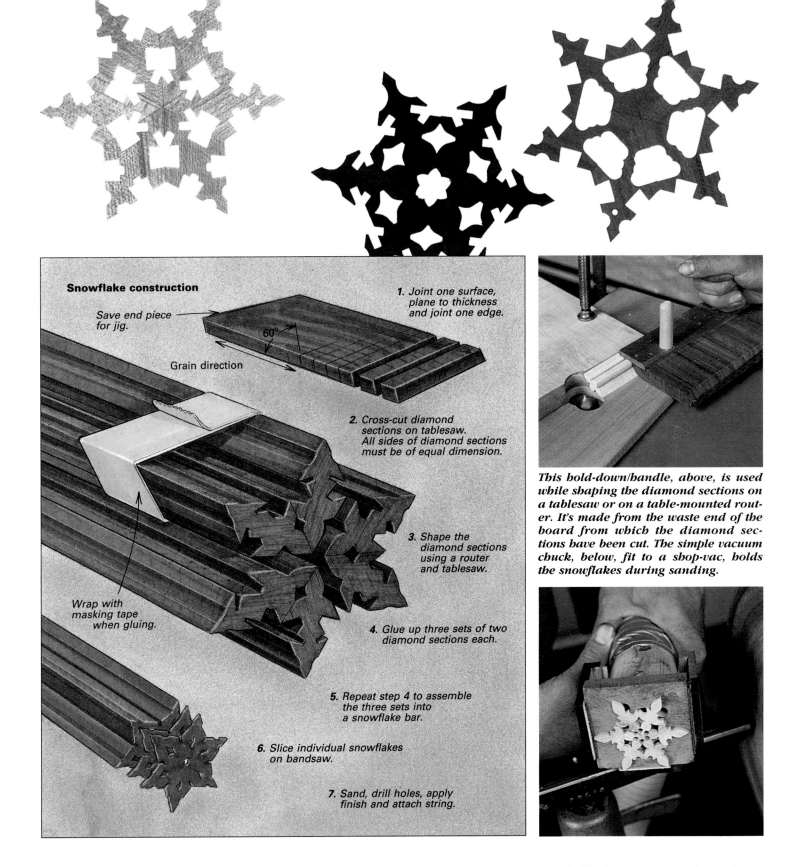

Snowflake construction

Save end piece for jig.

Grain direction

60°

Wrap with masking tape when gluing.

1. Joint one surface, plane to thickness and joint one edge.

2. Cross-cut diamond sections on tablesaw. All sides of diamond sections must be of equal dimension.

3. Shape the diamond sections using a router and tablesaw.

4. Glue up three sets of two diamond sections each.

5. Repeat step 4 to assemble the three sets into a snowflake bar.

6. Slice individual snowflakes on bandsaw.

7. Sand, drill holes, apply finish and attach string.

This hold-down/handle, above, is used while shaping the diamond sections on a tablesaw or on a table-mounted router. It's made from the waste end of the board from which the diamond sections have been cut. The simple vacuum chuck, below, fit to a shop-vac, holds the snowflakes during sanding.

After making a few cuts, I hold the six sections together to see how the pattern is developing. I repeat this until I'm satisfied. Don't remove too much wood from the mating edges, or you'll risk having insufficient gluing surface and a weak joint. Individual cuts should not be made too deeply, because an identical cut will be made in the facing edge, and a weak spot may result.

Before gluing the parts together, I remove rough edges with medium sandpaper so the sections will mate cleanly. I've tried to glue all six sections at one time, but I don't seem to have enough hands to accomplish this easily. So, I do them in two steps. I first glue up two diamond sections, and when I have three sets of these ready, it's fairly simple to glue them together to form the snowflake bar. Masking tape holds the sections together and provides adequate clamping pressure while the glue sets up. Excess pressure results in misalignments.

I slice the individual snowflakes on a bandsaw using an L-shape scrapwood carrier mounted on the miter gauge. The horizontal section raises the bar off the table to prevent the tips of the snowflakes from getting caught and broken in the blade slot. The vertical piece backs up the bar to prevent tearout. A third scrap piece clamped to the table acts as a depth stop for cutting off uniformly thick snowflakes. I grasp the partially sawn-through snowflake as it emerges on the exit side of the bandsaw blade to prevent it from flying off as the cut is completed. While doing

Photos of finished ornaments: Michele Russell Slavinsky; drawing: Bob La Pointe

this, I'm careful to keep my fingers back from the blade, well-clear of the cutting edge. Because the cut is being made *with* the grain, troublesome formations of "fuzzies" do not occur (as they might if crosscutting), so edge cleanup—which could be a messy problem with the snowflakes because they have a large amount of exposed edges—is eliminated.

Devising a way to sand the snowflakes on my disc sander was a little tricky. My solution was to fashion a vacuum-clamp attachment for my shop vacuum. As shown in the bottom photo on the previous page, holes drilled in the flat plate provide suction, and the three adjustable stops securely hold the snowflake. I have to

reduce the vacuum, by drilling additional holes in the side of the clamp, so the snowflake won't be "pulled" uncontrollably into the sander. Sanding is now straightforward: Just ease the snowflake into the sander steadily, keeping it parallel to the disc.

After drilling a small-diameter hole in one of the outer tips (I drill up to 10 snowflakes at a time), I finish the snowflakes with Watco oil. When the snowflakes are dry, I thread each hole with a decorative, metallic gold string. □

Steven Gray and his wife, Debbie, operate a woodworking shop in Bozeman, Mont., specializing in kaleidoscopes.

Turning inlaid balls

The wooden, hollow-turned Christmas-tree decorations I make reflect my machinist background: They require a fair amount of precision to build. Also, a number of the turning tools I use are custom-shaped for a particular operation. Nevertheless, while specific tools may simplify the job, the ornaments can be made just as well with commonly available wood-shaping tools. Since each ornament is custom-made—the design evolves as I build them—and assembled piece by piece, they take quite some time to make. Making these ornaments is not for everybody, but it's an interesting process, and I hope you try it.

Spindle-turning wood spheres isn't difficult, but the solid spheres will quickly weigh down the sturdiest evergreen bough. I use a variety of Pennsylvania-grown hardwoods, such as dogwood, as well as many exotic woods. These turn well, but they are dense and heavy, so I needed a reliable method to hollow the spheres. I borrowed the idea of using a compression chuck made up of two turned donut rings, as shown below. The sphere is sandwiched between the rings and held in place by three threaded bolts with wing nuts. My chuck can handle 2-in.- to 4-in.-dia. ornaments, but they've got to be reasonably round; otherwise, they'll slip in the chuck. The chuck is mounted on a lathe faceplate while I bore a 1¼-in.- to 1½-in.-dia. hole about one-third of the diameter deep. This allows me to reach in and remove wood with a modified roundnose chisel bent 90°. I reduce the wall thickness to about ⅟₁₆ in. I reposition the sphere and repeat this operation 120° in both directions from the first hole. Now I need to fill the three holes in the hollowed sphere's surface.

Simple wood discs with contrasting color or grain pattern are

okay; I like to create different patterns that feature the wood's characteristics and give the ornaments a light, festive touch. I use my tablesaw, scroll saw and sometimes my milling machine (for swirl patterns) to shape sections from ¼-in.-thick wood. Then I assemble and glue the pieces one at a time, using a disc sander to make adjustments as I proceed. When the glue is dry, I center the assembly on my lathe, butting it against the end of a ¾-in. dowel chucked in the headstock. The workpiece is held by the pressure of the cone center in the tailstock. I use a parting tool made from an old file to cut the disc roughly to size and follow-up with a skew chisel to precisely match the holes in the spheres. I like to use a different pattern in each hole. After the discs are glued in place, I remount the sphere in the compression chuck using the cone center as a guide to correctly align the disc. The disc is face-turned flush to the sphere surface; sometimes I create a concave or recessed pattern in it for added interest.

Adding a finial to the top, and often the bottom of the sphere completes the ornament. The compression chuck is used again while I drill ⅜-in. holes in the sphere for the finial's tenoned end. The finials are made from solid wood or laminates and are turned on the lathe. I drill a hole for attaching a supporting string in the end of the top finial, and I shape the eyelet using hand tools.

I finish the decorations with at least two coats of a clear sanding sealer. Sanding between coats is done with Scotch-Brite pads, and I use a hand-rubbed wax for the final coat. □

The turned sphere is drilled and hollowed out on the lathe using a compression chuck to support the work, left. Decorative discs are turned to fit the drilled holes; the pressure of the tailstock center supports the disc while it's being turned, right.

Dave Hardy is an active member of the American Association of Woodturners. He lives in Sellersville, Pa.

Three examples of the author's sliding-lid boxes: The smallest box houses an antique mouth harp. The box is carved and painted—a functional little sculpture. 'The Illustrated Box,' center, has chip carving on its edges and interior. The old man's face creates the illusion of depth. The domino box (7⅛ x 2¼ x 1¼ in.), right, was the author's first. Its lid is decorated with simple incised carving.

Sliding-Lid Boxes
Hand carved, top to bottom

by John Heatwole

I made my first carved box a number of years ago to house a set of old-bone tavern dominoes. Since that time, I've carved 20 to 30 sliding-lid boxes. I've always worked my boxes out exclusively with hand tools, not because I think this is the only way they should be done, but because handwork has been a tradition in my family for more than 200 years, and I'm very comfortable with it. By roughing out these boxes by hand, I feel I'm in total control, that the tools are an extension of my hands and mind. I love the sound of wood being peeled or carved, and as I work, I can hear the creative wheels turning. Besides, a beginning carver with limited financial means can produce a truly unique item with a very small investment. I've sold many pieces through galleries during my career, and I'm sure the fact that my work is done entirely by hand has not been a disadvantage.

In this article, I will describe how to make a small sliding-lid box by hand from solid stock. I will show you how to lay out the areas to be carved away, using beveled stop cuts to help preserve crisp edges, and I'll explain how to make the beveled slide channels in the box to receive the lid's runners. If you like, you can add decorative carvings to your boxes, but I'll leave that whole process up to you. I sometimes do figurative carvings in the interiors, as well as on the lids, as you can see from the photos above. Once you've mastered the basics, only your imagination and carving skills will limit what you can do.

Wood selection and tool kit—All the techniques I discuss can be applied to almost any wood. Inexperienced carvers should note that more pressure needs to be applied with harder woods and thus more caution. I recommend basswood, or linden as we call it in my part of the country, for your first few boxes. It is easily

From *Fine Woodworking* magazine (January 1989) 74:47-49

Photo this page: Michele Russell Slavinsky

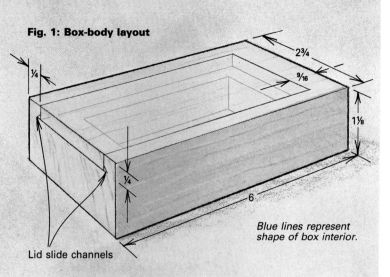

Fig. 1: Box-body layout

2¾

9/16

¼

1⅛

¼

6

Lid slide channels

Blue lines represent shape of box interior.

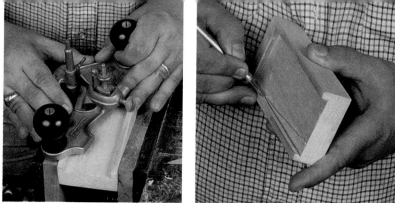

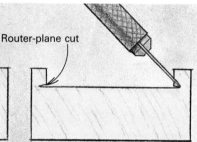

Above left: To make the beveled slide channels, turn the router at an angle and let the point cut into the base of the sidewall about ⅛ in. Push or pull the router to the front of the box, taking care not to go too deeply and weaken the sidewall. Take the blank out of the vise and draw a line 3/32 in. up from the lid opening. Above right: With your finger as a guide, cut at a 45° angle along the line to meet the router cut. Repeat this and the router cut until the wedge breaks free. Cut at the rear wall to release the wedge.

Fig. 2: Cutting the lid opening and slide channels

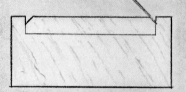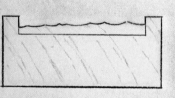

Router-plane cut

A. To create a stop cut for hollowing out the lid opening, make vertical cuts ⅛ in. deep on layout lines. Then, make 45° angle cut to meet vertical cuts and remove wedges.

B. Use gouge to remove wood down to stop cuts.

C. Repeat steps A and B to within 1/16 in. of layout line. Remove waste to line and flatten bottom with triangular blade in router plane.

D. To form the slide channel, make cuts, ⅛ in. deep, at base of sidewalls with router plane. Holding X-acto knife at a 45° angle, make cuts to meet router cuts, and remove wedge. (See photos above.)

Fig. 3: Lid-blank layout

3/32

13/16

2⅜

5 7/16

3/32

Pare the wood away from the lid's sides with a 20mm chisel. The beveled stop cuts reduce the chance of tearout beyond the line. When this wood is removed, the runners along the bottom of the lid will remain. Choke up on the chisel, as shown below, so if the chisel slips, your hand will hit the block before the chisel could cause injury.

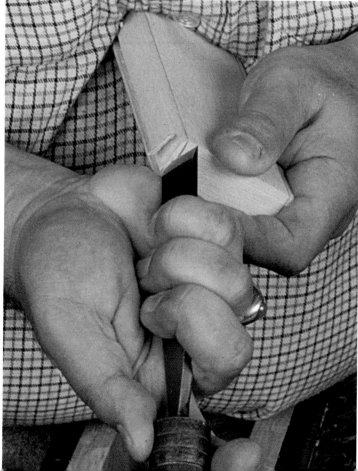

Fig. 4: Cutting the lid

Beveled stop cuts prevent tearout when removing waste.

Flat, 1/16 in.

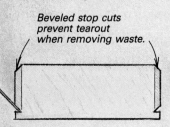

A. Bevel top edges along layout lines. Cut ⅛ in. deep along lines on edges, cut down to them at 45° angle and remove wedges.

B. Remove waste with chisel (see photo at right). Pare runners at 45° angle, leaving 1/16 in. flat at bottom edge.

worked but will maintain a crisp, strong edge, even in the small dimensions of the lid's runners. Basswood also takes stains and colors well. The following are the only tools you need: miter box, pencil, X-Acto knife with a #24 blade or a 6mm skew chisel (I've come to prefer the X-Acto knife for scoring lines because of its razor-sharp blade), 11mm straight gouge with a medium deep sweep, 20mm straight chisel, 8mm straight chisel, hand router-plane with triangular blade, and 150- and 220-grit sandpaper.

I begin by having a local cabinet shop mill two pieces of bass-wood, each about 3 ft. long. From these, I can make half a dozen boxes. The piece for the box body is 2¾ in. wide and 1⅛ in. thick. The piece for the lid is 2⅜ in. wide and ¹³⁄₁₆ in. thick. The lid stock should be as thick as the depth of the lid opening (¼ in.) for a flush fit, or thicker if you plan to do a high- or low-relief carving. The lid for the box discussed here is ¹³⁄₁₆ in. thick to allow for a high-relief carving.

Carving out the lid opening—Using the miter box, cut a 6-in. blank for the body from the 1⅛-in. stock. Lay out the lid opening by drawing lines on top of the blank (see figure 1 on the facing page). I draw the lines freehand, using my finger as a guide along the edge of the blank. The shoulders should be ¼ in. thick and as deep. The rear wall of the box should be ⁹⁄₁₆ in. thick. I sometimes leave the rear wall even thicker, say ⅞ in., so I can trim the corners and make the box into an oval after I've fitted the lid. If the front of the box is to be rounded, it must be done after the lid is in place, because the lid must also be shaped.

After laying out the opening, remove all the wood to a depth of ¼ in. between the shoulders and the rear wall. Clamp the blank in a vise, and with your X-Acto knife and a steady hand, score along the lines to a depth of about ⅛ in. Holding the knife at a 45° angle, make cuts ⅛ in. in from these lines and remove a wedge the full length of the cuts (see figure 2A on the facing page). These grooves act as stop cuts when you hollow out the lid opening. Now, take the 11mm gouge and make a series of cuts between the grooves. I usually pare the ridges left by the gouge with a 20mm flat chisel and then repeat the gouging and paring, down to a depth of about ³⁄₁₆ in. Take special care not to cut into the shoulders and rear wall; this is why the stop cuts were made. With a triangular blade in the router plane set to a depth of ¼ in., clean out any remaining chisel marks and take the lid opening the rest of the way down so you have a flat area ¼ in. deep.

Now you're ready to cut out the beveled slide channels. Without changing the blade's depth, turn the router to about a 45° angle with the sidewalls, and gently let the point of the router blade cut into the base of a sidewall at the back corner to a depth of about ⅛ in, as shown in the top, left photo on the facing page. With a light touch, push or pull the router plane to the front of the box, taking care not to cut too deeply and weaken the sidewall. Do this on both sides. Now take the blank from the vise and draw a line ³⁄₃₂ in. up from the bottom of the lid opening along the inside of both sidewalls. With the X-Acto knife at a 45° angle, cut along these lines so the blade meets the router cuts (see figure 2D on the facing page); steady your hand by running your fingers along the box's edges, as shown in the top, right photo on the facing page. You might have to repeat this cut and the router cut a couple times before the strip will break free from the slide channels, as shown in the photo. A cut with the X-Acto knife at the back wall will help to break the strip out. Clean up these channels by folding a square of 150-grit sandpaper once or twice and drawing it back and forth in each channel several times. This should be repeated with the 220-grit sandpaper, to make the channels smoother and thus easier for the lid to slide in.

The sliding lid—The lids in old sliding-lid boxes are often warped, probably because these boxes were used almost exclusively as containers in shops and barns, where they were exposed to extreme temperature and moisture changes. Boxes used as household containers or conversation pieces, however, are not likely to warp, if the wood has been kiln dried or sufficiently air dried.

From the 2⅜-in. by ¹³⁄₁₆-in. stock, cut a piece 5⁷⁄₁₆ in. long on the miter box. I always leave the lid about ¹⁄₁₆ in. too long, in case I need to trim a little for a better fit against the rear wall. Figure 3 on the facing page shows the layout lines for the wood to be removed to create the two narrow, beveled runners. The lines on the top are ³⁄₃₂ in. in from both long edges and extend down each end. The lines on each edge are ³⁄₃₂ in. up from the bottom and extend around the corners to meet the lines on the ends. With the X-Acto knife, make a cut along the bottom line on both edges and a 45° cut to meet these lines. Remove the wedges. Also, bevel the top corners along the layout lines at a 45° angle, as shown in figure 4A. Pare away the waste by eye with the 20mm straight chisel, as shown in photo at the bottom of the facing page. Finally, bevel the runners with the 8mm straight chisel tilted at a 45° angle away from the stock, leaving a scant ¹⁄₁₆ in. of flat on the long edge (see figure 4B). I choke up on the chisel and hold the lid blank so if the chisel slips, the heel of my hand will bump the end of the blank before I could cut myself.

Now, try the lid to the lid opening on the box blank. If it won't slide in easily, the lid is probably too wide or the runners are too thick. If the lid is too wide, sand both runners back and forth on a piece of 150-grit sandpaper flat on the workbench until it fits. If the lid fits, but is tight, fold a piece of 150-grit sandpaper and sand the bevels of the runners a few times, trying the lid until the runners slide in the channels easily. The lid should not fall out by itself, but it should move without requiring much pressure. Keep in mind that a wax finish on the boxes will make the fit a little more snug.

Hollowing out the box cavity—Once you have a box blank with a nicely fitting lid, you can hollow out the box interior. For a standard, straight-wall box, I proceed as I did with the lid opening. I mark out the area to be removed, score the lines and make stop cuts. Then I use a gouge to take away most of the waste wood and flatten the bottom with the router, leaving the bottom about ³⁄₁₆ in. thick. Be careful not to round over the top edge of the box cavity or the lid opening by levering the back of the gouge on them as you work. To keep the walls straight and vertical, it helps to repeat the scoring, gouging and routing process several times as you go deeper.

As an alternative to hollowing the whole box, you can also lay out an oval, two circles or a combination of shapes, gouge them out to a depth of ½ in. or ⅝ in. and smooth them with sandpaper. It may look like you don't have enough room for your jewelry, special stones or whatever with this type of depression, but try your object first to see if it fits before you gouge too deeply.

The photos of the finished boxes on p. 121 reflect several variations: straight walls utilizing the whole area below the lid opening as in the domino box; a carved recess, custom fitted for a mouth harp; and an egg-shaped recess smoothed and painted in the interior of "The Illustrated Box."

Any hand-rubbed oil finish, such as Watco or tung oil, will work fine on these boxes. I sometimes add a final coat of hard paste wax. If you want to add color to your box, try mixing artist's oil paint with boiled linseed oil and applying it with a small brush.☐

John Heatwole is a professional sculptor living in Bridgewater, Va. The Delaware Art Museum selected his wood sculpture "Crawdad" as the first piece for its new American Fantasy Art collection.

Casual Pig

When he's not shaping and painting Christmas ornaments, Tolone works on larger, equally colorful creatures.

Deck the Halls
Curious Christmas creatures

by Robert Tolone

I am a painter and a sculptor, and in addition to my regular work, I have for years been making wooden Christmas ornaments for my family and friends. Occasionally I thought about making some for sale, but had never really done anything about it. Two years ago, some friends encouraged me to show my ornaments to a gallery owner. So, I carved 27 different ornaments, figuring that if she wasn't interested, I'd at least have my Christmas list filled for the year. Fortunately, she was very enthusiastic and ordered some for sale.

Encouraged, I sent a set of slides of the ornaments to the Los Angeles Craft and Folk Art Museum. The next morning, the museum director called. "They're enchanting," he said. "We love them. We'll take 63 dozen."

That success spurred me on and more slide sets were mailed. A week later I was on a plane to New York and meetings with galleries there.

Falling Boy

Falling Girl

Ram's a' Running

From *Fine Woodworking* magazine (November 1986) 61:92-93

Carousel Horse

Caroler Head

Giant Anteater

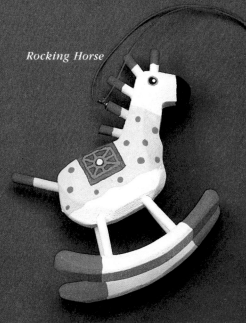

Rocking Horse

"How many did the Craft and Folk Art Museum buy?" asked the director of the American Folk Museum galleries. "Sixty-three dozen," I told her. "Well, we can do better than that," she said. "We'll take 85 dozen."

Six weeks after finishing the original set, I had sold more than 4,000 ornaments to fifteen galleries nationwide. I was euphoric. Never had anything I'd made gotten so overwhelming and favorable a response. On the strength of my orders I got a loan from my father for some necessary tools, and two weeks later had added a Hegner jigsaw, radial-arm saw, compressor and spray equipment, bandsaw, and assorted small tools to the shop, along with several hundred board feet of jelutong and alder.

"How many $\frac{1}{8}$-in. dowels do you have in stock?" I asked my lumber dealer. "More than you can possibly use," he said. "Good. I'll need

four thousand feet." "That's more than three-quarters of a mile of dowel!" he exclaimed. "What do you need it for?" "I make Christmas ornaments," I told him. He shook his head, "Lotta ornaments."

He was right. It was a lot of ornaments. I sat down at my workbench and figured out my cutting lists. Some of my designs were simple, only one piece. Others were very complex, up to 23 pieces in one ornament. It came out to more than 12,000 individual parts, all hand carved, hand sanded, hand painted. Into all those pieces holes had to be drilled and more than 20,000 assorted lengths of dowel inserted, ranging from $\frac{1}{4}$ in. to 2 in. My early euphoria subsided as I began to take realistic measure of the work before me. It was an enormous task. I was most concerned about quality. It's easy to make something well when you need do it only once, but how can you maintain craftsmanship when a job needs to be repeated thousands of times? Quality control became the summer's theme.

I had exactly four months to fill the orders. Still, I was confident I could deliver on time. All I needed to do was work 18 hours a day, seven days a week, and enlist every friend I had to help whenever they could. All told, more than 27 friends volunteered their time. We held doweling bees, like the old-time quilting bees, where friends came over and hammered thousands of dowels into thousands of holes. It was a wild, exhausting summer.

In the end, the deadline was met, the orders filled on time. Quality was maintained by dividing each job into simple, easy steps. We split up re-

petitive tasks so that each job got done before the monotony became unbearable. Most importantly, we enlisted my mother as Quality Control Officer, and she became as ruthless a nitpicker as ever bedeviled a production line. In every case, the production ornaments were better crafted than the prototypes, and of this I am quite proud.

"What about next year?" my friends all asked. "Are you going to do it again?" I sure am. As an artist, I am all too familiar with the struggle to succeed financially, and making my studio profitable has been tremendously exciting. Interestingly, showing the ornaments has led to many offers from galleries to do shows of my larger sculptures, as well as several commissions for large pieces. All in all, it's been a wonderful year. □

Robert Tolone is a painter and sculptor in Venice, Calif.

Index

L

Lacing, birch-root, 38-39
Lacquer, for turnings, 78-79
Lamination:
    glues for, 97
    helical, 84-87
Lap desks, making, 22-25
Lathe chucks, male bowl, collared, 83
Leather, source for, 20
Lettering, incised:
    gilded, 64, 67
    technique for, 64-67
Lynch, Carlyle, plans from, 17

M

Malavolta, Steve, on jigsaw puzzles,
    114-17
Marble rolls, making, 32-35
Marcoux, John, on whistles, 28
Marquetry. *See* Inlay.
Mehler, Kelly, on lap desk, 22-25
Menard, Edmond, bird carving
    by, 48-50
Message center, making, 44-47
Milling machines, for clock gears, 110

N

Nutting, Chester, bird-carving
    method of, 48

P

Parting tools:
    clean-cutting, 72-73
    machinist's, making, 87
    thin-kerf layout, 72
Pencils, mechanical, making, 70
Penetrating-oil finishes, fast-setting, 94
Pens, ballpoint, making, 68-70
Pepper mills:
    making, 92-94
    mechanisms for, 94
Pinch dogs, source for, 75
Pine, David Ray, on Moravian
    footstool, 16-17
Plastic, rod, source for, 97
Plywood, homemade, 105
Pool cues, making, 97-99
Puzzles, layered, making, 114-17

R

Rivets, from escutcheon pins, 42, 43
Routers:
    gear cutters for, 106, 107
    gears with, clock, 112-13
    grooving setup for, 69
    indexing jig for, 112
    on lathe cross-slide, 106, 107
    production runs with, 93
    surfacing with, 83

S

Saltshakers, making, 92-94
Sanding:
    of lathe work, 89
    production runs of, 93-94
    reference table for, 83
    rubber discs for, sources of, 31
    vacuum holding device for, 119, 120
    See also Turning.
Sanding sealer, aerosol, source for, 94
Sandpaper:
    for delicate turned boxes, 73
    15-micron polishing, 87
    Scotch-Brite pads for, 91
Schneider, Richard, on mosaic
    bracelets, 84-87
Schools. *See* Woodworking instruction.
Seaton, Jeffrey, on bandsawn
    boxes, 29-31
Shoes. *See* Klompen.
Shuler, Michael, on segmented
    turning, 80-83
Siegel, Anne, on Bob Siegel's work,
    61-63
Signs, carved, business of, 64
Slim, Colorado, on pool-cue
    construction, 96-99
Snowshoes:
    making, 57-60
    book on, cited, 60
Spindles, sectioned, screw
    connectors for, 98-99
    See also Pool cues. Turning.
Spoons:
    carving, 54-56
    finish for, 56
Springs, small, making, 68
Stacking, for bowls, turned, 74-79
Starr, Richard:
    on marble rolls, 32-35
    Woodworking with Your Kids, source
      for, 35
Stave construction:
    book on, 78
    formula for, 79
    for turnings, 78-79
Steam bending:
    of basket handles, 42-43
    See also Bending.
Steel, high-carbon, source for, 87
Sterba, Robert, on bricklaid bowls,
    74-79
Stirt, Alan, on carved bowls, 88-91
Stools, Moravian foot-, making, 16-17
Surfacing:
    with router, 83
    See also Finishes. Sanding.

T

Tablesaws:
    crosscutting jig for, 23
    finger joints on, 23-24
    sliding-cradle jig for, 92, 93
    taper jig for, 25
    wedge-cutting jigs for, 81
    See also Hold-downs.
Tapers, on tablesaw, 25
Threads, metal, on lathe, 97, 99
Tolone, Robert, on tree ornaments,
    124-25
Tongue-and-rabbet joints, on
    tablesaw, 25
Tool rests, lathe-steady, 97, 99
Toys:
    complex, planning of, 8-9
    fire engine, building, 12-15
    Mack truck, making, 8-11
    wheels for, commercial, 9
Tung oil, source for, 87
Turning:
    of balls, 95
    of balls, hollow, 120
    burn protection for, 83
    of cylinders, tiny hollow, 68-69, 70
    faceplate, mounting for, 89, 91
    of greenwood, 88-89
    heatgun for, 89
    lead-wool weighting of, 31
    microwave drying for, 88, 89
    sanding of, 73, 89
    weighting handles for, 83
    See also Boxes: turned. Lathe
    chucks. Spindles. Stacking. Stave
    construction. Tool rests.

V

Vaillancourt, Henri:
    Making the Attikamek Snowshoe,
      cited, 60
    on shoeshoes, 57-60
Valentino, Luca, on making a message
    center, 44-47

W

Wedges, cutting jigs for, 81
Westphale, Wayne, on clocks, 106-13
Whistles, making, 26-27, 28
Wild, J. Malcolm, *Clock Wheel and
    Pinion Cutting,* 105
Woestemeyer, F. B., on stave
    construction, 79
Woodworking instruction:
    in carving, 53
    in Norwegian crafts, 39
Workbenches, for shoemaking, 61

If you enjoyed this book, you're going to love our magazine.

A year's subscription to *Fine Woodworking* brings you the kind of practical, hands-on information you found in this book and much more. In issue after issue, you'll find projects that teach new skills, demonstrations of tools and techniques, new design ideas, old-world traditions, shop tests, coverage of current woodworking events, and breathtaking examples of the woodworker's art for inspiration.

To try an issue, just fill out one of the attached subscription cards, or call us toll-free at 1-800-888-8286. As always, we guarantee your satisfaction.

Subscribe Today!
6 issues for just $29

The Taunton Press
63 South Main Street
P.O. Box 5506
Newtown, CT 06470-5506
